Intelligent Machine Series

Volume I

Microprocessor
Based
Robotics

Mark J. Robillard has been actively involved in micro-computing for 10 years. He is currently involved in the research and development of advanced color graphics systems and voice recognition peripheral design.

Intelligent Machine Series
Volume I

Microprocessor
Based
Robotics

by

Mark J. Robillard

Howard W. Sams & Co., Inc.
4300 WEST 62ND ST. INDIANAPOLIS, INDIANA 46268 USA

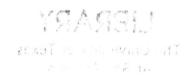

International Standard Book Number: 0-672-22050-4
Library of Congress Catalog Card Number: 83-60160

Edited by: *Welborn Associates*
Illustrated by: *R. E. Lund*

Printed in the United States of America.

PREFACE

In recent years, the microprocessor or "computer on a chip" has captured the heart of the designer and revolutionized the entire electronics industry. Today we utilize at least one such computer every day of our lives in some form. In a very similar way, robotics is becoming the new revolution. Soon the mechanical slaves of science fiction will become a reality.

This book serves to prepare the designer, experimenter, or scientist-to-be for the new challenges. Robotics is a science that mixes mechanical, electrical, electronic and computer engineering into one. In view of this, I have chosen to divide the book into five sections. Each section answers to one discipline, be it electronic or mechanical. Under these sections are individual chapters covering specific subjects. In all chapters, actual construction hands-on projects are included along with any necessary programming information.

MARK J. ROBILLARD

ACKNOWLEDGMENTS

The first person I should thank is my wife Angie. Thanks for the hours you spent on the word processor and putting up with me. Next are my children, Nichole and Valerie, who, for the most part, were excellent when I needed them to be.

Throughout the book I make reference to many suppliers and manufacturers. Although I never asked them for help in preparation of the book, I extend a word of thanks to them for providing such fine products. And there has to be a special thanks to Carl Helmers, editor of *Robotics Age* magazine, who helped me get into the writing business. Much of the material included here is adapted from my series of articles which appears in that publication.

To my Dad
The many blocks of paper
and the trip to the MIT open house
made all the difference in the world.

CONTENTS

Section I
MECHANICAL

Chapter 1

Chapter 2

Section II
ELECTROMECHANICS

Chapter 3

Chapter 4

Chapter 5

Section III
ELECTRONIC SENSORS

Chapter 6

Chapter 7

Chapter 8

Section IV
COMPUTER CONTROL

Chapter 9

Chapter 10

Chapter 11

Chapter 12

Section V
ROBOT COMMUNICATION/CONTROL

Chapter 13

Chapter 14

Appendix A

Appendix B

Appendix C

Section I:
MECHANICAL

Chapter 1

Hand Mechanics

In most publications on robotics, the hand or end effector is most neglected. You will see many articles about arms, rolling bases, control systems and even programming languages, but very few hands. This is unfortunate because the hand tends to be the business end of the robotic system. It is where the application of the system must be considered seriously.

Mechanically speaking, hands are a good entry point when learning about robotics. They can be made as simple or as complex as you wish. In this chapter we will explore the mechanisms behind several types of mechanical hands.

When we think of hands, we tend to model the appendage at the end of our wrist. Although a very adaptable, efficient unit, the human hand does not lend itself to easy representation. Our hands are the only end effectors we own so they have to fit with all the applications we apply them to. Robots, on the other hand (excuse the pun), may be suitably equipped so as to have removable hand units. Each unit could be designed for a specific application.

Look at Fig. 1-1. Here we have two end effectors designed for specific applications. These particular hands fit onto the UNIMATE ®* Robot designed by Unimation of Connecticut. Notice how most of the designs are patterned after a two-pincer or two-fingered mechanism. This design emulates a pair of pliers which, in most applications, is probably all you would need. It is certainly the easiest mechanism to emulate and control.

*Unimate is a registered trademark of Unimation, Inc.

TWO-FINGERED HANDS

Let's consider the design of a simple two-fingered hand. Fig. 1-2 shows a complete hand unit constructed mostly of wood. This particular design uses a kind of relay-motor called a *solenoid.* Solenoids will be discussed in detail in Chapter 4.

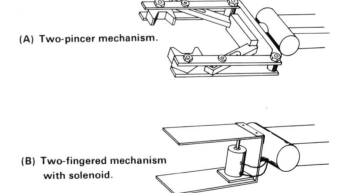

(A) Two-pincer mechanism.

(B) Two-fingered mechanism with solenoid.

Fig. 1-1 Sample hand designs for the Unimate robot.

The place to begin is to design the fingers. There are a number of things that must be considered in order to design them efficiently. Some of these are:

1. Overall length from the palm—
   This is determined by the shape of the object you

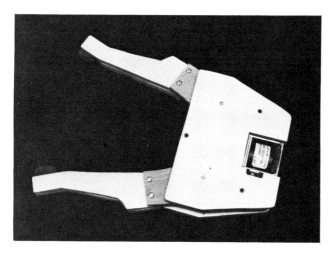

Fig. 1-2 A typical wood-constructed hand.

wish to manipulate. For instance, if you are lifting a wine carafe by the neck, you would want long slender fingers. If the object is a rectangular block, then short wide fingers, perhaps, might be better.

2. Width/length of finger contact area—

The force with which you manipulate the object will determine the width/length ratio. If the rectangular block is relatively heavy, it would need to have contact over a greater surface area than a pair of tweezer-like fingers would allow. In fact, the contact, or *pad area*, as it is called, is a very critical consideration when designing the hand.

Let's look at Fig. 1-3 and consider the following: When a hand is grasping an object, there are two forces acting on the object. Gravity exerts a force downward and the fingers exert a force inward. When the arm connected to the hand moves, another force is present. This force tends to make the object slip from the grip applied by the fingers.

The acceleration or deceleration of the arm might exert twice the normal pull of gravity. If the arm moves horizontally, the force exerted on the object-hand contact points is twice the weight of the object. Vertical motion nets a force three times the weight because of the normal gravity pull plus the factor of two for the forces exerted during motion.

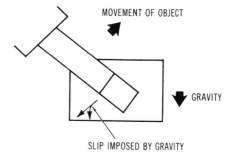

Fig. 1-3 Forces involved in gripper design.

Then there is friction to consider. When the hand-arm unit is lifting the object, gravity tends to pull the object parallel to the finger contact areas. This results in *friction* or *slip*.

If the center of gravity of the object is 6 inches above the points where the fingers make contact, there is a factor called a *friction coefficient* that is equal to 0.06. This number must be used along with the overall weight of the object times the distance between contact points on each pad of each finger to obtain the force needed to grasp, hold, and transfer the object successfully.

This is all well and good if you know where the *center of gravity* is located. Usually the center of gravity of an object is the center of its mass. Notice that I said usually. This is because some objects, like human bodies, have varying amounts of mass distributed throughout the body area. Assuming that the object you wish to manipulate has a constant mass, like a block, rock, bottle (unfilled), etc., we can locate the approximate position of the center of gravity by drawing intersecting lines from the corners of the object (Fig. 1-4). The point where

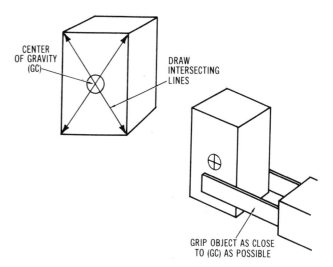

Fig. 1-4 Diagram showing procedure for finding the center of gravity.

the lines meet can be assumed as the center of gravity.

Getting back to the pad width problem, we have laid the basis for our first mathematical equation to be applied when designing hands. The following relationship may be used when figuring the force necessary to grip an object:

$$\text{Force Necessary} = \frac{\begin{array}{c}\text{weight} \\ \text{of} \\ \text{object}\end{array} \times \begin{array}{c}\text{distance between} \\ \text{points of contact} \\ \text{on pad}\end{array}}{\begin{array}{c}\text{friction coefficient (distance} \\ \text{from C. G. of contact} \div 100)\end{array}}$$

When you are engaged in the design of robot systems, frequently it helps to have a personal computer handy to call up design calculations. As you progress through this book, you will be building a library of these design calculations. They have been converted into short BASIC®† subprograms that can be used on most popular personal computers. These subprograms fit together into one main program which is discussed in Chapter 12. Listing 1-1 contains this hand force formula.

areas of these fingers are straight. The rest of the finger doesn't really matter . . . or does it?

4. Relationship between finger contact pads—
Perform the following experiment:
Take two popsicle sticks and place them on a flat surface so that the long dimension projects away from you (Fig. 1-5). Place both sticks approximately two inches apart and keep them parallel. Making sure the bottom of the sticks remains fixed like a pivot point, move the sticks together until

```
200 CLS: PRINT"GRIPPER FORCE EQUATION"
210 PRINT:PRINT"TO FIND GRIP FORCE REQUIRED:"
220 PRINT:PRINT"ENTER WEIGHT OF LIFTED OBJECT:"
230 INPUT"LBS";A
240 PRINT:PRINT"ENTER DISTANCE BETWEEN POINTS OF CONTACT ON FINGER PAD:"
250 INPUT"(INCHES)";B
260 PRINT:PRINT"ENTER DISTANCE FROM CENTER OF GRAVITY OF CONTACT:"
270 INPUT"(INCHES)";C
280 C=C/100:G=(A*B)/C
290 CLS:PRINT"GRIP FORCE= ";G;"POUND-INCHES"
295 PRINT:PRINT"<ENTER> FOR MENU,<SPACE> FOR ANOTHER"
297 A$=INKEY$:IF A$="" THEN 297
298 IF A$=" " THEN GOTO 200 ELSE GOTO 10
```

Listing 1-1 Gripper Force Equation

At this point, you may be wondering what force has to do with finger length. Well, if the grip force necessary to hold your particular object is calculated to be more than a thousand pounds, you've got a problem. The required actuator for that hand would be enormous! Don't change objects, however, just play with the size of the area of contact.

The grip force necessary can be reduced by either grasping the object closer to the center of gravity, or extending the contact pad length or area. Looking at the equation, you can see that by increasing either of these factors the gripping force will be reduced. Of course, there comes a time when that 200,000 pound object will definitely have to go.

3. Finger shape—
Our fingers are tubular, three-jointed masterpieces. One finger of a pair of pliers, by contrast, is rather rounded, rigid, and usually toothed. Yet both designs can open a screw-on bottle top equally efficiently. To grasp the neck of a bottle you would definitely want a finger that had a contour which is shaped the same as half the diameter of the neck. The reason for this is because the opposing finger would complete the circle and therefore sufficiently restrain the cap.

On the other hand, a rectangular block may only require two flat pad surfaces, and thus the contact

they touch. Notice that you have successfully made an inverted "V," or the top of a triangle. Consider a square object placed between the sticks before you move them inward. If the object is to be grasped by the sticks, the area of each pad on each finger is

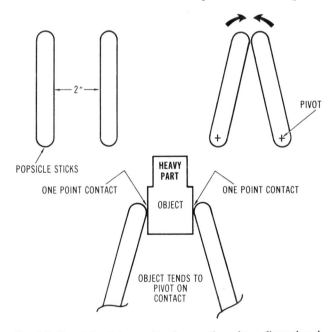

Fig. 1-5 Popsicle sticks used to show action of two-finger hand design.

† BASIC is a registered trademark of the trustees of Dartmouth College.

extremely small. In fact, the area constitutes only one point. When both fingers contact on one point you have provided the object with a pivot. This could have disastrous consequences if the object is heavier at the top, because it would topple and hit the surface when the hand raises it.

The way to ensure that there are two contact points per pad is to design the fingers so that they are what is called *self-aligning*. In this type of mechanism, both finger pads remain parallel throughout their journey from outer edge to inner contact. Fig. 1-6 shows the design of a self-aligning finger. Notice the pivot points of the pad area and how they are mechanically interlocked with the movement of the finger structure.

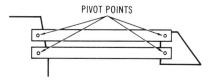

Fig. 1-6 Design for self-aligning finger.

In general, self-aligning jaws can be used effectively in most applications that require gripping an object. However, there are cases such as the manipulation of extremely tiny parts or objects where the tweezer effect works better.

The action of the popsicle sticks illustrates this approach although rather crudely. In cases where tweezer-like fingers are necessary, they are usually designed so that the end of the finger is cone shaped or at least tapers into a point.

5. Finger material—

Last, but certainly not least, is whether or not the finger you design can withstand the forces necessary to grip the object. Typically, experimental hands are built from plywood and small metal parts. These materials will be used extensively throughout this book. However, this is not to imply that wood will hold true in industrial applications. In fact, a thorough study of the forces exerted and applicable materials should be made, keeping in mind that the weight of the material directly affects other systems that we will learn about in subsequent chapters. The general rule of thumb should be to keep the weight at a minimum without jeopardizing the ability of the hand to perform its function.

That about covers finger design except for the placement of the pivot point if there is to be one. How can the finger perform a grasp operation without a pivot? Let's examine how this is done.

FINGER MOVEMENT

The National Bureau of Standards has been doing research on robotics for some time. Several years ago they developed an arm with an attached hand that used a unique finger-closing mechanism like that shown in Fig. 1-7. The jaws of the hand remain parallel at all times, yet they do not pivot. They simply slide toward each other on individual tracks.

The tracks on which the fingers move are provided with movement through a gearing arrangement called a *rack and pinion*. You might have heard of rack and pinion gearing in relation to automobile steering mechanisms. Basically, as you can see in Fig. 1-7, as the pinion gear turns, the flat gear called the *rack* moves linearly back and forth depending on the direction of movement (clockwise or counterclockwise) of the round gear called the *pinion*.

This type of movement is extremely simple to implement and it only requires one controllable motion element (pinion). The relationship between the number of teeth in the pinion gear and the number of teeth in the rack determines the force available at the finger and the speed at which the fingers close.

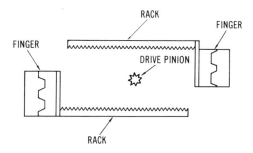

(A) Exploded view.

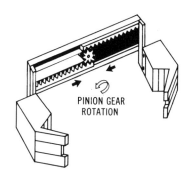

(B) Operational view.

Fig. 1-7 National Bureau of Standards design for hand using rack-and-pinion movement.

BASIC GEARING

Before we go any further, it is necessary to cover the concept of mechanical gear linkages. The relationship between size, number of teeth, and gear types must be understood for the proper design of hand movement mechanisms (Fig. 1-8).

In the previously described rack and pinion case, if the number of teeth in the pinion gear (which has teeth ground into a cylindrical shaft and parallel to the shaft) is 10, and the number of teeth in the rack (which is a flat bar with teeth ground perpendicular to its length) is 100 then the speed of movement of the finger unit will be $\frac{1}{10}$ that of the pinion. In addition, the force available at the finger will be ten times that transmitted by the pinion.

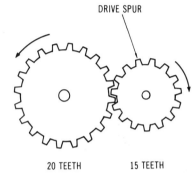

DRIVE SPUR

Fig. 1-8 Basic spur gear design relationships.

20 TEETH   15 TEETH

RELATIONSHIP BETWEEN DRIVE AND DRIVEN SPUR

20/15 = 1.5

(DRIVEN) 1.5 TIMES STRONGER (TORQUE)
(DRIVEN) 1.5 TIMES SLOWER

As you can deduce, by reducing the speed of the finger you increase the force. In a situation where you need more pressure on an object, yet cannot afford to increase the size of the motion element (motor), you could adjust the gear ratio between the *driver* (pinion) and the *receiver* (rack).

has two jaws that move toward or away from each other by turning a rather large screw with a handle. Notice how the rotation of the screw makes the jaws move as illustrated in Fig. 1-9. This is accomplished because of two things. First, the hole that the screw fits through in the jaw is threaded to accept the particular size thread of the screw so that it acts as a nut and, secondly, the jaws are prevented from turning (as a nut would) by yet another shaft arrangement. Therefore, the jaw has nowhere to go except in a linear motion forward or backward. As you can see, this accomplishes the same action as the rack and pinion while maintaining only one controllable motion element (the screw).

In mechanical terms, the screw is called a *lead screw* and the jaw would be a form of a *lead-screw carriage*. Of course, the design of your carriage can take any shape

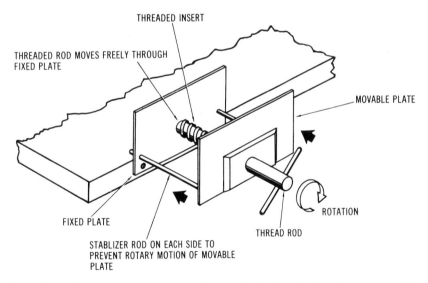

THREADED INSERT

THREADED ROD MOVES FREELY THROUGH FIXED PLATE

MOVABLE PLATE

Fig. 1-9 Action of shop vise as it relates to lead-screw mechanics.

FIXED PLATE

STABLIZER ROD ON EACH SIDE TO PREVENT ROTARY MOTION OF MOVABLE PLATE

THREAD ROD

ROTATION

Other gearing schemes work similarly. Anywhere that there is a gear-to-gear mesh, the number of teeth will determine the speed/force ratio. Let's look at another example of performing the finger movement similar to the rack and pinion.

LEAD-SCREW MECHANICS

If you do any type of shop work, you are probably familiar with the standard bench vise. This is a tool which

necessary as long as it is threaded and restrained from rotating.

Calculating the torque and force of a lead-screw mechanism is not quite the same as the other gears discussed so far. In fact, the ratio between driver gear and screw is usually so high that a very small input force can produce a large output force. The key is the length of the screw. When driving the screw, use a 1:1 ratio of gearing. That is, if the lead-screw driver gear (Fig. 1-10) has 10 teeth, drive

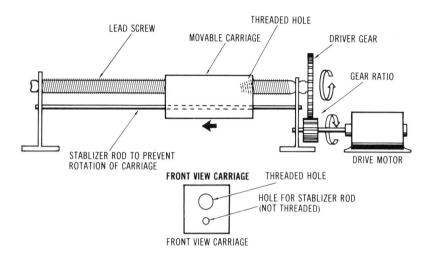

Fig. 1-10 Lead-screw design diagram.

it with a gear of 10 teeth. This makes the calculation simple. If it's impossible to use a 1:1 ratio go ahead to the section on spur gears to learn the relationships between them. The formulas used to design gearing systems is presented in Chapter 2 where gears as they are used in the design of various arm systems are discussed.

SPUR GEARS

Spur gears are your basic everyday "garden" variety gears. They are used to drive lead screws (unless the motor has a worm screw built into the shaft), they are the pinion portion of the rack and pinion gear, and basically interact as was previously discussed. The ratio of teeth from driver gear to receiver gear determines the speed and force (Fig. 1-8).

WORM GEARS

The *worm gear* acts very much like the lead screw in that the driver gear is a screw-like shaft. However, here the similarity ends (Fig. 1-11). The output, or receiver gear, simply meshes with the worm screw to provide rotational motion from the linear motion of the worm. Later in this chapter, we will investigate a hand design that uses worm gears.

In the last few paragraphs, we briefly touched on gears and their relationships. We will return to the design of gear systems in Chapter 2. However, it is necessary for you to know what action each type of gear perfroms before we investigate several hand designs.

CONSTRUCTION OF A HAND

There is no better way of learning a subject than to jump in and get your hands dirty. Well, we can do without the dirt, but let's begin the construction of a two-fingered hand. Mind you, this hand is designed to illus-

trate construction techniques and not to perform any specific duty other than as a prop for the illustration.

Fig. 1-2 is a photograph of a hand. Notice that the two fingers pivot about a hole and the jaws are not designed to be self-aligning. Fig. 1-12 is an outline drawing of the basic finger shape chosen for my example. The material is $1/2$ in. plywood cut with a scroll saw. The base structure material is $1/4$ in. plywood and also cut on the scroll saw table. Gears for the hand are provided out of the LEGO®‡ Advanced Builders spare parts kit carried at most toy stores.

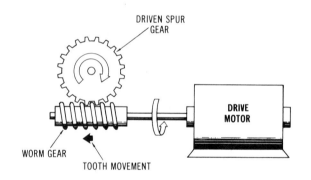

Fig. 1-11 Action of a worm gear.

Speaking again of gears, let's investigate the method used in this particular hand. Fig. 1-13 shows the gearing system which the author designed for this hand. Basiit does , the reverse of a rack and pinion in that when the rack block is moved outward, the gears rotate. As can be seen, by putting a rack on each side of the block, the two gears tend to turn opposite to each other which performs the necessary opening or closing of the fingers.

The rack block is moved linearly by a solenoid, but can be mounted on a lead screw if the block is threaded and some method of preventing the block from rotating is

‡ LEGO is a registered trademark of Interlego A.G. EXXON of EXXON Corp.

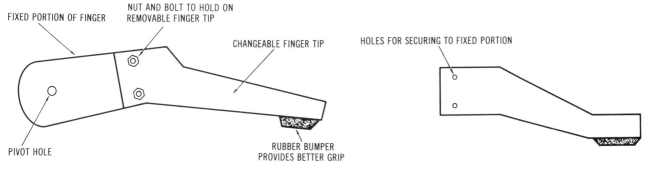

FIXED PORTION OF FINGER

NUT AND BOLT TO HOLD ON
REMOVABLE FINGER TIP

CHANGEABLE FINGER TIP

HOLES FOR SECURING TO FIXED PORTION

PIVOT HOLE

RUBBER BUMPER
PROVIDES BETTER GRIP

(A) Finger assembly.

(B) Removable finger tip.

Fig. 1-12 Finger design for wood-constructed hand.

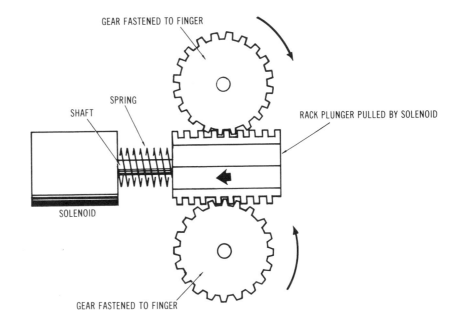

GEAR FASTENED TO FINGER

SPRING

SHAFT

RACK PLUNGER PULLED BY SOLENOID

SOLENOID

GEAR FASTENED TO FINGER

Fig. 1-13 Gear design using solenoid and rack plunger for wood-constructed hand.

provided. Figs. 1-14 through 1-16 provide other views of the hand which will aid you in understanding the construction of the hand. Specific details of any construction in this book are limited by the purpose of the book which is to teach design rather than provide kit instructions.

STUDY OF HAND DESIGNS

Mini Mover

Fig. 1-17 depicts a design currently in use on the *Mini Mover*®§ Robot from Microbot, Inc. Although small in size, this two-fingered approach accomplishes most of the design criteria outlined earlier. The jaws are self-aligning and are made of lightweight metal. Closure action is accomplished via a cable that, when pulled, draws the jaws together. A spring called a *torsion spring* relaxes when the cable is loosened, thus restoring the jaws to their open position.

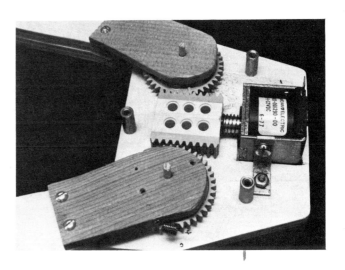

Fig. 1-14 Photograph showing plunger design.

§Mini Mover is a registered trademark of Microbot, Inc.

Fig. 1-15 Photograph of finger construction.

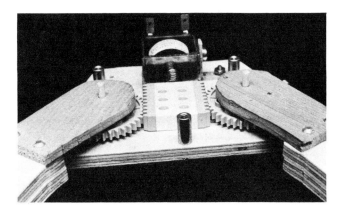

Fig. 1-16 Constructed hand showing interaction between rack plunger and worm gears.

Therefore, in this example, you also have to provide force enough to overcome the pressure of the torsion springs. If the springs exert little force themselves, they will not hold the hand open; yet, on the other hand, the greater their force is the greater is the force required of the hand closure system.

Cable-driven systems have many disadvantages. Most of these apply to the way in which you must attach and align the cable itself. However, the one main advantage of cable-driven systems is that they do not require the controllable motion element to be physically located in the hand, thereby reducing the overall weight. You can route a cable from this type of hand all the way down to the base of a robot system.

Armatron

Figs. 1-18 and 1-19 show both the outside and inside details of the two-fingered hand designed for Armatron®**, the toy (what a toy!) mechanical arm from TOMY Toys (California). This hand uses the worm gear arrangement discussed earlier. Note how the turning of the worm moves each finger gear in the opposite direction.

Examining the mechanics of this hand, the Mini Mover, and the author's design in Fig. 1-13 clearly show that there are numerous approaches to the same problem.

Each design was chosen for specific reasons. Our hand will be powered by a linear motion solenoid, therefore the rack block. Mini Mover was to be operated via cable so the idea of a pulled cable working against torsion springs looked best. In the Armatron design power is transmitted via shafts connected elsewhere to a very sophisticated

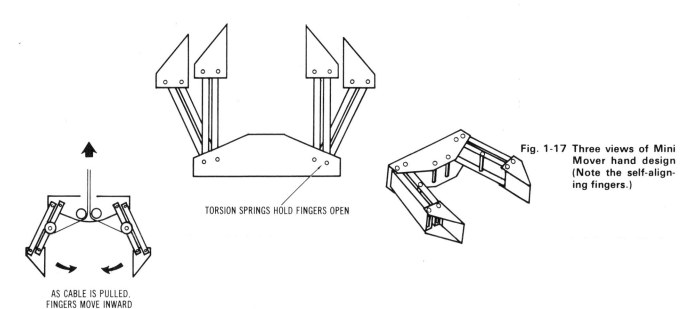

TORSION SPRINGS HOLD FINGERS OPEN

AS CABLE IS PULLED, FINGERS MOVE INWARD

Fig. 1-17 Three views of Mini Mover hand design (Note the self-aligning fingers.)

** Armatron is a registered trademark of Tomy Toys.

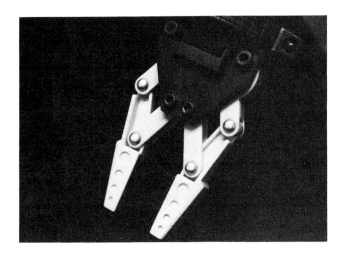

Fig. 1-18 Photograph of Armatron hand.

three joints much like our own fingers. The outer structure of these fingers is also tubular, therefore allowing the hand to become highly adaptable to a variety of object shapes.

Since each joint pulley is actuated by a single drive motor, it is possible to position the fingers in any direction regardless of the state of the other fingers. This type of individual control gets complicated when you get into building control systems.

Another three-fingered system, although not as versatile as the last, is shown in Fig. 1-21. This hand was developed by F.R. Erskine Crossley and F.G. Umhotz, both of the University of Massachusetts at Amherst. Their design also utilizes cable drive; however, the cables are not connected to pulleys!

The design emulates the human thumb, index, and ring fingers. The operation is such that the object is grasped first by the thumb and ring finger, then the index finger is operated independently, providing stability. Mechanical movement of the finger joints is extremely unique and quite interesting. Looking at Fig. 1-21, locate the joint gear. This gear is what is called a *turnbuckle*. It is threaded at both ends with right- and left-hand threads.

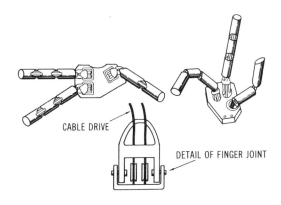

Fig. 1-20. A cable-driven three-fingered hand.

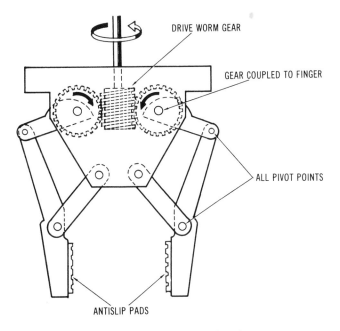

Fig. 1-19 Design drawing of Armatron hand.

gearing system (more on this later), hence the worm gear arrangement.

MULTIPLE FINGERS

There are times that two fingers just won't do the job. A third finger can add so much stability! Imagine what five can do!

There are a number of experimental three-fingered hands in operation. Most of these designs, however, use a kind of cable-pulley arrangement. Fig. 1-20 illustrates a three-fingered hand developed by Dr. Tokuji Okada from the Electrotechnical Laboratory in Japan. These three fingers shown are structurally similar to the human thumb, index, and middle fingers. Each finger has

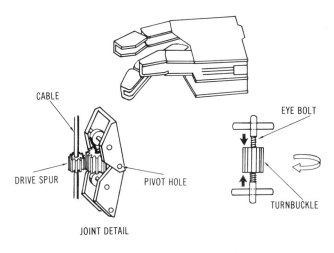

Fig. 1-21 Three-fingered hand using turnbuckle mechanism.

Both joints, which are simply formed metal flanges connected to this turnbuckle through eye bolts screwed into the gear. Turning this gear right or left results in the eye bolts moving outward or inward by screw action. This, in turn, moves the joint because the eye bolts are connected to the joints by a shaft, as shown.

The turnbuckle of each joint is activated by another gear attached to a flexible cable. This cable rotates much like the drive cable of a remote power-tool shaft. Of course, if you were to redesign this hand, you could add as many fingers as you think necessary.

CONSTRUCTING A FIVE-FINGERED HAND

Multiple-fingered hands do not have to employ individually movable fingers. Let's look into constructing a four-finger plus thumb hand that operates much like the two-fingered variety. Fig. 1-22 shows the completed hand after assembly. Primarily made of wood, this hand exerts a tremendous gripping force.

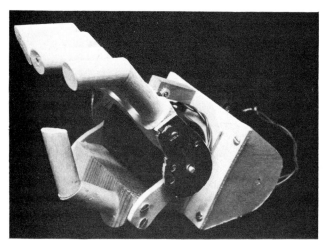

Fig. **1-22** Photograph of five-fingered hand constructed of wood and a small motor.

The fingers of this unit are made from wood dowel cut at angles and glued together. The four fingers are then glued to a thick piece of oak cut to the shape of a knuckle assembly. The dowels are inserted into the knuckle by first drilling a shallow tunnel at an angle into the oak.

The thumb is mounted into another oak structure designed to act as the palm of the hand. This portion of the hand is fixed to the motor base and not movable. The knuckle assembly is fitted with two end structures which act as pivot guides. One of these end plates is mounted to the shaft of a motor mounted in the palm of the hand. The other is positioned so as to pivot about a small shaft. Fig. 1-23 illustrates the mechanical details of the construction. The motor used is an Edmund Scientific #C41,331 which is rated at 31 inch-ounces of torque (more on motors in Chapter 4).

You can see that when the motor turns, the hand either opens or closes. Pick a motor with a small stall current as you will end up stalling the motor in order to grasp an object with any force.

Another method of accomplishing the five-fingered hand motion with greater control of position is detailed in Fig. 1-24. Here, linear motion out and in will cause the hand to open or close. The mechanical linkage used to convert the in and out to up and down is called a *bell crank*. Pulling the actuator shaft in causes the bell crank to rise on the driver side, and the opposite is true if we push on the drive shaft.

This shaft can be representative of a number of mechanisms discussed earlier. The lead screw could be used if the carriage becomes the drive shaft (Fig. 1-25). The rack of a rack and pinion system can be made to become the drive shaft. We will explore linear motion mechanisms more in the discussions on motors in Chapter 4.

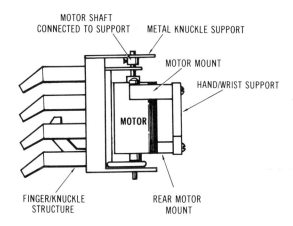

(A) Finger view.

(B) Palm and thumb view.

Fig. **1-23** Construction details for a five-fingered hand.

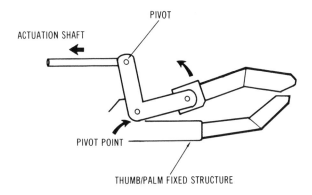

Fig. 1-24 Diagram of linear actuation to open and close hand.

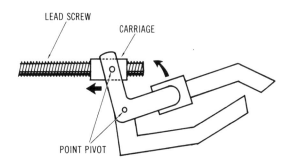

Fig. 1-25 Lead screw application in hand design.

OTHER HAND DESIGNS

Would you believe there is a host of other hand designs we have not touched on yet? There are hands that grab or pick up objects, yet have no fingers!

How about a hand based on the motion of a rotating belt? Don't read any further! See if you can think of a design for a hand that actually grasps objects using a rotating belt! Then read on to see if you got it.

In 1974, John Birk wrote in the *IEEE Journal* an article titled "Transactions on Systems, Man and Cybernetics" on a rotating belt hand. Fig. 1-26 discloses the mechanical details. Note that as the belt traverses the pulleys, it actually can grab anything poised at the opening of its "jaw." The object would then tend to rotate within the chamber and might even slip out; therefore, you might design the control system to move the belt until the object is in the chamber. Reverse action of the belt will eject the object. Pretty clever design! The top pulley support is made movable to accommodate various sized objects.

This hand wins my award for simplicity of design and ease of control.

A HAND THAT IS OUT OF THIS WORLD

Another hand that grasps, yet has no finger is used on the Remote Manipulator System aboard the space shuttle. This hand has some unique design pre-conditions.

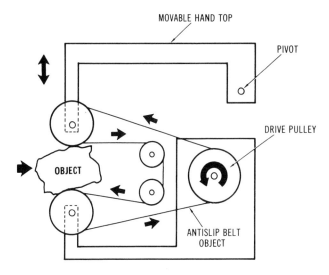

Fig. 1-26 Rolling belt hand design.

The objects grasped basically will be shafts or have shaft-like protrusions for grasping.

Fig. 1-27 depicts the mechanical details of the space-shuttle hand. Notice in the figure that there are two gripping actuators. The outer gripper bars act like the aperture of a camera. The shaft of the object to be grasped is positioned inside the opening of the aperture mechanism. Motor action then twists the bars which slowly close on the shaft.

After the object is secure within the first gripper, the whole gripper assembly is then pulled inward until the

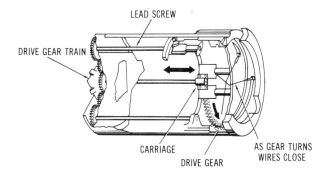

(A) Cut away view.

(B) End view.

Fig. 1-27 Design for space shuttle hand.

body of the object contacts the outer ring of the hand shell. This assures a firm lock on the object.

COULD THERE BE MORE?

We have only touched the surface of a subject that is an engineering discipline by itself. Of course, there are other robotic end effectors. There are magnetic hand plates and vacuum units. Welder, drilling, and paint spraying attachable hands are also available, but to cover all these would not leave room in this book for other critical design mechanisms. With the knowledge you now have, you can learn about more complex mechanisms. So, let's move on up the arm.

A Study
Of Arm Design

When a robot is in a position where it cannot pick up an object that it is meant to grasp, typically it will have an arm or some other reaching mechanism. We are familiar with the normal humanoid structure with two arms, and many of Hollywood's robots have been designed as such. And, undoubtedly, you have seen the robots that are only an arm, such as the Unimate industrial type. In this chapter, we will investigate several design approaches for manipulating remote object.

WRIST DESIGN

For the purpose of discussion, we will treat the wrist mechanism as an integral part of the arm. The ability to position the hand in any attitude proves useful when manipulating objects through irregular openings. The wrist provides up-down motion commonly called pitch, as well as turning, or roll. Some complex mechanisms also allow side to side motion called yaw. Fig. 2-1 shows their relationship. Let's investigate the simplest of these three motions—roll. In order to provide the hand with the ability to rotate, it must first be mounted on a pivot or shaft. The hand will now rotate about the shaft. Look at Fig. 2-2 which shows a simplified example of how to mount the hand to a roll wrist device. Notice that when the motor is energized, the hand turns. In fact, this design is not unique to robot wrists, and is the basis for most rotating department-store display stands. Because the weight is distributed about the hand, and there is no

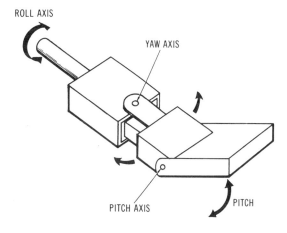

Fig. 2-1 Diagram showing pitch, roll, and yaw relative to robot, wrist/hand mechanisms.

distance horizontally from the motor, nearly any size motor will work (provided the hand is oriented vertically, as shown in Fig. 2-2). Moving the wrist up and down provides pitch. Fig. 2-3 depicts a simple way to construct a pitch mechanism. Here, you need to be careful of the motor rating, as the motor must be powerful enough to lift the hand. If suitably strong, it will raise the hand until it is physically stopped by the forearm structure. Similarly, it will be stopped when it meets the structure while traveling in the downward direction.

Yaw motion utilizes the same concepts as pitch except the motor is mounted so that the hand rotates about a large arc limited only by the forearm structure. So, in

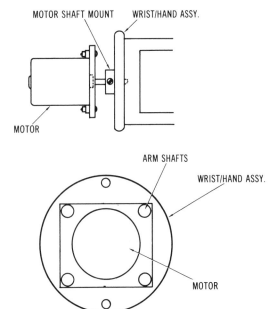

Fig. 2-2 A simple roll mechanism.

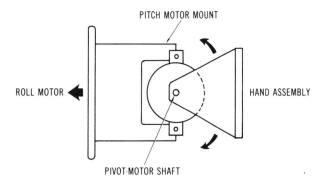

Fig. 2-3 Motor control pitch mechanism design for robot wrist.

effect, the yaw mechanism is almost a combination of the pitch and roll devices. Figs. 2-4 through 2-6 show the construction of a wrist that provides both roll and pitch.

Now that we have investigated the basic motions of a wrist, let's look at a few design constraints. After all, simply putting motors on mechanical supports does not a wrist make!

When designing the roll mechanism, take into consideration the construction of the hand. Are there electrically actuated devices present on the end effector? If so, you will quickly find that rolling the hand through 360° more than once will tangle any control wires that pass through the wrist and into the hand. You may never need the wrist to rotate through a full circle, therefore just leave enough slack in the cable to accommodate turning. However, if you are going to emulate a screw- or nut-driver action with the hand, and it must rotate continuously in one direction or the other, watch out! It would

not be appropriate to leave slack for "42" rotations. Yes, you could do it, but sometime the cord would become knotted, brittle, and broken.

If you are faced with this problem, there is a way out. Years ago, the electronic industry had such a dilemma where surveillance cameras were required to rotate yet had to avoid cable crimping. They developed a special type of contact called a *slip ring*. This device, as shown in Fig. 2-7, consists of metal bands or rings located on the base (immovable) portion of the unit. Control wires were connected to these rings to form one side of the connection. The movable assembly had metal or wire brushes attached to controller mechanisms to form the other side of the connection. When the unit is rotated, electrical contact is maintained because pressure holds the brushes in contact with the rings, thus the brushes simply drag across the rings.

As you may have guessed, there are a lot of problems associated with slip-ring technology. First, there is dirt. Whenever bare contact surfaces are exposed, they do attract dirt which inevitably leads to performance problems. Slip rings can now be purchased that are sealed to prevent dirt from being a problem, however, the price is not inexpensive. There are instances where there is no other way to accomplish control in the hand without them, so if necessary do investigate their availability. On the other hand, there are pure mechanical methods for solving hand motion using roll joints that will be discussed later.

WORK FORMULATION

Work is a word with which we are familiar. Without it nothing gets done. This is definitely the case in robotics. Work is the amount of energy needed to produce certain actions. In many instances, it will be expressed in pounds. At this time, let's discuss work without reference to specific motor units because that is covered in depth in Chapter 4.

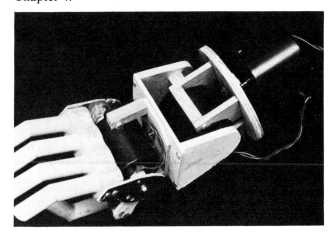

Fig. 2-4 Five-fingered hand and integral pitch, roll wrist constructed of wood and hobby motors.

26

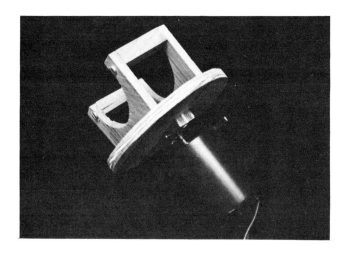

Fig. 2-5 Roll mechanism.

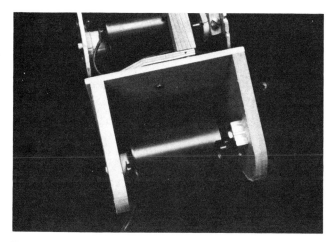

Fig. 2-6 Photograph of pitch mechanism.

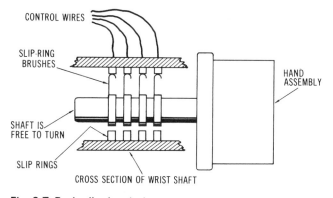

Fig. 2-7 Basic slip-ring design.

When providing a pitch mechanism for a robot wrist, one consideration is the force or amount of work necessary to lift the hand. Let's assume the hand mechanism alone weighs one pound. You have attached it directly to the shaft of a motor like the diagram in Fig. 2-3. How much force will it take to lift the hand?

Let's look at another formula:

$$Work = (weight\ of\ hand + lifting\ weight) \times distance$$

Notice that we must add the weight of the object we intend to lift to that of the hand. This is logical because if we design the wrist to lift the hand effectively without any payload, we have designed a practically useless mechanism. The term "distance," in the equation, refers to the amount of distance horizontally that this weight will be present. For instance, let's assume the object we want to lift in the hand equals the weight of the hand, or 1 pound, and the center of that weight is 6 inches away from the shaft of the pitch motor (Fig. 2-8).

The equation becomes:

$$work = (1\ lb + 1\ lb) \times 6\ inches$$

$$work = 12\ inch\text{-}lbs$$

It is surprising how the distance increases the amount of work, but we owe that to the same force that keeps our feet on the ground. Listing 2-1 is another part of our robot design program in which a computer can solve the preceding equation for us.

WRIST MECHANICS

It is now time to investigate several types of wrist mechanisms. You will notice, as we go on, that there are numerous approaches to solving the roll, pitch and yaw problems. A different design is dictated by the controllable motion system used.

Fig. 2-9 shows another method with which to achieve a wrist roll mechanism. Notice that the motor controls a gear which meshes with another gear that is parallel to the controlled gear. These gears are called spur gears and they are designed to mesh in this way. By taking into consideration the amount of teeth in each gear, it is possible to increase the force from a small motor. Notice in Fig. 2-9 how the driver gear attached to the motor is relatively small where the wrist gear that would be mounted under the hand is larger, hence, more teeth, therefore, slower speed, and more strength.

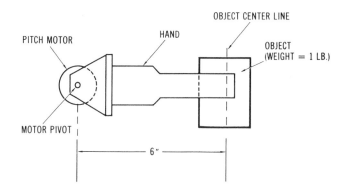

Fig. 2-8 Object weight and distance from pivot point of motor are important when designing pitch mechanism.

```
300 CLS:PRINT"WORK FORMULA"
310 PRINT:PRINT"ENTER WEIGHT OF HAND ASSY:"
315 INPUT"LBS";A
320 PRINT:PRINT"ENTER WEIGHT OF OBJECT TO LIFT:"
330 INPUT"LBS"; B:W=A+B
340 PRINT:PRINT"ENTER DISTANCE BETWEEN DRIVER SHAFT AND OBJECT:"
350 INPUT "INCHES";C
360 WK=W*C:CLS
370 PRINT"WORK = ";WK;" POUND-INCHES"
380 PRINT:PRINT"<SPACE> FOR ANOTHER,<ENTER> FOR MENU"
390 A$=INKEY$:IF A$="" THEN 390
395 IF A$=" " THEN GOTO 300 ELSE GOTO 10
```

Listing 2-1 Work Formula

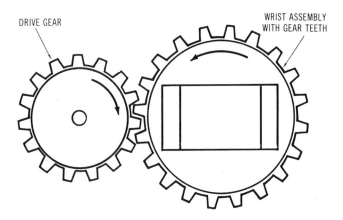

Fig. 2-9 An approach to roll design using an outside-spur drive gear.

Other mechanisms that may be used to provide roll directly are shown in composite Fig. 2-10. Here we see another application of the gear mesh scheme (Fig. 2-10A). The motor may be mounted inside the wrist structure utilizing a ring and drive gear. Fig. 2-10B depicts the use of a worm-gear drive to achieve roll, and Fig. 2-10C doesn't use any gears. Instead, pulleys driven by a belt work just fine. This system is used in your car to power the generator. Here the size difference between pulleys determines the speed reduction and force increase just as the number of teeth in a gear system do. Some consideration must be made to prevent the possibility of belt slip. There are several timing belts with teeth available to reduce the possibility of wrist slippage.

Moving along, let's consider the bevel gear. Arrange two bevel gears with a miter gear and you have a differential gear mechanism. Seems confusing? Look at Fig. 2-11. Here is a wrist that can roll over 360° and can pitch, too, all with only two control cables. These cables drive each of the bevel gears located on the sides of the wrist. Moving each gear in the opposite direction causes the wrist to turn or roll. Switching the direction of both gears reverses the direction of wrist rotation. If you allow the gears to be driven in the same direction, you get up or down pitch. This mechanism is used in many robot arms. An entire

differential gear assembly can be purchased from several sources. Of course, direct motor drive can be used to power the gears if you don't want a cable-driven system.

Fig. 2-12 depicts one of the most clever wrist designs that the author has encountered. The wrist is part of the Armatron Robot Arm from TOMY Toys and is driven

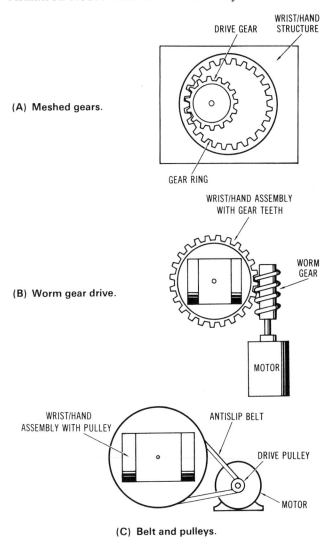

(A) Meshed gears.

(B) Worm gear drive.

(C) Belt and pulleys.

Fig. 2-10 Other approaches to roll design.

28

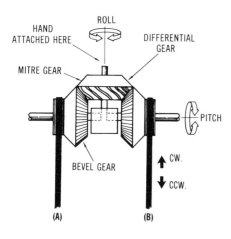

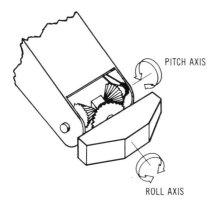

CABLE MOTION			
A	B	HAND	MOTION
CCW	CCW	RAISES	(PITCH UP)
CW	CW	LOWERS	(PITCH DOWN)
CCW	CW	CCW	ROTATION (ROLL)
CW	CCW	CW	ROTATION (ROLL)

Fig. 2-11 Wrist design using differential gear. Design is used in the Mini Mover robot.

by two shafts, each with an associated spur gear. The roll mechanism is controlled by this spur gear meshing with a gear having teeth perpendicular to itself (see Fig. 2-12). This second gear then meshes with a spur gear that is physically attached to the hand structure. When the shaft turns, so does the hand. At the same time, the hand is attached to the wrist structure through a shaft-like design that allows a second shaft to physically raise and lower the entire wrist structure, therefore providing pitch. Figs. 2-13 and 2-14 help to clarify the construction of this wrist design. You can also see from the photographs that the hand is controlled by a third shaft through the middle of the wrist gear mechanism, therefore providing a powered hand without the need for slip rings at the joint.

Wrist mechanisms provide another degree of freedom for the hand in a robot system. Thus the aim here has been to present a varied number of mechanical drive systems and propose several design constraints about which you need to be concerned. If, however, the object

you wish your robot to reach is still farther away, provide it with an extendable arm.

ARM DESIGN

When attempting to provide extendable reach in a robot system, there are several designs to take into consideration. One approach that comes to mind is the humanoid arm. Here we have a two part mechanism: forearm and upper arm, or biceps. Between these is the elbow. Other methods also involve extendable telescoping tubes.

The elbow is a complex joint. Mechanically it provides only pitch-like motion yet consider, if you will, that the same formula applies to the elbow that we used to determine work for the wrist. Consider also that a humanoid forearm is approximately 9 inches long, and that it is multiplied by the weight of the payload plus a hand and a wrist! The resulting inch-pounds necessary would take a rather large motor to produce movement. Move forward up the arm to the shoulder. Here is yet another 9 inches plus the weight of the elbow! Are we building a monster?

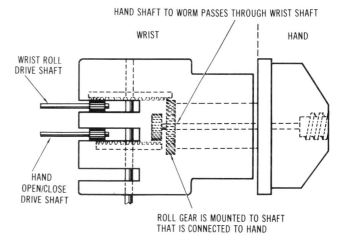

Fig. 2-12 Wrist design of Tomy Toys Armatron toy robot arm.

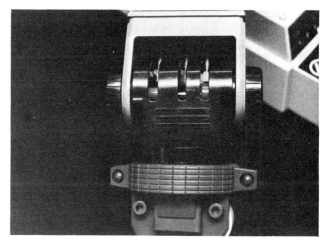

Fig. 2-13 Photograph of Armatron wrist.

Fig. 2-14 Another view of Armatron wrist showing internal gearing.

Not really! Let's look at methods of gearing in the elbow that can decrease the size of the motor. Your best approach for elbow operation is the worm gear method. Why the worm gear? Well, there is a phenomenon that occurs with motors when they are de-energized . . . they slip! If you use a spur gear to spur gear arrangement, however, to raise the forearm say 90°, when you stop the motor, the arm will drop. A worm-gear mechanism, though, doesn't allow the driven gear to move when the worm stops.

Physically, the gear threads are at right angles to each other. Thus, you have a locking mechanism. There are other methods to achieve locking that we will explore later.

Fig. 2-15 depicts a typical worm-gear-driven elbow mechanism. There is a different formula used to determine strength (force) and speed when using a worm gear. Let's explore the equation:

$$\text{Elbow Speed (rpm)} = \frac{\text{worm speed}}{\text{No. teeth in elbow gear}}$$

If the motor that turns the worm screw is rotating at 3600 rpm (typical slot car motor), and there are 50 teeth in the gear attached to the elbow joint, the elbow speed will be 72 rpm, much too fast! An elbow should raise and lower about three times faster than a clock second hand, or 3 rpm. Of course, if you could guarantee the elbow could halt on a split second, you might get away with a faster speed. The easiest way to reduce the speed in the elbow is to start with a slower motor. Chapter 4 has instructions for selecting motors that are already speed reduced for applications such as these.

The force needed to lift the arm is calculated for the worm gear using the following formula:

$$\text{Work} = \frac{\text{force (lbs)}}{\text{worm screw}} \times \frac{\text{radius of}}{\text{screw}} \times \frac{\text{TAN pitch}}{\text{angle}}$$

By now you may be ready to give up. Bear with it, there is more:

$$\frac{\text{Force (lbs)}}{\text{worm screw}} = 6.28 \times \frac{\text{radius of screw}}{\text{pitch of threads}}$$

Using the second formula, you can find part of the first, but you still need physical information about the screw. First, measure the diameter of the worm screw and divide it in half to get the radius. Then measure the distance between the threads of the screw to obtain its pitch. With this information, you can obtain the force that the worm screw can produce. To find the pitch angle, simply transpose the first equation, as follows:

$$\frac{\text{TAN Pitch Angle}} = \frac{\text{force (lbs)}}{\dfrac{\text{worm screw} \times \text{radius of screw}}{\text{Work}}}$$

Most of the physical information about worm screws can be found in catalogs containing stock gears. Begin by designing your robot arm using real weights of previously designed mechanical hands and wrists. Then, using appropriate catalogs, pick a worm drive system that matches your design numbers. It's as simple as that. Listing 2-2 is another section of the design program that provides the worm-gear calculations for your personal computer.

CABLE-DRIVE SYSTEMS

Another method for an elbow mechanism is a cable-drive system. As previously mentioned, cable systems are used in both hands and wrists. They offer the advantage of not having the heavy controllable motion elements placed out at the joints. As you can now appreciate, this saves on work, therefore reducing power and expense. Let's look at a typical cable-drive elbow in Fig. 2-16.

Notice that one end of the cable is fixed at the forearm, the other end is looped around and tied to a pulley

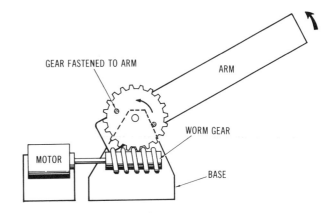

Fig. 2-15 Elbow mechanism using a worm-gear technique.

```
400 CLS:PRINT"WORM GEAR DESIGN"
410 PRINT:PRINT"SELECT THE FOLLOWING:"
420 PRINT:PRINT"1) WORM SPEED"
425 PRINT"2) WORM WORK FORMULA"
430 PRINT"3) PITCH ANGLE FORMULA"
440 A$=INKEY$:IF A$="" THEN 440
450 IF A$="1" THEN 500
455 IF A$="2" THEN 600
460 IF A$="3" THEN 700
470 GOTO 400
500 CLS:PRINT"WORM SPEED"
510 PRINT:PRINT"ENTER WORM DRIVE SPEED:"
520 INPUT"RPM";A
530 PRINT:PRINT"ENTER NUMBER OF TEETH IN DRIVEN GEAR:"
540 INPUT B:S=A/B
550 CLS:PRINT"WORM DRIVE SPEED=";S;"RPM"
560 PRINT:PRINT"<SPACE> FOR ANOTHER,<ENTER> FOR MENU"
570 A$=INKEY$:IF A$="" THEN 570
580 IF A$=" " THEN GOTO 400 ELSE GOTO 10
600 CLS:PRINT"WORM WORK FORMULA"
610 PRINT:PRINT"ENTER DIAMETER OF DRIVE SCREW:"
620 INPUT"INCHES";A:R=A/2
630 PRINT:PRINT"ENTER PITCH OF THREADS:"
640 INPUT"INCHES";P
650 FW=(6.28*R)/P
660 PRINT:PRINT"ENTER PITCH ANGLE:"
670 INPUT"DEGREES";PA
680 W=FW*R*TAN(PA)
690 CLS:PRINT"WORK=";W;"INCH-POUNDS"
692 PRINT:PRINT"<SPACE> FOR ANOTHER,<ENTER> FOR MENU"
695 A$=INKEY$:IF A$="" THEN 695
697 IF A$=" " THEN GOTO 400 ELSE GOTO 10
700 CLS:PRINT" PITCH ANGLE FORMULA"
710 PRINT:PRINT"ENTER DIAMETER OF DRIVE SCREW:"
720 INPUT"INCHES";A:R=A/2
730 PRINT:PRINT"ENTER PITCH OF THREADS:"
740 INPUT"INCHES";P
750 PRINT:PRINT"ENTER WORK AMOUNT:"
760 INPUT"INCH-POUNDS";W
770 PA=(((6.28*R)/P)*R)/W
780 CLS:PRINT"PITCH ANGLE=";PA;"DEGREES"
790 PRINT:PRINT"<SPACE> FOR ANOTHER,<ENTER> FOR MENU"
795 A$=INKEY$:IF A$="" THEN 795
797 IF A$=" " THEN 400 ELSE GOTO 10
```

Listing 2-2 Worm-Gear Design

attached to a motor. As the motor turns, the forearm raises or lowers. The distance the arm moves depends not only on how much cable the motor takes in or lets out but on how tight the cable tension is. Other types of cable systems that use either bands or chains are shown in Fig. 2-17. When cables or bands are used in this type of mechanism, slip must be considered just as was with the wrist. Timing belts or V-grooved bands should be considered. If you expect a very large load on the arm, chain and sprocket drive may be best. This type drive is what is used extensively in bicycles. You can purchase all the necessary belts, bands, and drive chains from distributors of several manufacturers. I have included names and addresses in the appendix under "Parts Suppliers."

ARM STRUCTURE

This may seem an inappropriate time to get into body work but before we abandon the elbow style arm let's consider the shape of the arm and the structure of the elbow. Keep in mind that material strength is most important ahead of weight and cost. Fig. 2-18 depicts one type of forearm-elbow structure. This author tends to use dowel-like arm construction. The arm shown in Fig. 2-19 uses a powerful stepper motor to raise and lower the

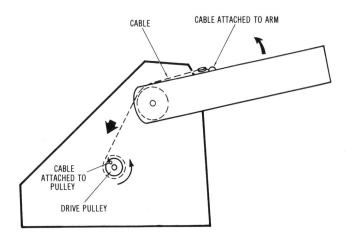

Fig. 2-16 Tethered cable design approach for raising the elbow.

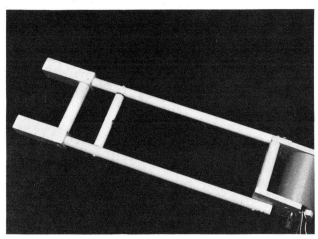

Fig. 2-19 Photograph of pine and dowel biceps. (Notice stepper motor in lower right corner.)

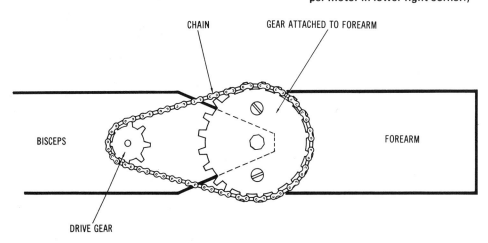

Fig. 2-17 Chain and spur-gear elbow design.

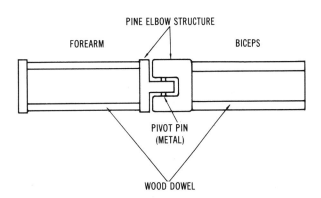

Fig. 2-18 Elbow pivot using wood dowels and small strips of pine.

elbow. Notice how the motor, mounted at the elbow, will fit together with the biceps.

Other design concepts can now be considered. Let's look at various mechanical solutions for the arm structure design problem. Fig. 2-20 shows the structure of a cable-driven arm using metal tubes. It might be cautioned

here that this structure may not hold up under some stress situations. However, the structure is light, sound, and economical.

Fig. 2-21 depicts the structure of the Mini Mover arm by Microbot. This structure is made of lightweight metal bent into an inverted "U" shape. Pulleys and cables are therefore neatly hidden from view. Stepper motors mounted in the base provide drive to the cable system.

The space shuttle utilizes the tube structure (Fig. 2-22) to accomplish its design as well. In fact, the weight of the shuttle arm is so heavy, compared to the lightweight material that makes up its structure, that it would crush itself here on earth! This is another example of design by taking into account the environment of operation. In the case of the shuttle, the environment is gravity-free and, therefore, the ratio between structure strength and payload weight is practically irrelevant.

The SANDHU Rhino®* XR-1 arm structure is fabri-

----

* RHINO XR-1 is a registered trademark of Rhino Robots, Inc.

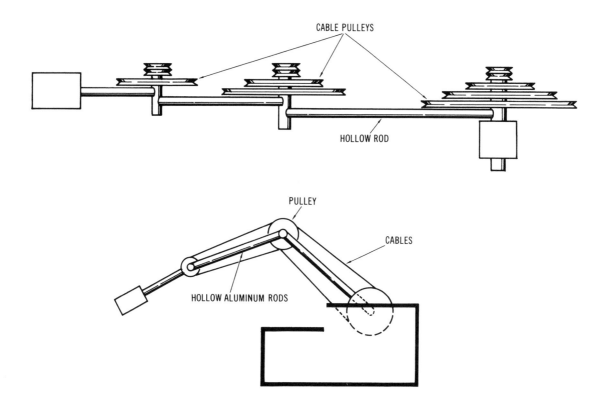

Fig. 2-20 Arm using pulleys.

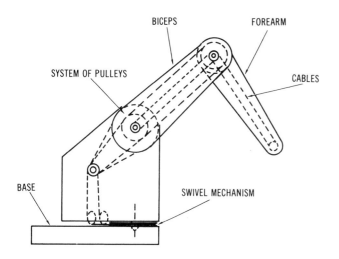

Fig. 2-21 Mini Mover arm design uses tethered cables.

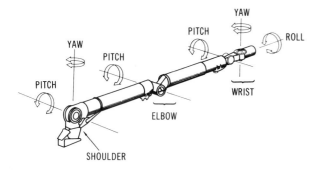

Fig. 2-22 Space Shuttle arm design.

cated from lightweight aircraft aluminum (Fig. 2-23). Here we see that both the chain and cable-drive methods have been incorporated simultaneously. Once again, the drive motors are located in the base assembly.

Finally, the Armatron robot from TOMY Toys incorporates a unique yaw mechanism for an elbow (Fig. 2-24). Here the elbow does not lift or lower the forearm. It works, instead, in the horizontal axis to provide a sort of yaw to the wrist-forearm structure. Hard plastic rectangular tubing is used as the structural component.

Arms that contain elbows are very popular. They seem to possess the greatest amount of freedom of movement. If your design doesn't require this amount of freedom, there are other methods that can achieve elbow-like extension.

TELESCOPING ARM DESIGN

Many of the Unimate-class robots seen on television being used in factories around the world consist of an arm with a shoulder that rotates. The robot picks up parts from one surface, rotates 90° and places them on another. Needless to say, these are called pick and place robots!

The hand on these pick and placers is extendable by a telescoping forearm. This forearm is maneuvered much like the hideaway antenna on an automobile. There are many ways to accomplish this action so let's investigate some of them.

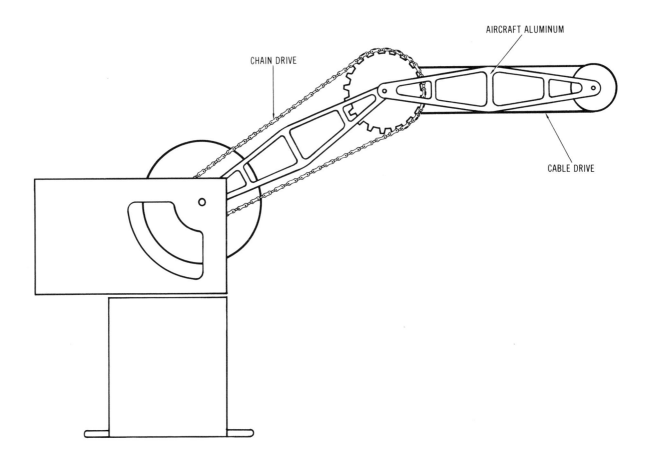

CHAIN DRIVE

AIRCRAFT ALUMINUM

CABLE DRIVE

Fig. 2-23 The Sandhu arm uses a combination chain- and cable-drive system.

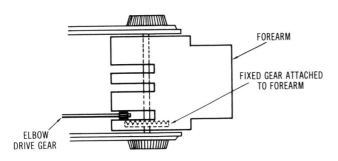

FOREARM

FIXED GEAR ATTACHED
TO FOREARM

ELBOW
DRIVE GEAR

Fig. 2-24 Elbow design for Armatron toy robot arm.

Remember the lead-screw mechanism briefly discussed in Chapter 1? We saw a screw-threaded shaft turned by a motor device. A carriage threaded with the same screw thread rode on that screw. Taking this one step further, let's mount the carriage inside a tube (Fig. 2-25). The carriage and tube become one piece. Now, fit a slightly larger tube over the carriage tube. Attach the larger tube and call it the biceps. The carriage tube now becomes the forearm. This by itself will not work because as the lead screw is turned, so will the carriage. In order for the carriage to travel, we must restrict its rotary movement (remember the shop vise?). This can be accomplished in a few different ways.

Restricting motion of the carriage can be accomplished if you provide a pin that protrudes out of the carriage tube into a slot that runs lengthwise along the outer tube. Because this slot would decrease rigidity of the outer tube, it is not recommended. Another method is to mount another two-tube mechanism along side the first and fasten the two inner tubes together at the wrist point, as shown in Fig. 2-25B.

Lead-screw mechanics requires yet another formula to determine the force necessary to provide the work. Consider the relationships in Eq. 2-1. Here the distance to travel will be the length you wish the forearm to extend or retract. The number of revolutions the gear or lead screw must travel can be obtained by finding the thread of the screw. If you are using a $1/4 \times 10$ screw, it has 20 threads to the inch. The last part of the equation is 2π which is equal to 6.28 (look familiar?). Let's assume a distance of 9 inches for travel and enter the equation with a 3 pound total for the hand, wrist, and payload. Fig. 2-26B illustrates what transpires.

The 0.382 inch-ounce torque required is well within the range of most motors. Now you can see the advantage of lead-screw mechanisms. It should be pointed out that these numbers are worst case in that we are designing for the maximum pull in the worst position (straight down).

Equation 2-1 Force Required

$$\frac{\text{weight of payload}}{\text{(hand, wrist, object)}} \times \frac{\text{distance}}{\text{to travel}} =$$

$$\frac{\text{force}}{\text{required}} \times \frac{\text{no. gear revs.}}{\text{to traverse distance}} \times \frac{2 \pi}{\text{(or 6.28)}}$$

$$\frac{3 \text{ lbs.}}{\text{(payload)}} \times 9 \text{ in.} =$$

$$\frac{\text{force}}{\text{required}} \times \frac{180}{(20/\text{in.} \times 9 \text{ in.})} \times 6.28$$

$$27 \text{ in.-lbs.} = \frac{\text{force}}{\text{required}} \times 1130.4$$

$$\frac{27 \text{ in.-lbs.}}{1130.4} = \frac{\text{force}}{\text{required}}$$

$$.024 \text{ in.-lbs.} = \frac{\text{force}}{\text{required}}$$

$$.024 \text{ in.-lbs.} \times 16 \text{ oz.} = \frac{\text{force}}{\text{required}}$$

$$.382 \text{ in. oz. } \dagger = \frac{\text{force}}{\text{required}}$$

† Typical unit of measure for small motors.

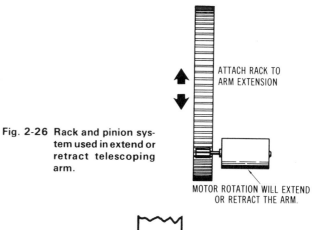

Fig. 2-26 Rack and pinion system used in extend or retract telescoping arm.

ATTACH RACK TO ARM EXTENSION

MOTOR ROTATION WILL EXTEND OR RETRACT THE ARM.

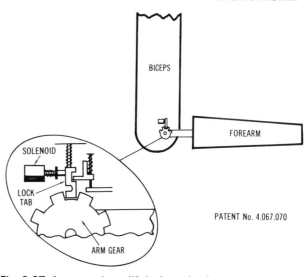

BICEPS

FOREARM

SOLENOID

LOCK TAB

ARM GEAR

PATENT No. 4.067.070

Fig. 2-27 A patented arm lift-lock mechanism.

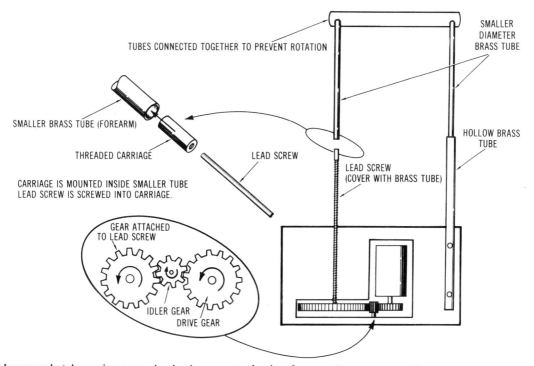

TUBES CONNECTED TOGETHER TO PREVENT ROTATION

SMALLER DIAMETER BRASS TUBE

SMALLER BRASS TUBE (FOREARM)

THREADED CARRIAGE

LEAD SCREW

CARRIAGE IS MOUNTED INSIDE SMALLER TUBE LEAD SCREW IS SCREWED INTO CARRIAGE.

LEAD SCREW (COVER WITH BRASS TUBE)

HOLLOW BRASS TUBE

GEAR ATTACHED TO LEAD SCREW

IDLER GEAR

DRIVE GEAR

Fig. 2-25 A homemade telescoping arm using lead-screw mechanism from reading pacer machine.

```
300 CLS:PRINT"LEAD SCREW MECHANICS"
310 PRINT:PRINT"ENTER WEIGHT OF PAYLOAD:"
315 INPUT"LBS";W
320 PRINT:PRINT"ENTER DISTANCE OF TOTAL TRAVEL:"
325 INPUT"INCHES";D
330 PRINT:PRINT"ENTER SCREW THREAD TYPE:"
335 INPUT ST
340 GR=ST*D
350 F=((W*D)/(GR*6.28))*16
360 CLS:PRINT"TORQUE REQUIRED=";F;"OUNCE-INCHES"
370 PRINT:PRINT"<SPACE>FOR ANOTHER,<ENTER> FOR MENU"
380 A$=INKEY$:IF A$="" THEN 880
390 IF A$=" " THEN 800 ELSE GOTO 10
```

Listing 2-3 Lead Screw Mechanism

This equation adds to our overall design program through the inclusion of computer Listing 2-3.

There are other methods for telescoping arms. You could use a stiff band which, when unraveled, serves to push the arm outward or, when the band is rolled up, it pulls the arm inward. This method is commonly used to position the magnetic read-write head of mini floppy-disc drives.

Another mechanism worthy of note is the rack and pinion gear system. The rack gear can mount on the forearm with the pinion gear powered by a motor. Fig. 2-26 shows an arm using the rack and pinion gear mechanism.

LIFT LOCKS

As promised earlier in this chapter, we will now cover other locking mechanisms for arms. Over the last few years, researchers have considered the problems of lift locks for artificial arms worn by humans. Out of this research have come a few patents. One such device called a "Prosthetic Joint Lock and Cable Mechanism" patent #4,067,070 has a solenoid-driven mechanical bar that engages a gear which stops the arm motion (Fig. 2-27). If you want to design a lock device and not violate any known patent, just provide holes in the structure of the forearm-elbow mechanism so that a lock shaft may be extended to serve as a detent. When designing the shaft and mechanism take into account the weight or stress that will be placed on the shaft.

As you probably know, there are many other arm mechanisms. New methods are being designed every day. With the information provided here, it is hoped that you are able to design the one that suits your needs. Separate space for the coverage of the shoulder was not provided because it is just another elbow. The same equations apply to both. With the manipulator mechanism defined, let's move on to the structure that supports all this . . . the base.

Section II:
ELECTROMECHANICS

Chapter 3

Base/Leg Considerations

This chapter will either be extremely important or worth skipping over. It really depends on what your robot will be like. If you intend for your machine to be immobile or to be just an arm, then you don't need to be concerned here. However, if your plans include the ability to travel across a room, or simply rotate between work stations, then you had best read on.

BASE

The base of the robot can assume many shapes. For example, a simple base structure for a robot that consists only of an arm could be a standard tripod with hardware on which to mount the arm unit. A base primarily serves as a mounting surface for the various mechanical components and sometimes the electronics.

There are no mathematical guidelines to follow for selecting a base structure except to keep in mind that the weight of the material used may add to the overall structure. If you intend for the robot to be mobile, this will be a greater concern. As always, never conserve weight if it means skimping on the structural ability of the base to perform its duty.

If you are a relative newcomer to robotics, it might be helpful to examine some of the base structures in use on today's robots. Let's start with the simple arm-structure units. Many of the robots "employed" in our factories only consist of an arm. Fig. 3-1 shows some details of several base structures.

Some of the bases in the figure allow rotational movement about the vertical axis. This gives the arm the ability to reach around a 360° area. Let's investigate a mecha-

nism that allows us to achieve this freedom of motion. The mechanism used in the rotational platform of Fig. 3-2 is very simple. Two small motors are physically mounted to a base that is basically a rotating disc or lazy susan. On the shafts of the motors are small rubber wheels that contact with the surface beneath the lazy susan. When the motors are turning in the same direc-

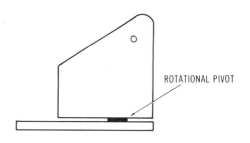

(A) Microbot base.

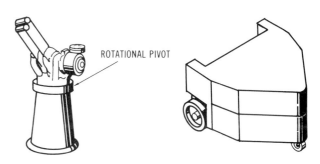

(B) Cincinnati Milacron T3 base.   (C) Hilare Robot (France).

Fig. 3-1 Various robot base designs.

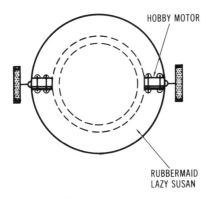

(A) Top view.

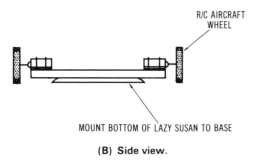

(B) Side view.

Fig. 3-2 Simple rotating-base design using two hobby motors and a lazy susan.

tion, they provide a means of turning the rotary base. Momentarily connecting the motors to rotate in opposite directions will provide a sort of break.

Fig. 3-3 shows a homemade rotation platform that uses a chain and sprocket approach. Notice that once again the lazy susan base mechanism is utilized.

Other methods of achieving rotary motion are outlined in Chapter 2. In particular, the roll-wrist designs provide a similar make-up to rotary bases. The methods include

Fig. 3-3 Home-constructed chain-drive rotating mechanism using plastic chain gearing and commercially purchased lazy susan by Rubbermaid.

the worm-gear drive and spur-gear drive covered in both Chapter 1 and Chapter 2.

Another device worthy of note is the ratchet and pawl drive. This method is new and was not included as a mechanism for either hands or arms because, in many instances, it does not make a reliable device. A closer look at how a ratchet and pawl mechanism operates will point out its deficiencies. Fig. 3-4 shows its inner workings.

The electromagnetic coil (solenoid), when energized, will pull the claw-like hook of the pawl in so that it effectively disengages the pawl. When the coil is de-energized, the claw will push the ratchet gear ahead one tooth. Rotary motion, or near nonstop turning, can be achieved by feeding the coil a constant stream of on-off-on pulses. Electronic control of this and other motion devices is covered in depth in Chapter 4.

Examine Fig. 3-4 closely and when you understand the principles involved, you will think of several uses for it. Some of its advantages are that it can move a precise distance with one pulse; when the pulse stops, so does the motion. Also, when it stops it is effectively locked in place

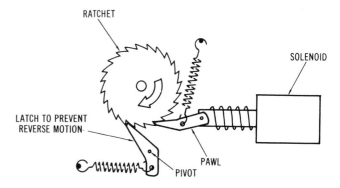

Fig. 3-4 Basic design of ratchet-and-pawl mechanism.

mechanically by the pawl, which gives it good holding stability without the need for holding power.

The main disadvantage is the fact that you cannot reverse direction. At least, in this particular design you won't be able to turn right, then left. If the ratchet had teeth designed to accept two pawls, one for forward and the other for reverse, it might work. In this case your mechanism would need two coils and a circuit that assumed only one coil would be energized at a time.

So much for rotation. I think you get the picture on the how's and why's of turning a base. Of course, you could leave the base stationary and use wheels to move the entire robot. We will cover "rovers" later in this chapter, but first, let's investigate the ability to raise and lower a platform.

LIFTING BODIES

Anyone opening the book at this point would think it might be about physical fitness. Actually, you do have to build some muscles into your robot if you want to give it the ability to raise and lower a platform. What use would this be good for? Well, if you were to build a housepainting robot, a stock-room robot, or an inspection platform machine, the ability to extend vertically could be useful. Let's stop thinking big and assume maybe you would like to raise a light sensor or extend an antenna. All these things require up and down motion. How should you go about it?

Remember what was learned about raising arms and extending fingers? Believe it or not, the same mechanism will lift and lower. There is one mechanism that works extremely well in a lifting platform—the jack screw.

Jack screws are used to lift cars in service bays to get to the underneath side. We can use them, too. Examine the mechanics of the jack screw illustrated in Fig. 3-5. The

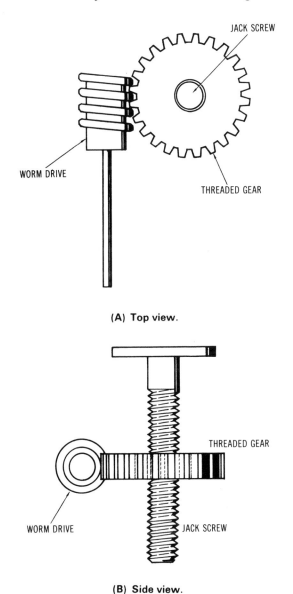

(A) Top view.

(B) Side view.

Fig. 3-5 Internal detail of jack-screw lift system.

shaft that is driven by a motor is a horizontal worm-like screw. The gear it meshes with is threaded inside and raises or lowers the screw-threaded shaft. A platform or sensor may be mounted to this shaft.

Other methods could be used to accomplish the same action. Try to design a lifting system using the rack and pinion gear described in Chapter 1. As you will see, in-out motion is accomplished with the same actuators. Learn one and you will understand the other. Keep in mind that gravity plays a big part in the weight you are lifting and design for worst-case situations.

Well, that about covers the ways we can move a stationary base about an axis. This base can take any shape that might be useful. Coverings and supporting structures, such as heads, arm coverings, and base shrouds, may be considered as parts of the body.

BODIES

It really doesn't matter what is used for cosmetic coverup. The body or outer shell of the robot may be as simple or as absurd as you wish. Some robot structures use the outer surface to mount sensors and electrical control panels. We'll not try to influence the outward appearance of your robot by applying any technical preconditions. There are cylindrical, triangular, square, tubular, and squat flat robots. The form fits the function.

You can use linoleum, aluminum, plastic, cardboard, foam core board, or even a household trash can. The skeletal structure beneath any of these coverings should be a firm mount for the arms—if used, the sensors (to be discussed in Chapter 5), and any electronics necessary to control these systems. The power source, be it battery, solar, or plug-in ac, should be considered during the design of the body shape. Try to keep the weight close to the ground—that is, if the robot is to be used on the ground. Sounds crazy? Examine the body structure of the ceiling mounted robot in Fig. 3-6. This design doesn't waste floor space, yet it is very versatile. The robot swivels 360° and has the capability to raise and lower its "hand" in a 180° arc. This particular robot is manufactured by KUKA, a European firm, that has an outlet here in the United States called Expert Automation of Michigan.

One last consideration, when designing the body, is whether it is necessary to carry the upper portion of the robot level at all times to the horizontal. In most cases, this will not be a necessity, however, in case you come across that requirement, you should learn about self-leveling mechanisms and shock absorbers. Admittedly, shocks won't keep your robot level, but they do smooth out the bumps. If commercial shock absorbers won't fit the requirement, look into shock-absorbing material, such as rubber, foam, and coiled springs.

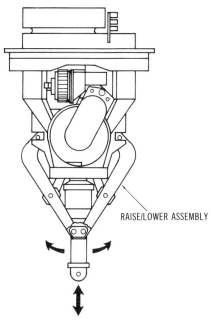

(A) Side view.

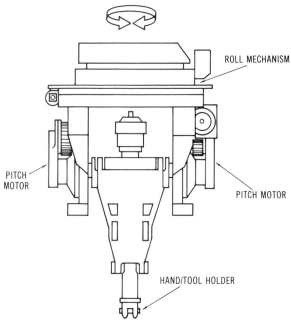

(B) Front view.

Fig. 3-6 Kuka ceilng-mount robot design.

MOTION

Giving a robot the capability to move about is not a trivial task. Many things have to be considered. The distance you expect it to have to travel and the way in which it travels that distance determines the method you will use. Let's consider a robot that must travel the length of a production line picking up parts and distributing them somewhere else.

There is no need for complex turn mechanisms as the motion is backward and forward. Why not just mount four wheels and a motor and call it even? There are many considerations to be made that involve the surface over which you wish to traverse. Why the surface? Because, like gravity, the surface of a floor can cause resistance to the movement of the wheel. When taken into account initially, you can design for this resistance and not encounter problems. Let's look at some methods of calculating this resistance.

First, let's assume the surface is a hard wooden floor. If the wheels are made of hard rubber, like the tires of a tricycle, and there is no wind blowing, then the slightest push of force will move the robot. This, however, is very idealistic. Introduce a half inch pile rug and much greater forces are required.

$$\text{resistance} = \frac{\text{force} \times \text{radius of wheel}}{\text{weight of robot}}$$

This formula can be applied to determine the resistance to a wheeled platform. Of course, you would have to know the force needed first. In that case, enter a force in pounds that you can achieve, given the motion you are expecting to use. If you don't know then don't worry about it now, because motors and the power required to make them move objects will be discussed in detail in the next chapter.

Let's move on to the mechanical aspects of a four-wheeled robot. Fig. 3-7 shows a typical two-wheel drive and two-wheel steering platform. Notice the gear train design of the rear wheels. This arrangement allows a small motor to achieve greater pushing power. Reverse motion is accomplished by simply reversing the power leads to the motor. In the case of our production line robot, the front wheels would be stationary, yet free to turn.

What if we want our robot to turn 90° left or right? The front wheels must be mounted on a pivot. This assembly will have to be controlled by yet another motor. This time some fancy mechanics must be designed to turn your wheels. Consider the approach used in Fig. 3-8. Here is a design using a steering system that has a spur gear arrangement. Although this approach will work, there are better ones. Rack and pinion steering has been used in cars for some time and the drawing in Fig. 3-9 illustrates how to use it effectively in your robot design.

Other approaches will work using the design information previously supplied on worm gearing. As you can see, whenever you need a turning action, just fall back on the basic mechanisms.

If you can achieve your design goal using three wheels, things get a little easier. After all, turning one wheel is

42

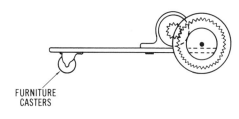

(A) Side view.

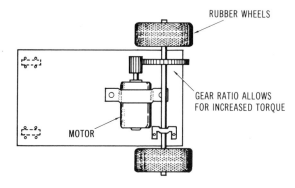

(B) Top view.

Fig. 3-7 Design of simple four-wheeled mobile cart, the front two wheels do not steer.

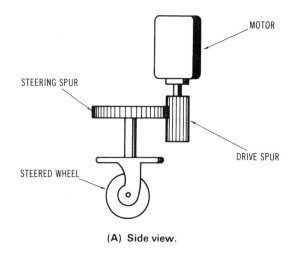

(A) Side view.

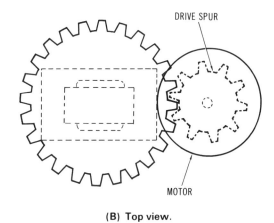

(B) Top view.

Fig. 3-8 Simple motor-driven steering mechanism using spur gears.

mechanically easier than two. Fig. 3-10 shows how a wheel mounted directly to the shaft of a hobby motor is used to steer a three-wheeled vehicle. After going over all these methods to steer a wheel or set of wheels, there is actually an easier way to control the direction of a two-wheeled rover without the use of any other powered wheels. Let's examine the tank.

TWO-WHEELED DRIVE

In actuality, the tank has many wheels. However, for the purpose of this discussion the treads of a tank act as two independent wheels. If we want to emulate the motion of a tank, we can do so with two wheels each one separate and each powered by its own individual motor. Consider the wheeled platform in Fig. 3-11. Notice, if you will, that when both wheels are moving in the same direction, the platform goes forward, or reverses, in a straight line. Reversing the direction of only one of the motors causes the platform to turn either right or left.

This type of vehicle is probably the most versatile of the roving designs. It is helpful if you provide a third wheel to balance the craft, otherwise it can tip. A simple motion platform can be constructed using slot-car motors and a piece of wood. Fig. 3-12 depicts one that was constructed by the author in an evening.

Directly attaching the motors to the wheels is not the most efficient means of transportation. Some gearing should be provided to reduce the speed of the motors to where the robot travels at a slow enough rate of speed for

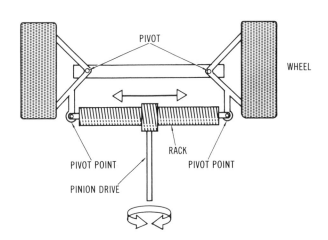

Fig. 3-9 Rack and pinion steering system.

stable control. It also helps to provide the starting strength to move the mass of the robot body. Let's investigate a commercial toy to see how the mechanical design is accomplished.

Figs. 3-13 and 3-14 show the gear box of Milton Brad-

43

Fig. 3-10 Photograph of simple motor-driven steering wheel.

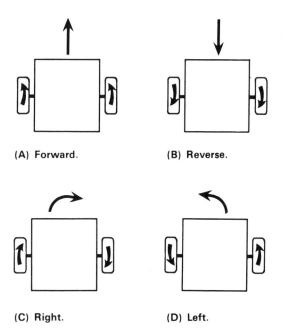

(A) Forward.

(B) Reverse.

(C) Right.

(D) Left.

Fig. 3-11 Basic mechanics of two-wheel drive.

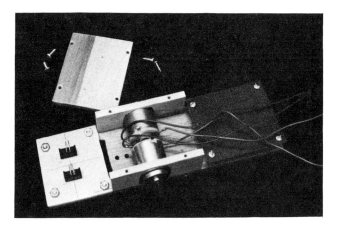

Fig. 3-12 Simple two-wheel roving mechanism using hobby motors and wooden construction.

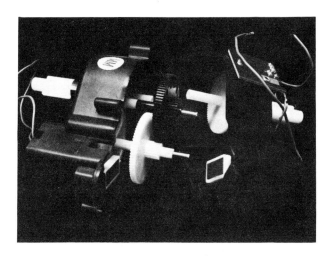

Fig. 3-13 Big Trak gear box.

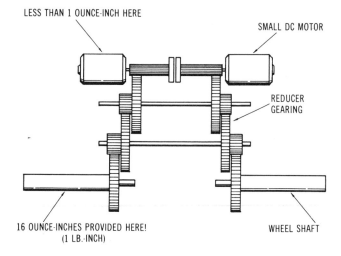

Fig. 3-14 Internal gearing system for the Big Trak drive train.

ley's Big Trak®*. This toy is essentially a two-wheel drive platform with sophisticated electronics to control its motion. The black gear in Fig. 3-13 is used for position sensing. The optical position sensor is located at the upper right in the drawing. Studying the gear relationships here will give you some good insight into the many ways to accomplish motion. The toy and its associated controller will be covered extensively in the chapter on motion control.

So far, we have been concerned only with motion over a flat surface, such as a road or floor. There are many more concerns when the need is to traverse a hill or a

*Big Trak is a registered trademark of Milton Bradley.

flight of stairs. If you need to accomplish this type of motion, you should look into the true tank traction method of the tread.

A treaded vehicle is basically a two-wheeled system where each side is covered with a long band equipped with cleats (see Fig. 3-15). Mechanical design of treads or treaded vehicles is beyond the scope of this book. In fact, it is not easy to obtain data or parts for tread systems. Therefore, if they can be avoided they probably should be. Other traversing mechanisms have been developed by NASA for use in harsh terrains. Some of these approaches involve wheels made of a sponge-like aluminum mesh, while others possess a much more familiar method of traction.

mine the order in which the legs walk. Consider the drawing and observations in Fig. 3-16.

The patterns of the feet, as they contact the floor, are known as the *gait* or the walk. These patterns have been analyzed to occur in the order presented in the diagram. It would seem, if we were to make a mechanical representation of this gait, that we would have a walker.

Let's look at some mechanical methods used in the university robots mentioned earlier. The Hexapod knee joint is basically a worm-gear system connected to the motor of an electric drill (Fig. 3-17). The action of this joint is illustrated also in the figure. Note the many states in Fig. 3-16 that each leg must go through to complete one stroke.

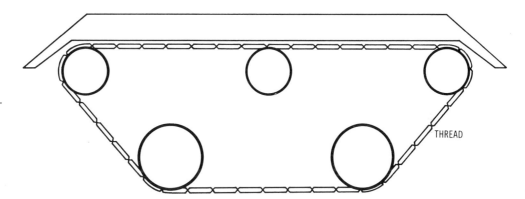

Fig. 3-15 Tank tread design.

THREAD

LEGS

This subject, as it relates to robotics, is quite controversial. You have seen science fiction movies of the robot that emerges from the space craft walking on two legs. Or perhaps you've marveled at the four-legged destruction machines of a recent *Star Wars* film. Is it actually possible to build a walking robot? The answer is yes, but not easily.

First, you must study the mechanics involved in walking. This includes not just which leg swings out first but the physical relationships between each leg during all phases of the walk. Human two-legged, or biped, walking is probably the hardest to emulate. The reason for the difficulty is found in the fact that a lot of balance must be accomplished between leg movements.

Let's start from the beginning. Some years ago several students at Ohio State University set out to build a six-legged walking machine they called Hexapod. Each leg had a few degrees of freedom and the whole assembly was controlled by a rather large minicomputer external to the legged unit.

Several quadrapeds (four-legged) have been constructed over the years since the Hexapod as have a few bipeds. For a first attempt, let's study the mechanics of a four-legged dog emulator. It will be necessary for us to deter-

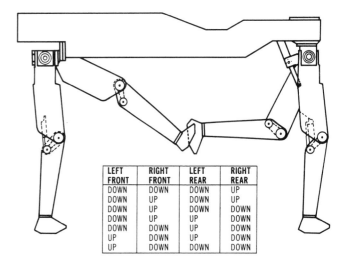

LEFT FRONT	RIGHT FRONT	LEFT REAR	RIGHT REAR
DOWN	DOWN	DOWN	UP
DOWN	UP	DOWN	UP
DOWN	UP	DOWN	DOWN
DOWN	UP	UP	DOWN
DOWN	DOWN	UP	DOWN
UP	DOWN	UP	DOWN
UP	DOWN	DOWN	DOWN

Fig. 3-16 Basic walker design patterned after a GE four-legged walking system.

You will find, quickly, that if you construct a system using sticks for legs, it will exert a very wobbly motion. This is because there is no give in the pelvic area. Look at your hips while you walk. They are actually moving up and down, forward and back. Roll an egg down a slight hill and record, if you can, the motion of the ends. This is

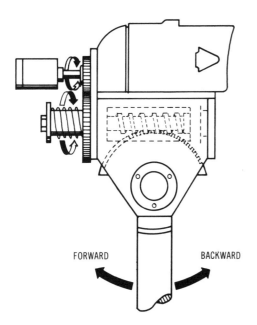

Fig. 3-17 Ohio State University Hexapod walker design showing worm-screw action of the knee.

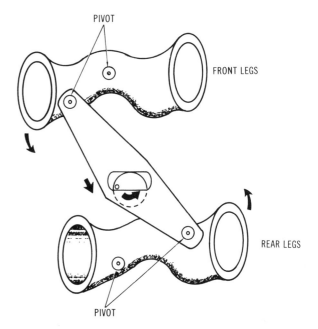

Fig. 3-19 Mechanical details of the walking turtle.

very close to the mechanical movements you should develop for the structure that is to hold the legs.

Walking is not easy. It is a highly complex mechanical system, however, there are short cuts. Have you ever bought one of those wind-up walking toys? Do so. The education you can get is amazing. Let's investigate three types of these toys in order to get some ideas for a walker design. We'll start with a quadraped.

Fig. 3-18 shows the inner workings of a toy turtle made by TOMY Toys. This toy, when wound up, actually walks across a table. It is very easy to scale up the mechanical design presented here for use in our robot systems. Fig. 3-19 discloses the mechanical aspects of the turtle. Notice how the simple rotary motion of the motor is transferred by a cam into the linear motion of leg movement. The legs actually scrape forward and reverse instead of lifting.

Fig. 3-20 shows two methods of accomplishing biped

movement. The first is a walking lion by TOMY Toys. The mechanism is similar to the turtle in that a cam is fitted to the shaft of a rotating motor and the cam moves the leg forward, around, and back. The second method, the two sneakers by TOMY Toys, is very simplistic in that they are connected to a suitably bent drive shaft. One sneaker contains the drive motor, the other simply follows.

These design examples are presented only to stimulate your mind when designing actual walking systems. It is suggested that you stay with the basic rolling platform

Fig. 3-18 Photograph of the inside of walking toy turtle from
Tomy Toys.

Fig. 3-20 Typical walking toys by Tomy Toys.

46

ideas until you are well versed in the ways of mechanics. Walker control is very complex and has been the subject of many a doctoral thesis. Perhaps, in a later book, we will go over the design in greater detail.

ROVING ROBOTS WITHOUT WHEELS

Nothing says the robot we design has to be either automobile-like or walk like a dog. There are other very usable motion mechanisms available.

It really depends on the floor or traveling surface that the robot must traverse. What about tracks? It sure is easy to guide our machine using the railroad technique; especially if the distance is short. A path for the machine to follow could be constructed using standard track design or the use of one track like that of the monorail could be considered.

Yes it still needs wheels, gears, and motors, but wait until you find out what it takes to keep a rover moving in a straight line. Tracks take care of that. You could also use a cable system like that in use on the trolleys in San Francisco to pull the robot along.

As you can see, once again, there is no right answer or one approach for developing robot mechanics. The number of physical combinations is limited to the imagination of the designer. The only real constraints encountered are weight, power, and available motion devices.

These controllable motion devices that have been mentioned since Chapter 1 are the subject of the next chapter. Many of the mysteries and questions you might have should be answered in Chapter 4. You will see how the mechanics in these first three chapters fit into controllable systems.

Controllable Motion Devices

Throughout these first three chapters, controllable-motion devices such as motors, solenoids or other electromechanical components were mentioned. This chapter will familiarize you with the actions of these very critical components and introduce you to the electrical interfaces required to control them. In this chapter, electronic circuits are used in the design of robot systems. For the rest of the book this will be the rule rather than the exception, because it is here in the development of robotics that the two fields of mechanical and electrical technology meet.

MOTORS

Basically speaking, motors convert electrical energy into rotary motion. Some motors are designed to convert rotary motion into linear travel. As you might have noticed, the motor plays a big part in the design of electric robots. So far, we have shown them used in hands, wrists, arms, wheeled bases, and legs. Later, we will investigate their use to position various sensors and scanners.

It is not intended to go over the actual physical theory of how motors work in this book. If you feel uncomfortable with your knowledge of the subject, you can find some excellent material on the theory of these devices at the library or possibly in the same store where you bought this book. We are going to cover, however, the action provided by the motor and how to specify the correct type of motor for the job. This brings us to the first of several characteristics which make motors useful—torque.

TORQUE

What is this strange word? It is the expression for the amount of rotational power the shaft of your motor can supply to any robot joint. Torque is usually expressed in units like *ounce-inches* or *pound-inches*. Sometimes you might see it advertised as inch-ounces or foot-pounds. Confusing, right? Let's get to the ground rules regarding torque to help you understand all this double-talk.

Torque is force that produces motion. Motion of a motor is normally circular about the armature axis. To find the torque required to lift or move an object simply multiply the required force times the distance to be traveled. For instance, if a hand/arm system weighs 1 pound, the total weight to be lifted at the shoulder is 2 pounds. Now, if the arm is 18 inches long between the pivot point of the shoulder to the payload center, then the torque required of the motor equals 2 pounds time 18 inches or 36 pound-inches.

Fig. 4-1 illustrates the forces involved and the equation to find torque. Look familiar? It is basically the same formula we used for work in Chapter 2.

After completing calculations using the formula, you can figure out the amount of torque required, but how do you know if the motor you have selected provides that torque?

Sometimes that's not very simple. If you are fortunate enough to have bought a new motor with specifications on the nameplate or you are ordering one from a catalog, the information on torque is usually supplied. However, if you are experimenting with surplus or bargain bag motors, the torque may not be so simply obtained.

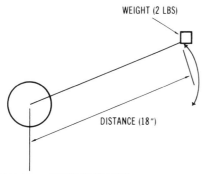

AMOUNT OF WORK = WEIGHT TO BE LIFTED × DISTANCE BETWEEN WEIGHT AND SHAFT
36 LB-IN = (2 LBS) × (18″)

Fig. 4-1 Work formula for designing with motors.

There is, however, one relatively easy way to measure the stall torque of the motor you have. It does require that you mount a pulley of some kind onto the shaft of the motor. This sounds easier than it is! The pulley with a string or cable will be used along with the motor as a winch-like device to lift a weight against gravity. Note that some of the inexpensive slot-car motors have a small $\frac{1}{8}$-inch shaft for which it is hard to find a pulley to fit. If you decide to make one, be sure to provide some sort of set-screw arrangement to lock the pulley wheel to the motor shaft.

Moving along . . . Fig. 4-2 describes the mechanical details of the torque-measuring system. A small box or pail is attached to the end of a string to carry the weight. The idea here is to turn on the motor and keep adding measured weight until the motor stalls. Be careful! These little motors spin very rapidly. Too little weight in the box can result in the box acting as a small windmill with your face being the wind!

When you have found the weight that actually stalls the motor, take this number and multiply it times the radius of the pulley. The radius is half the diameter or distance across the pulley through the center. The resulting number will be the torque of your motor. Fig. 4-2 has an example problem already worked out.

As has been the case throughout this book, the torque formula has been added to the design program with the inclusion of Listing 4-1. Listing 4-1 or Listing 4-2 is designed as a subroutine that fits into the master robot-design program. Full details of the program operations are covered in Chapter 12.

MOTOR TYPES

It's about time for us to look at what these torque producers are. Fig. 4-3 shows a variety of dc motors. Primarily, we will be concerned with the dc variety, however, the calculations for torque remain the same for either ac or dc motors. When specifying a motor, be sure to consider its weight. That is because the next motor up the line will have to move (lift) this one.

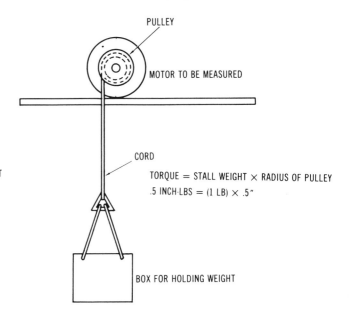

TORQUE = STALL WEIGHT × RADIUS OF PULLEY
.5 INCH-LBS = (1 LB) × .5″

Fig. 4-2 A system for measuring torque.

Fig. 4-3 Some typical dc motors.

DC PERMANENT MAGNET MOTORS

These motors are the most common units found in toys, hand-held motorized devices, and some appliances. They are probably the least expensive and most available to the experimenter. They run on dc voltages of 3, 6, 12, and 24, and range in torque rating from 0.65 ounce-inches to 2 pound-inches.

Most of these motors run fast. Speed of 3600 revolutions per minute (rpm) is not uncommon. Imagine a robot arm lifting a cup of coffee that fast and then coming to a "screeching" halt! That's why it is preferred to use slow, or relatively slow, motors. Remember our discus-

```
1000 CLS:PRINT"TORQUE MEASUREMENT SYSTEM"
1010 PRINT:PRINT"DO YOU WANT TO:"
1020 PRINT"1) FIGURE TORQUE"
1030 PRINT"2) MEASURE TORQUE"
1040 A$=INKEY$:IF A$="" THEN GOTO 1040
1050 IF A$="1" THEN GOTO 1100
1060 IF A$="2" THEN GOTO 1200
1070 GOTO 1000
1100 CLS:PRINT"ENTER WEIGHT TO BE LIFTED"
1110 INPUT"(LBS)";A
1120 PRINT"ENTER DISTANCE BETWEEN WEIGHT  AND SHAFT"
1130 INPUT"(INCHES)";B
1140 PRINT:PRINT"TORQUE MUST =";A*B;"POUND-INCHES"
1150 PRINT:PRINT"<SPACE> FOR ANOTHER,<ENTER> FOR MENU"
1160 A$=INKEY$:IF A$="" THEN 1160
1170 IF A$=" " THEN GOTO 1000 ELSE GOTO 10
```

Listing 4-1 Torque Measurement System

```
1200 CLS:PRINT"TORQUE MEASURER"
1210 PRINT:PRINT"ENTER DIAMETER OF PULLEY"
1220 INPUT"(INCHES)";A
1230 PRINT"ENTER STALL WEIGHT"
1240 INPUT"(LBS)";B
1250 PRINT:PRINT"TORQUE =";(.5*A)*B;"POUND-INCHES"
1260 PRINT:PRINT"<SPACE> FOR ANOTHER,<ENTER> FOR MENU"
1270 A$=INKEY$:IF A$="" THEN GOTO 1270
1280 IF A$=" " THEN GOTO 1200 ELSE GOTO 10
```

Listing 4-2 Torque Measurer

sions on gears in previous chapters mentioned that as the gear ratio changes so does the speed? Great!

It is obvious that a 0.65 ounce-inch motor at 3600 rpm won't help an elbow joint much, but what if we geared down that motor? By doing so, we can decrease the speed and increase the torque. It's like killing two birds with one stone. If we keep doing this gear conversion, we soon end up with a mechanical drive train larger than the elbow we initially designed. There is one way, however, to get this kind of gearing down to small size.

DC GEARMOTOR

Motors can be purchased that have fantastic gear ratios built inside their cases. These are called *gearmotors* . A typical gearmotor configuration is shown in Fig. 4-4. The gears are arranged so that you can have the shaft extend from any surface of the motor. You can get right angle gearmotors, straight ones, even motors that have two shafts!

Edmund Scientific Company, among others, is a source of some small lightweight plastic gearmotors. The motors used in the five-fingered hand in Chapter 1 are found in the Edmund Scientific catalog No. C41,331. The motors were geared down to provide a speed of only 2 revolutions per minute! The resulting torque supplied by this motor is 31 ounce-inches or roughly 1.9 pound-inches. You can get gearmotors that effectively increase torque by hundreds of times the actual rating of the motor encased within.

Gearmotors and regular dc motors work the same way. When power is supplied, the shaft rotates. Hook them up backwards and the shaft rotates in the reverse direction. When these motors start they physically jerk from inertia and stopping them results in a slow coast. Let's look into the electrical control of these motors.

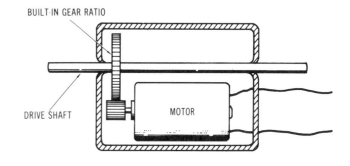

Fig. 4-4 Internal design for a typical gearmotor.

CONTROL

Turning any motor on and off is fairly simple. If you want the motor to turn in one direction only when energized, take a look at Fig. 4-5A. Here we have a motor shown whose power feed line is connected directly to +12 volts dc. The ground return line or negative side of the motor is switched. Although this example may seem overly simplistic, this arrangement is typically used throughout the industry. Now consider the conveyor belt that is turned on manually and switched off or stopped by an object that is riding along on the conveyor. In this case, the object trips a limit switch somewhere along the route. Fig. 4-5B schematically shows the two switch connections necessary for control of this kind.

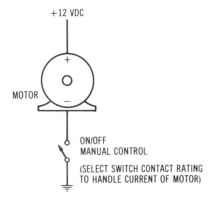

(A) Single-switch control.

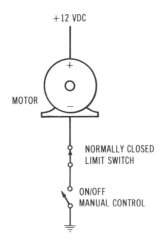

(B) Two-switch control.

Fig. 4-5 Basic On-Off switching of a dc motor.

Moving ahead a few years in technology brings us to Fig. 4-6. The switch mechanism in this figure is called a *relay*. Being an electromechanical device, the relay uses electrically induced magnetism to physically draw the switch contacts together. However, there must be some controlling device to apply power to the relay. You will

see that control eventually traces back to a switch similar to the ones shown in Fig. 4-5.

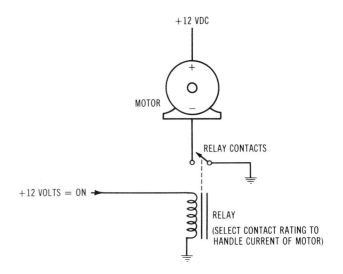

Fig. 4-6 Electromechanical relay switching of a dc motor.

Transistors can act as electronic relays when controlling motors. The advantage of transistors over relays is that they are smaller and consume less power. See Fig. 4-7. The transistor is enabled by a voltage applied to its base. There are several excellent texts on transistor theory that should be considered at this point, if you feel the need to brush up on the subject. The appendix includes the names of some books that have been helpful.

As you can see, there really is nothing to getting a motor to spin, either by manual or automatic control. If you stick to unidirectional motion, you've got much simpler design problems. However, robots which have arms that only go up could prove not to be very useful. That brings us to the subject of how to reverse the direction of the dc motor at will.

BIDIRECTIONAL CONTROL

As you may recall, it was said that to reverse direction you have to hook up the motor backwards. Well, what was meant is that you reverse the power and ground connections to the motor. Effectively, you are reversing the current when you do this. Let's go back to our switches and discover a way to accomplish this reversal with four of them. In Fig. 4-8A, when both switch 1 and 4 are closed, the motor rotates. Opening switch 1 and 4 and closing switches 2 and 3 will cause the motor to spin in the opposite direction. If you use this circuit, be careful not to close switches 1 and 2 or 3 and 4 at the same time. This will short out the power supply!

You can see that as simple as this circuit is, it has its drawbacks. Let's see how a relay can help give us some remote control. Fig. 4-8B shows how relay 1, when ener-

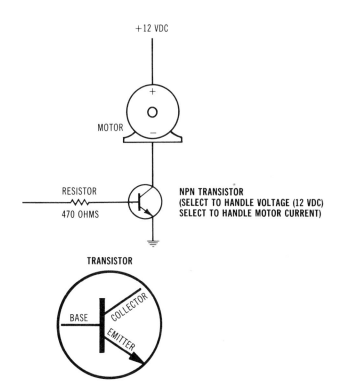

+12 VDC

MOTOR

RESISTOR
470 OHMS

NPN TRANSISTOR
(SELECT TO HANDLE VOLTAGE (12 VDC)
SELECT TO HANDLE MOTOR CURRENT)

TRANSISTOR

BASE

COLLECTOR

EMITTER

Fig. 4-7 Electronic switching of a dc motor.

gized, and relay 2, when left de-energized, can perform the same operation as switches 1 and 4. If we de-energize relay 1 and energize relay 2, the motor reverses rotation. The contact configuration of this circuit disallows the possibility of damaging the power supply.

When we move into electronic bidirectional control, things become more complicated. Each switch position must be replaced by a transistor, and each transistor must be selected by the position and use in the circuit. Fig. 4-9A is not intended to be an operational circuit. It does, however, show the connections of the four transistor switches and the types selected. The npn transistors selected are used to switch ground and the pnp types are used to supply power to the motor. The motor is connected between them similar to a bridge circuit. You can see that by activating alternate transistors, it effectively duplicates the action of the switches in Fig. 4-8. An operating circuit of this type is depicted in Fig. 4-9B. Here we have a single control-voltage input to the circuit.

A ground potential on the control input turns off the pnp 2907 power feed transistor, Q4, but will allow current to the ground switch npn 2222A transistor, Q3, by inverting the signal through the inverter. Conversely, transistor Q1 allows current to flow, and Q2 is disabled. Applying a positive signal to the input reverses all the transistor activities which effectively reverses the direction of the motor.

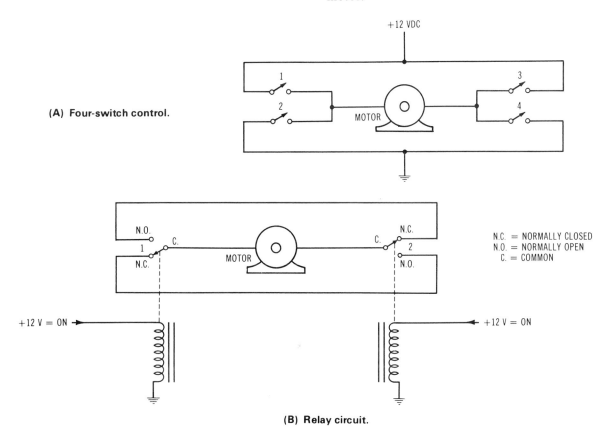

(A) Four-switch control.

N.C. = NORMALLY CLOSED
N.O. = NORMALLY OPEN
C. = COMMON

(B) Relay circuit.

Fig. 4-8 Basic bidirectional control.

53

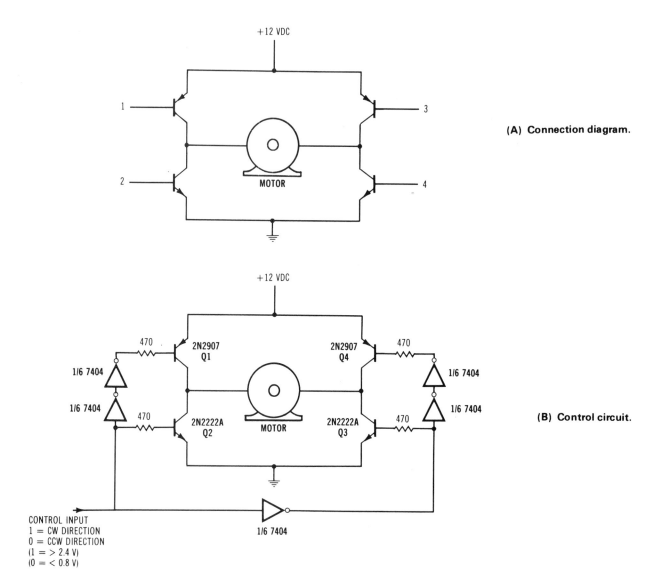

+12 VDC

(A) Connection diagram.

1

2

3

4

MOTOR

+12 VDC

470

2N2907
Q1

2N2907
Q4

470

1/6 7404

1/6 7404

1/6 7404

1/6 7404

(B) Control circuit.

2N2222A
Q2

MOTOR

2N2222A
Q3

470

470

CONTROL INPUT
1 = CW DIRECTION
0 = CCW DIRECTION
(1 = > 2.4 V)
(0 = < 0.8 V)

1/6 7404

Fig. 4-9 Electronic bidirectional control of a dc motor.

When you finish constructing this circuit, you will notice that four transistors and their associated resistors take up a lot of room. Are there no single part solutions to the problem? Yes, there are. Sprague Electric Company, who has been a leader in motor control products, has a single-component motor driver that provides for forward and reverse rotation. Fig. 4-10 shows the connections of the Sprague UDN-2949Z motor driver. Notice the technique used to cause the motor to reverse direction. A high voltage, twice the motor voltage, is applied to the driver and the motor is connected to the driver pin 4. The other side of the motor is connected to its normal voltage supply. When the motor driver supplies the higher voltage to the other side, the motor rotates because there is a difference in potential of 15 volts across the motor. Enabling the reverse direction effectively grounds the output of the driver which reverses the direction of the motor.

Well, now that we've got our motors or gearmotors turning, that should get the robots somewhat closer to operating. The On-Off control that's been covered is probably all that you'll need for most robotic applications. However, when you use motors in the base for moving the robot around, you might have to have some speed control. This subject is as vast as robotics. There are several methods to slow down motors electronically from lowering their voltage to switching them on and off at varying rates. A few books on the subject are listed in the appendix for further reading; however, let's investigate a few of the more simple speed-control approaches.

SPEED CONTROL

As said previously, the easiest speed control method is to vary the voltage applied to the motor. If you double the

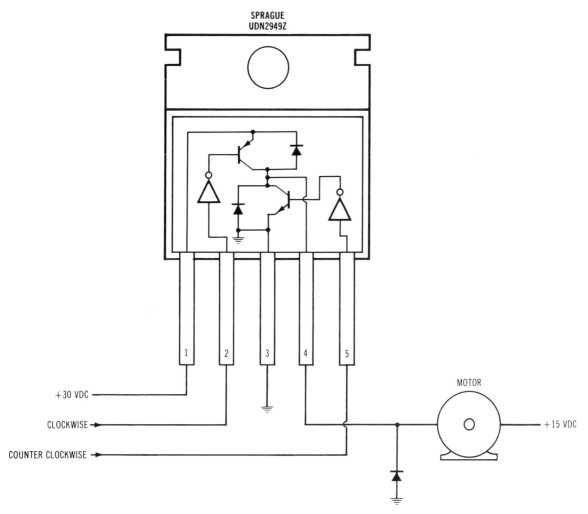

Fig. 4-10 Bidirectional one-chip motor-control IC from Sprague Semiconductor.

supply voltage, you will double the rotational speed; the torque, however, will drop to one-half. It works like the gear ratios we learned about earlier. Look at Fig. 4-11. Here is a potentiometer-controlled speed reducer. It will work, but how can you do it automatically? There are a few ways.

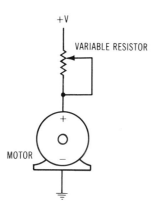

Fig. 4-11 Simple speed control for a dc motor.

One of the more common methods of automatic speed control is called pulse-width modulation (pwm). The term does not come from the motor-control field, nor does it apply only to speed control. It is simply a method of communicating information to a device. We will see it used in remote-control interfaces later in the book. As for motors, pwm is used selectively to switch full supply power on and off to the motor at some frequency using a varying duration (duty cycle) between them. When you want the motor to go slow, the duration of each "on" pulse is very short, therefore supplying a small amount of power to the motor at each pulse. The opposite is true for higher speeds. Fig. 4-12A shows the timing relationship of these pulses. As you can see, varying the "on" time will vary the speed of the motor.

Fig. 4-12B depicts a typical pwm circuit applied to motors. It uses a variable duty cycle oscillator and an external pass transistor. This control can be replaced with a varying voltage such as that found in a digital-to-analog converter. We will investigate computerized automatic speed controls later.

55

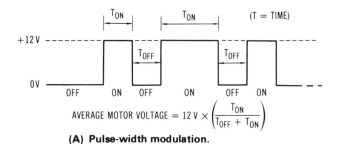

(A) Pulse-width modulation.

$$\text{AVERAGE MOTOR VOLTAGE} = 12\,V \times \left(\frac{T_{ON}}{T_{OFF} + T_{ON}}\right)$$

(B) Circuit for pwm control.

Fig. 4-12 Basics of pulse-width modulation (pwm) and a circuit to provide motor speed control using this method.

You will notice that all the speed-control circuits discussed thus far have involved unidirectional motors. When you attempt to control forward and reverse direction at different speeds, things get very complicated—that is, if conventional transistors are used. However, let's look again at the motor control IC that was used in Fig. 4-10 from Sprague. These components are designed to allow control by pwm! Look at Fig. 4-13 where two of the UDN2949Z devices are used along with some logic components to provide a bidirectional varying-speed drive circuit that is about the least complicated. Connect the output of the pwm oscillator circuit in Fig. 4-12B to the pwm input of the circuit.

An important subject that should be considered here is the current that the motor will draw during operation because it will directly affect the selection of the transistors or drivers you use. For example, most slot-car motors run at hundreds of milliamps while others draw a few amps. The Sprague ICs can handle peak currents of up to 3.5A which should be sufficient for most robot uses; however, pay attention to specifications. Realize that when a motor is first turned on, it will draw a surprising amount of current. Design to allow this initial surge. It will save you hours of work later and possibly save your components from destruction if you plan ahead.

After reading all this, you should have an idea about how to provide motion to the various joints in your robot

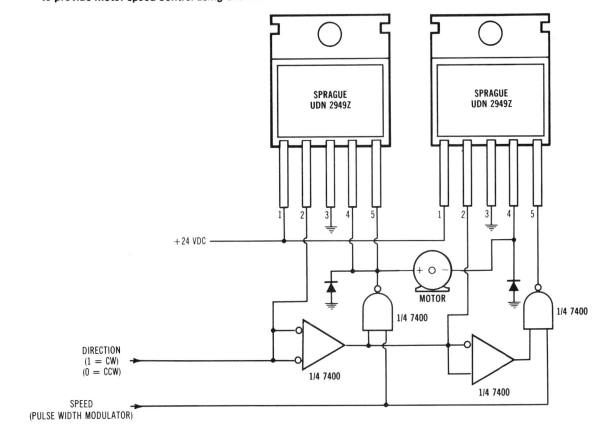

Fig. 4-13 Dual single-chip motor controller provides bidirectional control of motor with varying speed.

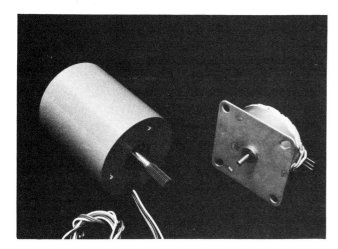

Fig. 4-14 Two typical stepper motors.

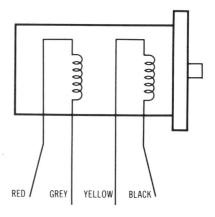

(A) Two-phase stepper.

system. Providing motion is one thing, controlling the precise position desired is another. We saw that these dc motors, when stopped, will coast to a halt. If you want the ability to place that robot arm repeatedly in the same place, you will need a different type of motor.

STEPPING MOTORS

The name *stepper* or *stepping* implies the action. Stepper motors actually step from one position to the next. Remember our discussion of the ratchet and pawl mechanism in Chapter 3? It stepped one exact amount with each on-off electrical pulse. The stepper motor works similarly; however, it does not use a mechanical linkage to perform the steps (Fig. 4-14).

Unlike the ratchet and pawl, the stepper can go forward and backward provided you purchase the bidirec-

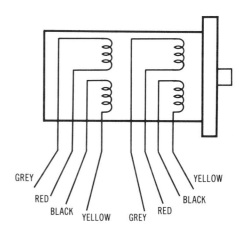

(B) More common four-phase stepper.

Fig. 4-15 Internal wiring of stepper motors.

Fig. 4-16 Phases necessary to control a stepper motor.

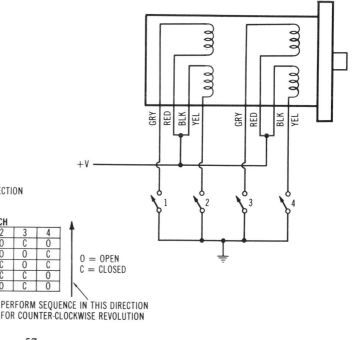

PERFORM SEQUENCE IN THIS DIRECTION FOR CLOCKWISE REVOLUTION

SWITCH				
STEP	1	2	3	4
1	C	O	C	O
2	C	O	O	C
3	O	C	O	C
4	O	C	C	O
1	C	O	C	O

O = OPEN
C = CLOSED

PERFORM SEQUENCE IN THIS DIRECTION FOR COUNTER-CLOCKWISE REVOLUTION

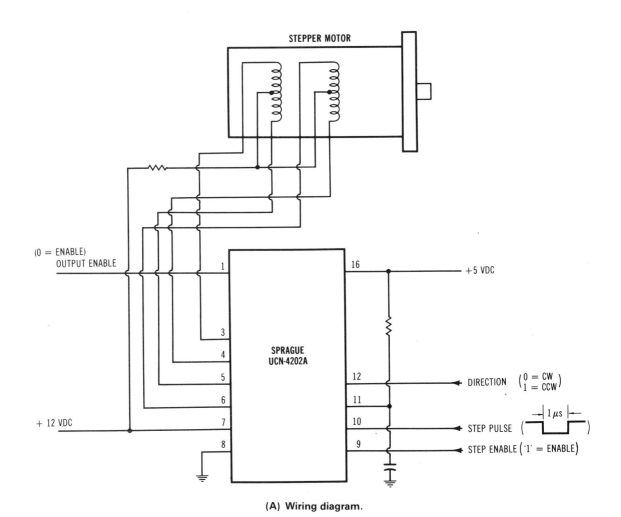

(A) Wiring diagram.

SPRAGUE UCN 4202A

(B) Pinout of IC.

Fig. 4-17 Sprague UCN4202A stepper-motor controller IC diagrams.

58

tional type. You see, it is possible to get unidirectional types, also. The connections and control of this type of motor differ significantly from the conventional dc motor. Applying full voltage to the winding results in one small step, then nothing. In fact, while the voltage is still applied to the winding, it acts as a lock on the shaft.

Different types of steppers have a different number of turns on their windings. See Fig. 4-15. A typical unidirectional stepper may have two windings shown schematically in Fig. 4-15A. This is called a two-phase stepper. There are 3-, 4-, and 6-phase type steppers available. The most common bidirectional type is the one with four windings (Fig. 4-15B).

We say they step. That is, the shaft of the motor will turn some fraction of a full 360° per step. Typical step angles are 7.5°, 15°, and 18°. Of course, you can get custom step angles in just about anything from 0.72° to 90°. Each pulse will move the shaft a precise amount. When we say each pulse, we don't mean to the same winding. There is a specific sequence that must be followed. Look at Fig. 4-16. Notice how we have to go back to switches to relate the control necessary. Follow through the table in Fig. 4-16 and realize that it is not easy to provide the sequence automatically. That is if there had not been Sprague Electric there before us to design their stepper motor control ICs.

Fig. 4-17 shows the connections required to get the Sprague UCN-4202A stepper motor translator/driver to work. That sure takes the edge off of things! You provide a direction signal and step pulses, and it does the rest. The sequence we went over in the previous figure is done automatically in the on-board circuitry of the IC. They even provide an enable signal to allow you the ability to disable the circuit. Another useful IC is the SAA1027 that is available from many suppliers, including some stepper-motor manufacturers. It is shown connected in Fig. 4-18. The "trigger" input acts like the "step" input of the 4202. The "set" input will set the motor outputs to a known state and the "direction" input allows control of cw or ccw rotation.

LINEAR MOTION

Steppers provide a controllable rotation about an axis. Remember when we were designing earlier with the lead screw? Well, take a stepper motor, attach a lead screw, then hollow out a shaft, and thread it. Screw this shaft over the lead screw and provide pins on either side of the shaft to counteract the rotation. Mount the entire assembly in a case so that only the shaft protrudes, and you have just built a linear actuator.

Fig. 4-19 shows a few of the linear actuators available. These devices are basically stepper motors. They are

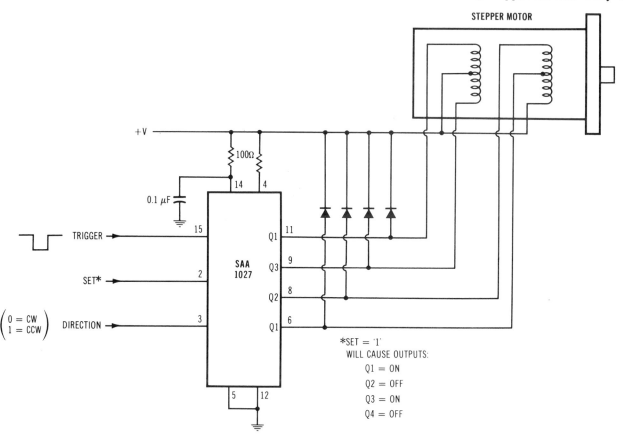

Fig. 4-18 Diagram of the SAA1027 single-chip stepper-motor controller.

59

Fig. 4-19 Typical linear actuators-stepper motors from Airpax Corp. with built in lead screws.

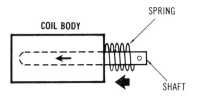

(A) Energized coil holds shaft in against the spring.

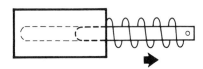

(B) De-energized coil allows spring to return the shaft.

Fig. 4-20 Design and electromechanical action of typical solenoid.

controlled by the same circuitry and are just as precise. However, remember that you will have to convert that rotary step angle into linear travel. Fortunately, the linear actuator manufacturer will provide you with this. They are useful in a variety of applications from hand control to vision scanner movement.

Other less precise methods of linear motion can be accomplished through the use of solenoids. These are electromagnetic devices with a hole through the middle of the coil. An iron shaft is inserted into this hole and held out, slightly, by a spring. Fig. 4-20 shows a drawing of a solenoid. This is the device we used to provide linear motion for the hand in Chapter 1. When power is applied to the solenoid coil, it will pull the shaft into the coil body, thereby providing linear motion. You cannot control the speed at which the shaft moves nor the position. Also, you cannot stop the shaft half way because the spring will return it to the out position.

It was decided to explain solenoids last because, as you can see, they have limited application. Where they work well is when you must fully open or close a small door or lift an object, then retract it. Solenoids are used to punch print hammers on a printer and used in conjunction with mechanical valves to control the flow of fluids. They can be controlled using the same On-Off circuits we described for unidirectional motors.

The use of motors in robot systems adds another dimension to the intelligent machine. The ability to manipulate its environment brings the robot closer to the human and, therefore, becomes more useful as a tool to augment our life. The motion that the motors provide helps our system to perform. There is, however, one facet of motion control we must still require. The ability to sense the position of our arm or to determine how far the robot has traveled along a path is the subject of the next chapter.

Chapter 5

Position
of Feedback
Mechanisms

The motor controls of the preceding chapter give us the ability to position our robot anywhere we please. When we exercise this type of control without actually checking on the movement of the device automatically, we are performing what is called *open loop control*. The loop is the resulting action if we go too far.

Consider, if you will, an arm that is commanded to raise. When it reaches the point where we want it, we simply turn it off. What if we are not there? After all, a robot is supposed to perform some duties independently. Therefore, we need a way to close that loop and perform an automatic shutdown when the correct position is sensed. Providing this loop will require some means of mechanical connection to the mechanism being moved, and an electronic sensor to read the amount of movement effectively. We will get into that later; however, let's back up for the moment.

LIMIT FEEDBACK

Probably the most important piece of information we need to gather when controlling an appendage—be it a hand, an arm, or a foot—is whether or not it has reached any physical limit. After all, it might be dangerous or damaging to have an arm crushing into the body. We need a sensor to trigger when we have reached that point. Let's look at a few ways to accomplish this important function.

The easiest method is to mount a small switch, such as a microswitch, to the place on the body or movable unit that is the limit. When the unit reaches this limit point,

the switch closes. Fig. 5-1 shows a profile of a typical microswitch and some mounting ideas so as to actuate a signal when the physical limit has been reached. These switches can be wired into the motor circuit in much the same way that the end of the conveyor limit switch is applied in Fig. 4-5B. However, conventional approaches connect the sensor to some higher intelligence controller which functions to shut down the motor. This controller will be covered along with the interface between it and the limit sensor in Chapter 11.

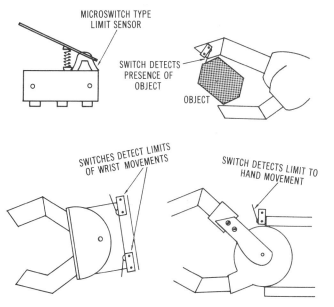

Fig. 5-1 Microswitch uses in limit sensing.

Determining that the robot arm has gone too far can be helpful except in cases where we are trying to pick up an object. If we need to know where we are at any given time, the limit sensor doesn't afford us much help.

MOVEMENT FEEDBACK

When we say *movement*, we don't mean the sensing of motion. This will be covered in detail in Chapter 7. This particular movement means the arm or hand is moving now and this is how long it has been moving. There is a difference between *sensing movement* and *sensing distance*. Let me illustrate by example (see Fig. 5-2). The devices used here are optoelectronic. A light-emitting diode or even a simple lamp is pointed directly at a phototransistor or other light-sensing device. When the light is allowed to strike the lens surface of the detector, a circuit is completed. In the case of the phototransistor, the output assumes a ground potential. If this beam of light is interrupted, the circuit opens and the switch output voltage rises. This parameter makes this a suitable no-contact limit switch. If you mount the detector on the upper arm and the emitter on the lower arm so that when they are close to their limit the two are opposite each other, you have a perfect limit switch.

Going further, we can apply this type of sensor to tell us when the arm is moving. Consider the wheel in Fig. 5-2. It has tiny holes drilled around the circumference approximately $\frac{1}{4}$ inch from the edge. This wheel, when mounted on the pivot shaft of a joint, rotates as the joint is flexed. Positioning an optical sensor so that the holes in the wheel make and break the circuit as the wheel rotates results in a stream of On-Off pulses. If these pulses are counted, we can set a relative motion measurement from the last count. This may be converted into actual distance traveled by measuring the distance the joint must move to pass each hole through the sensor and multiplying this times the number of holes (pulses) counted.

By using two sensors, cleverly mounted, we can determine direction. Look at the drawing in Fig. 5-3 which shows the arrangement of two sets of detectors. The first one to generate a pulse tells us the direction the wheel is moving. If we alter the slots and add another row and

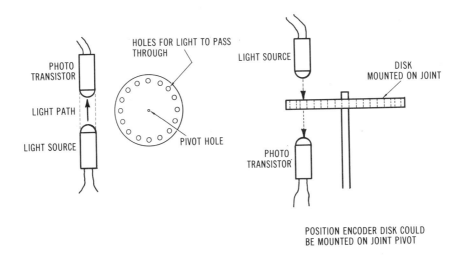

(A) Encoder disk detail.

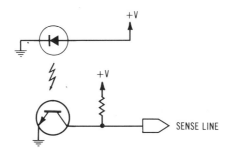

(B) Timing diagram.

Fig. 5-2 Diagram showing construction of an optoelectronic disk encoder using small holes to detect the position of an arm.

remount the second sensor we can achieve the same result. In this instance, the holes are 90° out of phase or, in English, the second slot is placed above and between the first row. Fig. 5-3 shows both approaches and gives the hole layout for the two wheels.

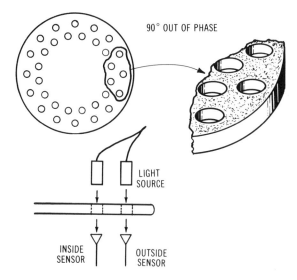

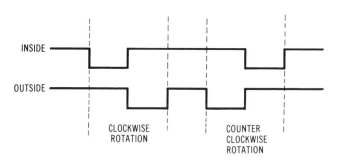

(A) Optical encoder detail.

(B) Timing diagram.

Fig. 5-3 Using 90° offset holes gives added dimension of direction to optical encoding.

The initial hole-pattern type of movement sensor shown in Fig. 5-2 is used effectively in Milton Bradley's Big Trak. In Fig. 5-4, we see the photo sensor used. It consists of an infrared emitter and phototransistor positioned opposite each other. Fig. 5-5 shows the sensor mounted as it is in the drive gear box so that it counts the holes in the gear. This information is fed to an onboard computer which counts the sensor detections and determines distance. You can make one of these sensing devices very simply from available materials such as wood, or even using the plastic lid from an instant frosting container. Emitters and detectors are standard LEDs and phototransistors stocked by many electronics supply stores including Radio Shack.

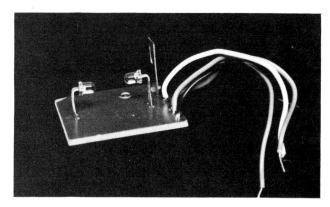

Fig. 5-4 Optical sensor from Milton Bradley's Big Trak.

Fig. 5-5 Internal view of gear box showing the optical sensor in action.

REFLECTIVE DETECTION

If you position a light source and a detector at an angle such as that shown in Fig. 5-6, you will discover that the light from the source is reflected off of the object and returned to the detector. This is not very easy to build because you must position these devices precisely for the effect to work. Typically, the distance between the object and the sensor must be very small to obtain detection.

There are, however, several emitter-detector pair devices available. The Texas Instruments TIL 139 (Fig. 5-7) is a plastic assembly that has both parts mounted in such a way that a reflective object approximately 0.15 inch away will trigger the detector. This particular device has no other electronics associated with it except the emitter and the detector. It should be used instead of trying to mount the devices properly yourself. Other devices available such as the Hewlett Packard HED-1000 have built-in lenses which help resolve smaller reflective objects.

To complete your reflective movement detector, you will want to apply reflective dots or strips to the wheel. This can be done first by painting the wheel black, or

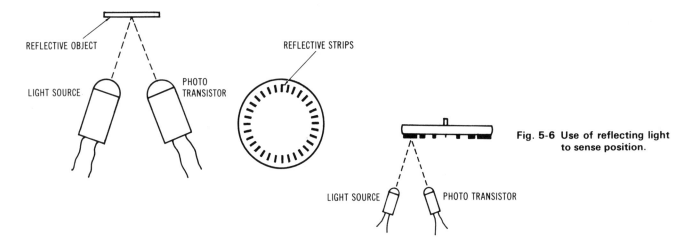

Fig. 5-6 Use of reflecting light to sense position.

Fig. 5-7 Picture of Texas Instruments TIL 139 emitter detector pair module.

making sure that the basic background is not reflective. Small strips of adhesive-backed foil may be applied along the circumference much like the holes that were drilled in the previous wheel. Because the strips can be placed closer together than holes, we are able to resolve finer distances. If you find it hard to place reflective strips securely, consider the reverse. Paint the wheel with reflective paint and scribe or paint thin nonreflective lines in places along the circumference.

MAGNETICS

There are other methods of achieving a reflective-like sensor without the use of light. You can sense the presence, or absence, of a magnetic field using a device called a Hall-effect sensor. In 1879, a man named E. H. Hall discovered that a magnetic field placed near a semiconductor that was carrying current and perpendicular to it produced a voltage that was perpendicular to both the magnetic field and the semiconductor current. Today you can purchase tiny IC packages that contain all the circuitry needed to detect a magnetic field and to produce a voltage to trigger a transistor.

Consider the diagram in Fig. 5-8. Hall-effect sensors, such as the Texas Instruments TL172 and the Sprague Electric UGN-3020T, will mount the same way that regular transistors do and they are also easy to apply. Some sensors, like the Sprague UGN 3201M, are actually 8-pin mini-dip packages that mount like typical ICs. They can be used in most places where opto devices can, yet the source won't wear out. Some typical applications are shown in Fig. 5-9 to spark your imagination. Fig. 5-9A shows a typical pitch-limit sensing arrangement and Fig. 5-9B shows an application for a Hall-effect position sensor.

As we have seen, both optoelectronic and magnetic sensors can work effectively as movement detectors.

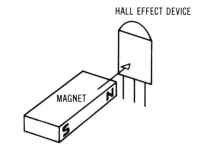

(A) Pitch-limit sensing arrangement.

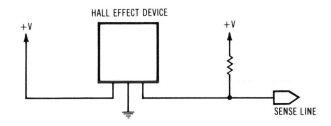

(B) Position sensor.

Fig. 5-8 Diagram showing Hall-effect device and associated schematics.

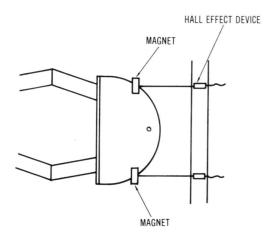

(A) Pitch-limit sensing arrangement.

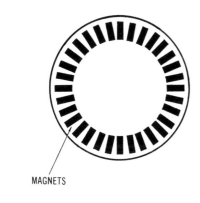

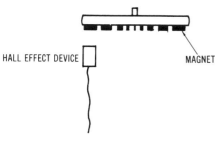

(B) Position sensor.

Fig. 5-9 Two applications of Hall-effect device in robotics.

Together with some intelligence, they can also relate distances in coarse measure. But, what if we want precise position feedback? What if we want to limit the amount of intelligence demanded for the job of position feedback? There are methods available.

SERVO CONTROL

A servo-control system is a combination of devices. First, there is the motor, of course, This motor should actually be the one moving the part of the robot whose

position we want to check. Another component in the system is a potentiometer, or variable resistor. The shaft of the potentiometer and the shaft of the motor should be connected mechanically so that any movement of the motor results in a change in resistance of the potentiometer. If the motor is required to rotate more than 360°, then the potentiometer must be of a continuous-turn type. Typically, some type of control circuit is added that allows the motor to rotate until the resistance of the potentiometer equals some desired value.

Of course, there is not a resistance-measuring system in the controller. No need; this is how it functions. A voltage is supplied to a comparator through the variable resistor, and when the voltage from the potentiometer equals that of an incoming signal, the circuit de-energizes the motor. See Fig. 5-10. There are numerous ways to accomplish this control with both discrete and integrated circuits. Let's look at a few popular one-chip approaches to servo control.

The Signetics NE544/644 device is very easy to apply. In Fig. 5-11, we can see that there is a minimum of components associated with this device. Input is a pulse-width modulated information signal that tells the IC where to position the motor. Pulse-width modulation is used to determine both direction and speed, depending

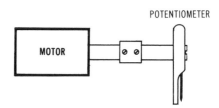

(A) Mechanical coupling.

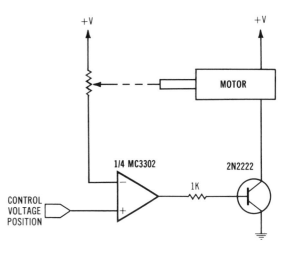

(B) Schematic.

Fig. 5-10 Basic servo mechanism and the mechanical coupling necessary between the motor and the position feedack potentiometer.

65

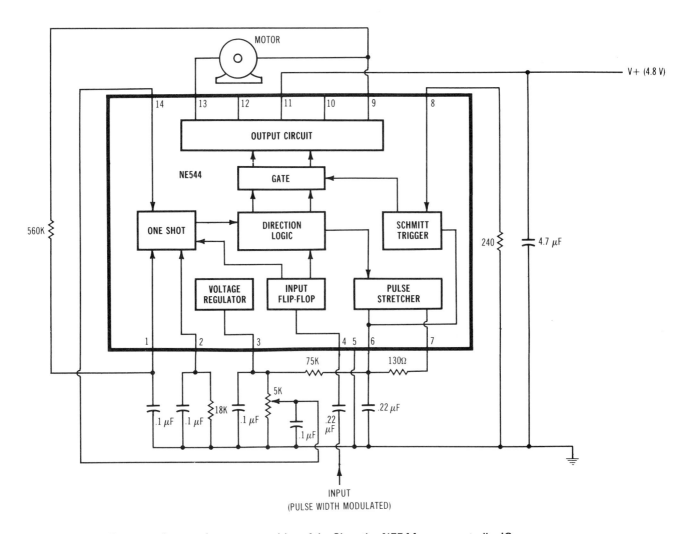

Fig. 5-11 Block diagram and external component wiring of the Signetics NE544 servo-controller IC.

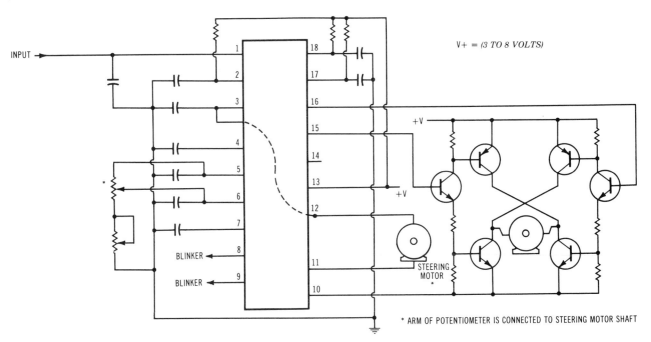

Fig. 5-12 External component wiring diagram for the Exar XR2266 motor-controller IC.

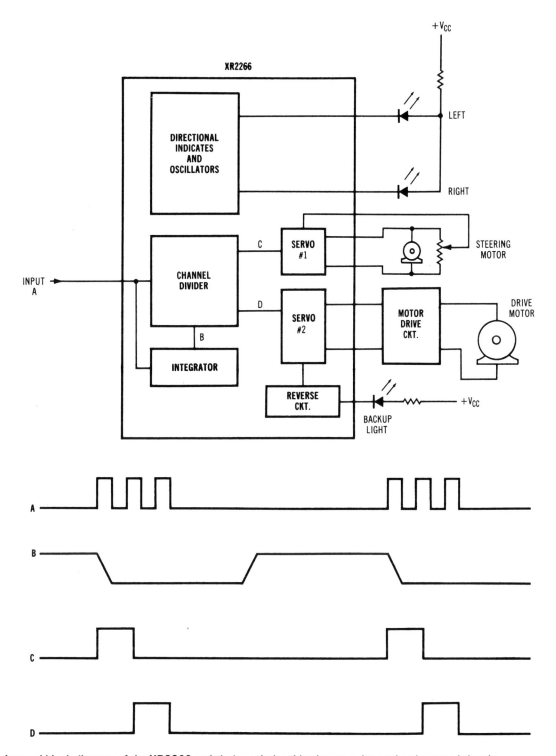

Fig. 5-13 Internal block diagram of the XR2266 and timing relationships between internal and external signals.

on the width of the signal. We can understand the system a little better if we investigate yet another type of servo controller.

The EXAR 2266 servo controller is a marvel of electronic design. It includes the capability to drive two motors, one for drive and the other for steering. Also provided are blinking outputs for direction signals and a reverse, or back-up, light indicator. This device functions ideally to control the base of a roving robot.

Fig. 5-12 shows the required connections. This IC also uses pulse-width modulation, but its operation is more well defined by the supplier than the Signetics device. Looking at Fig. 5-13, we see that the input signal first goes to a channel divider. This splits the signal into a drive signal and a steering signal. Looking at the waveforms of the signal, you can see that the input is split into two signals, C and D. Waveform B is used to reset the channel-divider circuitry. This channel divider triggers on the leading edge of the input signal pulse and provides two outputs—one for speed and the other for steering. The width of each pulse determines the amount of travel.

Consider, if you will, that even though the signal is constantly being sent to the device, this pulse width is stored, then the motor is moved so that the potentiometer produces a pulse width comparable to the input. How does the potentiometer produce a pulse width? Well, if it is connected to an oscillator where the resistance of the potentiometer controls the duty cycle of the oscillator, it will produce a pulse width!

Servos have been used for several years, even before transistors were developed. You'll find them useful for determining position whether you use one-chip solutions or go the home-built route. Combining both the limit sensors and servo control can give you the precise control desirable for the limbs of your robot. Experiment with different sensing methods and construct a few of your own.

Section III:
ELECTRONIC SENSORS

Chapter 6

Tactile Sensing

With motion comes direction and with direction there is a need to know. This required knowledge consists of measures and attitudes. In robotics these quantities are assimilated through a myriad of sensors. We have investigated ways of determining how far we are reaching. Now let's look at the how and why of measuring touch.

Tactile sensing can be extremely important in a robotic system, if the machine has to manipulate objects. Without knowing how hard to grasp an object, the robot may either drop it or nearly crush it. This type of feedback is generally associated with the hand, although bump sensors around the base may also be classified as tactile. In either case, the technology used can be the same. Let's consider a simple touch sensor.

Fig. 6-1 shows a simple system of touch switches connected to a hand. The hand shown is assumed to have five fingers with integral palm just like its human counterpart. Each switch shares a common ground line while the other contact is connected to some main controller, Notice in Fig. 6-1B that this contact potential is pulled up through a 1K resistor which tends to force the output to a logic 1 when the switch is open. Closure of any one of the switches assumes that it has touched something which effectively grounds the output and sends a logic 0 to its controller.

Using mechanical switch mechanisms, such as the microswitch, we can obtain the vital information from the hand that it has made contact with an object. By placing a number of these sensors around an area, you can determine a rough shape. Consider the outputs obtained in Fig. 6-2B. Here the object is a child's block. The sensor switches in the index and second fingers (f_1 and f_2) detect the straight edge of the block by showing their outputs at a logic 0. The thumb sensor, T_1, also detects the presence of the block and activates the switch. All other sensor positions are maintained at logic 1s. A round object would activate only some of the switches.

Microswitches require a certain force to operate them. They require some pressure exerted by the hand before they will close. This can be detrimental, especially if the object might be damaged by this force. A piece of fruit, such as a peach or bunch of grapes, could be ruined. There are other methods of determining touch which are not so destructive.

OPTICAL TOUCH

Remember, in Chapter 5, we found that mechanical sensing of position can be emulated through optical switches. Here again, the use of light can enhance the application. Finger-tip sensors equipped with photo emitters and receptors not only can detect touch, but can measure the amount of it. Look at the example portrayed in Fig. 6-3.

In the figure the reflective method of light sensing is used. Here an optical reflection point is provided by extending a rubberized skin-like material over the sensor. Therefore, the phototransistor in the finger will always be providing an output. This output, however, will vary depending on the position of the skin. If we measure this light amplitude, a force-like number can be obtained. One way to do this is shown is Fig. 6-4.

Amplifying the light-detector output of the phototransistor yields a varying voltage and this voltage can be

(A) Five switches mounted on hand.

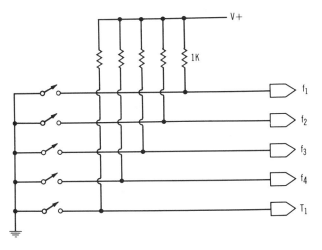

(B) Equivalent circuit.

Fig. 6-1 Use of microswitch limit sensors on a five-fingered hand.

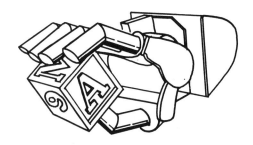

(A) First two fingers and thumb.

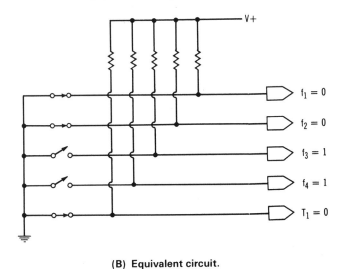

(B) Equivalent circuit.

Fig. 6-2 Schematic of outputs activated if the hand in Fig. 6-1 grasped a square block using two fingers and thumb.

converted into a numerical quantity by several methods. If we place an analog-to-digital converter on the output of the amplifier, we will get a digital representation of the touch. Another method (see Fig. 6-4) converts the voltage into frequency with a voltage controlled oscillator. The changing frequency can be measured by conventional means and a force calculated.

The circuit in Fig 6-4 uses the voltage to frequency method. The output is connected to a frequency counter which displays amounts of force.

Other methods of optical sensing could be discovered through experimentation. If we do not place a skin-like material over the sensors, the proximity of an object will be reported. When a surface is close enough to reflect the beam, the phototransistor will be activated and provide an output. From this point, the amount of force can then be measured by those means discussed previously.

Well, we have found that both mechanical and optical switch methods may be used to give us effective tactile sensors. We have treated these objects as components which may be applied to a hand surface. Let's digress for a moment and investigate the design of a skin-like hand covering which is an integral tactile sensor.

In many products today, we see that the traditional

pushbutton is rapidly being replaced by the *touch surface*. These panel areas are actually mechanical switches that are made with a combination of mylar and conductive paint. Pushing on the contact area, which is usually identified by some legend printed on the surface of the panel, will cause two conductive surfaces to make contact, therefore completing an electrical circuit. Fig. 6-5A shows the construction of the touch or *membrane* switch.

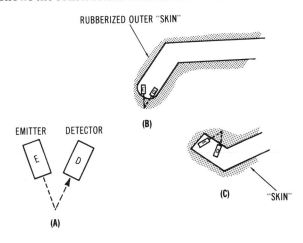

Fig. 6-3 Use of optical reflectance for tactile sensing.

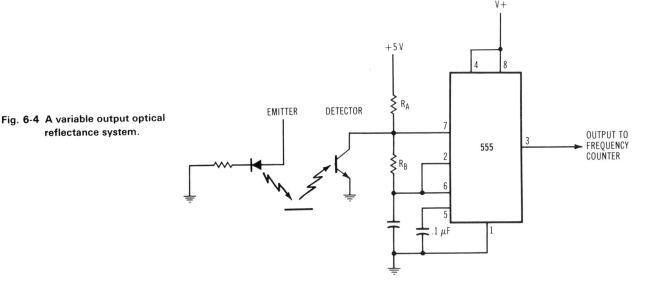

Fig. 6-4 A variable output optical reflectance system.

The contact surfaces of a membrane panel are printed on much like a newspaper or book. The ink is made up of conductive materials such as silver or copper. Contact areas and the interconnections between them are printed at the same time. Both contact surfaces are printed on the mylar, then the plastic piece is folded to produce a top and bottom layer. In between the two surfaces, another piece of mylar is placed to act as a separator from the others. Holes are punched where the contact surfaces lay above and below this mylar separator. When a force pushes down on the back side of the top conductor, the surface physically protrudes through the hole in the separator and contacts the lower conducting surface. Fig. 6-6 shows a section of a commercially available membrane switch.

So what has all this got to do with robots? Consider making a membrane switch that is in the form of a glove. Every quarter inch or so we could place contact surfaces so that we can get good resolution when grasping an object. Of course, you could lessen the distance between contact areas to get added sensitivity, but even at a quarter inch there would be numerous outputs. Using strips for contact area, instead of square or circular pads, allows thousands of sensors.

What do we do with all these outputs? Let's look at yet

MYLAR INSULATOR

WIRE #1

FOIL OR CONDUCTIVE TAPE

MYLAR SPACER WITH HOLE

FOIL OR CONDUCTIVE TAPE

WIRE #2

MYLAR INSULATOR

(A) Construction detail.

(B) Schematic.

WIRE #1 WIRE #2

Fig. 6-5 Basic construction diagram of a membrane-style switch.

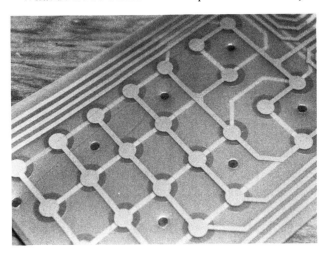

Fig. 6-6 Photograph of the underside of a commercially available membrane switch panel.

another technology and see where the two fit together here. Electronic keyboards (keypads) that are used to enter data into computers sometimes use the membrane switch. In any case, a switch is a switch. Let's look at how a keyboard reports which switch is being pushed, and try to apply this method to our mechanical hand. After all, a keyboard is actually a tactile sensor for a computer. It detects the touching of your fingers.

TOUCH ENCODING

A simple key switch encoder may take the form of an IC circuit known as a *priority encoder*. This device (Fig. 6-7) transforms the closure of one of eight switches shown into a 3-bit binary code. Ideally suited to a small number of hand sensors, the 74LS148 has provisions for cascading to make a larger array and strobing which allows for selectively activating the touch sensing area. When there are more than 8 or 10 contact areas, this system loses its effectiveness.

In larger keyboards where there are from 16 to 126 keys, a different technique of coding is used. By arranging the switches into a matrix so many high by so many deep,

we can use a technique called *scanning*. The block diagram in Fig. 6-8 points out the various stages of this system. An oscillator, running at approximately 200 to 500 Hz, clocks the column counter. The outputs of this counter are decoded into one of 'n' active low outputs, where 'n' is the number of possible output states. These low going pulses are sent down each column sequentially. The switches are arranged in a matrix as shown in the figure. When a switch is closed, either by finger pressure in the case of the keyboard or by the detection of an object in the robot's hand, it serves to route one of the column strobes into the row multiplexer.

The row multiplexer selects each row in sequence as determined by the row counter. The order of scanning is: row 1, column 1, 2, 3, ... n; row 2, column 1, 2, 3, ... n, etc. For each row that is selected, every column is strobed. The column strobe is sent via the closed keyswitch to the row multiplexer, the output of which is connected to one side of a gate which can stop the oscillator. When this output goes low, it does just that which locks both the row and column counter outputs to their present state. At this time, a 'key down' signal is generated and the binary counter outputs are strobed into

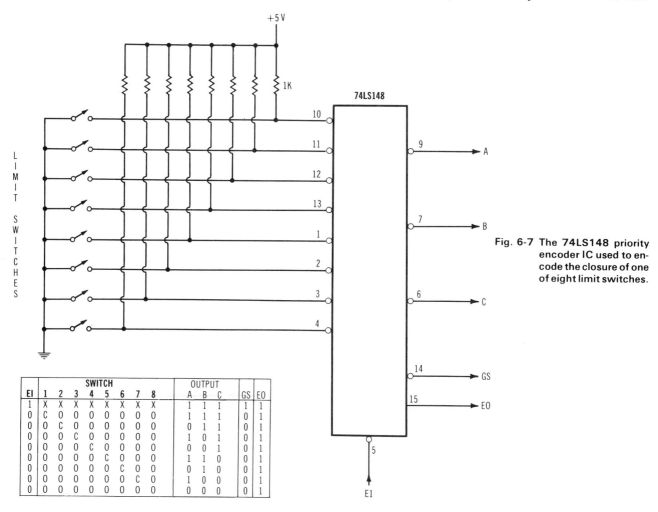

Fig. 6-7 The 74LS148 priority encoder IC used to encode the closure of one of eight limit switches.

EI	\multicolumn{8}{c	}{SWITCH}	\multicolumn{3}{c	}{OUTPUT}	GS	EO
	1	2	3	4	5	6	7	8	A	B	C		
1	X	X	X	X	X	X	X	X	1	1	1	1	1
0	C	0	0	0	0	0	0	0	1	1	1	0	1
0	0	C	0	0	0	0	0	0	0	1	1	0	1
0	0	0	C	0	0	0	0	0	1	0	1	0	1
0	0	0	0	C	0	0	0	0	0	0	1	0	1
0	0	0	0	0	C	0	0	0	1	1	0	0	1
0	0	0	0	0	0	C	0	0	0	1	0	0	1
0	0	0	0	0	0	0	C	0	1	0	0	0	1
0	0	0	0	0	0	0	0	0	0	0	0	0	1

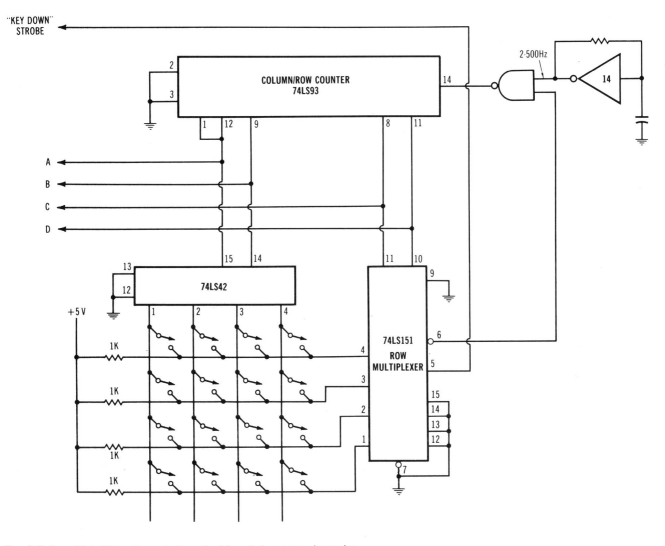

Fig. 6-8 A multiple IC implementation of a 16-switch scanner/encoder.

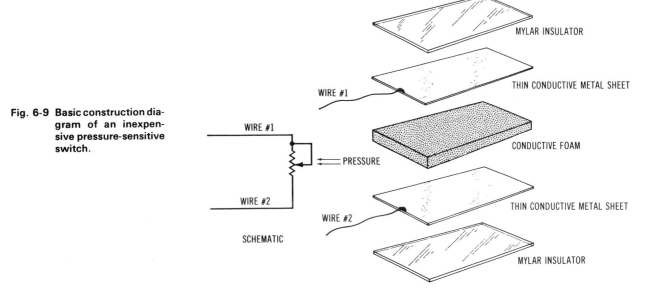

Fig. 6-9 Basic construction diagram of an inexpensive pressure-sensitive switch.

another latch for safekeeping. The master controller, which in our case is the robot brain, would be notified of a switch closure by the presence of this strobe. At that time, it interrogates this latch to determine the switch that is activated.

That is basically how keyboards are encoded. One disadvantage to this method is that it allows the reporting of only one switch at a time, and the scanner does not continue looking for other closures until the previous one is released. We need a method for determining how many switches are active and where they are positioned simultaneously. In the chapter on manipulator control, we will present a complete arm controller design.

PRESSURE SENSING

If you are familiar with integrated circuits, you must have, at one time or another, come across what is known as *black foam*. This is a material used to ship ICs. The devices are inserted into the foam which acts as an electrical shunt between all the legs of the IC. This foam is impregnated with a conductive material. If you place the test leads of a multimeter into each end of a piece of the foam, you will measure a resistance, not an open circuit which is the case for other foams.

These foam pads can be used as a sort of pressure sensor. Through experimentation I have found that pressure on the foam compresses the cells together which tends to lower its resistance. If we measure the change and convert this into a digital number, we have effectively emulated the optical measuring device discussed earlier. Fig. 6-9 shows the construction of a foam pressure sensor. In Fig. 6-10, you can see one that the author constructed. Metallic surfaces are mounted to the outer and lower areas of the foam. Pressure applied from top to bottom tends to decrease the distance between the plates which changes the resistance reading obtained by placing test probes on each surface. Applying this sensor where the photo transistor was in Fig. 6-4 yields the same result.

There are commercial pressure sensors on the market. National Semiconductor has a number of relatively low cost IC-type sensors. Other products that you may not think of as pressure sensors may also be used. Let's take, for instance, a device called a *piezoelectric element*. These devices have been used recently as speakers in hand-held electronic games. They are flat metallic components usually connected by two wires.

Fig. 6-11 shows a variety of piezo elements. In actuality, these devices are crystals much like the ones that set the frequency of your CB radio. However, this particular type of crystal, when mechanical pressure is applied, produces a voltage at its leads. This piezoelectric effect was discovered long ago. You probably have connected its use with other circuits already given in this book. For example, we could connect it to the variable frequency

Fig. 6-10 Photograph showing homemade version of the pressure switch detailed in Fig. 6-9.

Fig. 6-11 Photograph of various piezo sound elements.

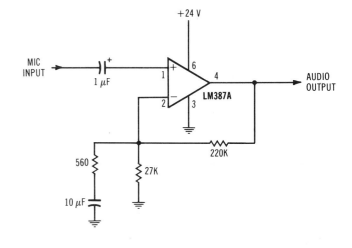

Fig. 6-12 A simple microphone amplifier.

76

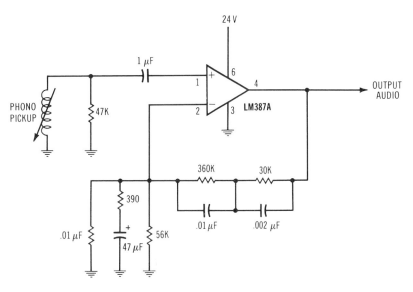

Fig. 6-13 A simple phono cartridge amplifier used as a tactile sensor by creating a sensing pad connected to the phono element as shown in Fig. 6-14.

circuit of Fig. 6-4. One word of caution here, though. The piezo element is an extremely fragile device! It would not stand repeated hand pressure without some form of support. Experiment with these devices and see if you can construct a combination piezo-black foam pressure-pad sensor!

FEELING WITH SOUND

There is another interesting method for tactile sensing. The use of sound to determine texture would certainly be beneficial if the robot system will be involved in handling many different materials. It would also be a good *slip* sensor. Let's look at a few ways to construct this type of sensor.

Fig. 6-12 shows a simple inexpensive microphone connected to an audio amplifier. The output of this amplifier is sound. Have you ever noticed that dragging a microphone over a rough surface produces bumps and grinds proportionate to the surface? Mounting a small microphone on each finger tip would yield an enormous amount of information about the texture and position of the object grasped. Of course, a microphone typically does not lend itself well to mounting in the small area of a finger. Some miniature electret-type mikes are small enough; however, they tend to be rather expensive. Another sound transducer, which we all have had some contact with, is the phono cartridge.

In all record players, the phono cartridge mounts into a finger-like support called a tone arm. They come equipped with easy-connect push-on electrical connections and are very simple to use. The schematic in Fig. 6-13 shows a simple amplifier for a phono cartridge. The output may

Fig. 6-14 Photograph of a standard stereo phono cartridge outfitted with a small metal sensing pad connected where the diamond stylus normally goes.

be converted to a digital signal by using an A-D converter. Fig. 6-14 shows an inexpensive phono cartridge that is outfitted with a finger sensor plate.

An attempt was made, in this chapter, to show that there are a number of approaches that can be taken to add tactile sensing to a robot system. In covering these methods, we have only touched on their interface to a master controller or brain-like device. As has been indicated, the subject of tactile sensing intermixes so heavily with an external controller that to get into such detail here would be pointless. Suffice it to say that these are the methods and the devices to use. Later, as you begin to grasp the control aspects of master computers, you will learn how to use them effectively.

Chapter 7

Motion, Attitude Sensing

As we complete our daily chores, be it at home or at an office or factory, we do not generally find it necessary to know exactly where we are. Certainly, if we did not recognize our surroundings, we'd feel lost. But what about those times that you drove to work wondering how you got there without remembering having seen the normal landmarks? There are times that an automatic guidance system seems to take over.

If we do need help to find ourselves, there are many signposts and maps available to assist us. Most direction determining aides used at present by humans require vision to interpret. So far, our robot is more blind than a bat! It can't even hear. In cases where a locating capacity is desired, other methods must be devised to sense direction. There are a number of them, so let's begin.

Direction is the angular difference measured in degrees from some reference point. On a magnetic compass, this reference is the magnetic north pole. Although it would be possible to build a magnetic compass into a robot and detect with tiny light beam sensors the direction of the needle, it would not be accurate enough. Try holding a compass and walking in a straight line. Notice how the needle bobs and weaves. Now imagine the phototransistor outputs going on and off between readings.

Let's assume that we are to build a material-handling robot—one that rides down a corridor delivering mail to each doorway. If you build a motor-driven platform that has the capability to steer around corners, where should the steerable wheel be located to assure straight movement down the corridor? You might place it exactly parallel to the drive wheels. This being the case, what about the possibility of a slightly crooked hall? It would require that you judge the distance between the robot and the wall and keep it constant as the robot travels the length of the hall.

This type of guidance system can be accomplished using a combination of many technologies. A bump sensor made up of a microswitch connected to a long spring rod could serve the purpose well. Consider a case where the rod is 12 inches long. As long as the switch is closed, we know the robot is one foot from the wall . . . or do we? What if it is drifting closer to the wall? The switch remains closed. Of course, we could provide another switch connected to a shorter rod, perhaps 10 inches long. In that case, we could steer until the longer rod made contact but not until the switch on the shorter rod closed. If it closed, we would have to reverse the steering direction.

This back and forth driving motion not only looks silly, but it requires much of the master controller's time. After using the wall-sensor technique for a while, you will notice unsightly marks scribed by the rod on the wall along the entire route the robot travels. This unfortunate side effect is aggravating to anybody not caring to repaint or repaper their walls every six months. We will have to come up with a better alternative.

MOTION DETECTION

Before we get into the nitty-gritty of determining how many inches from the wall we are, let's first determine if we are moving. This sounds easier than it is. Consider the fact that you can hold a glass of water perfectly steady in a

Fig. 7-1 Commercially available bicycle speedometer.

Fig. 7-2 A two-directional shop level bought at a local hardware store.

car while driving at 90 miles per hour down a road. How do you detect the motion of a body?

There are some clever devices available called *accelerometers*. An accelerometer measures the pressure on a surface as it travels through the air. In our case, it could give a reading of how fast you are traveling. You might assume that this is what gives the speedometer reading in our automobiles. Well, not exactly because accelerome-

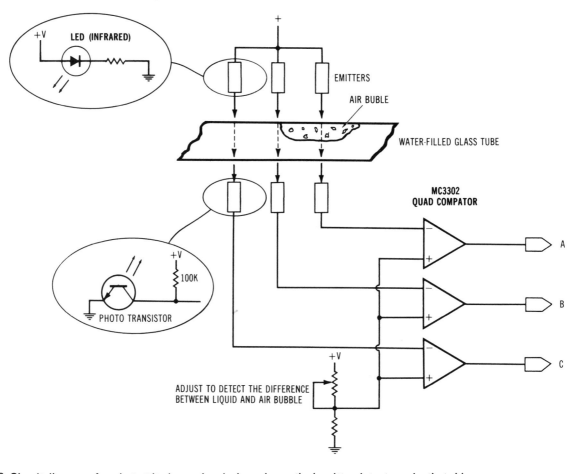

Fig. 7-3 Circuit diagram of a robot attitude-sensing device using optical emitter detector pairs that shine light through tubes of a shop level such as that shown in Fig. 7-2.

ters are not inexpensive and they are not easy to build, either. Their use in a home robot would be costly. There is another method.

Getting back to the automobile, let's investigate how to convert the rotary motion of the wheels into speed information. First, never measure speed from the rotation of the driving wheels. This is because, if the body becomes stuck for some reason, the drive wheels connected to the motor may be turning while the body is actually standing still. So, let's look at the steering wheels or, maybe, the idler wheels that provide balance in a two-wheeled approach. These wheels will only move if the entire robot is moving.

The easiest method is to attach a slotted wheel to the one to be measured and a detector to read the presence of the rotating holes as we did in Chapter 5. This would give us direction as well as distance. We can measure the time period between pulses to determine speed because the distance between holes would be known. The only sensor circuitry required has already been described and there is little else to add. Besides being easiest to implement, the slotted-wheel design is also the most inexpensive to build.

Other methods for measuring speed or motion use a device called a *tachometer*. This device is a motor-like unit that is coupled to the rotational element being measured. When it turns, it produces a voltage proportional to the speed at which it is turning. It is a straightforward task, generally, to connect this device to some type of analog-to-digital converter for determining speed. Although relatively inexpensive tachometers may be purchased through industrial supply houses, it may be easier, from an experimenter's viewpoint, simply to purchase a bicycle speedometer. These assemblies consist of a metal transducer that converts the rotary motion of the front wheel to turn a long flexible shaft. This shaft enters a meter-like housing where it is converted to electrical current that moves the needle of the meter calibrated to indicate speed in miles per hour. Fig. 7-1 shows a typical bicycle speedometer. To install the speedometer on a robot, simply mount the transducer so that its wheel physically contacts the wheel you wish to measure.

These speedometers are rugged and very reliable. If you should purchase an industrial tachometer, chances are it would be a small plastic-encased unit with a 1/8 inch shaft. You would have to ruggedize it yourself.

ATTITUDE SENSING

Now that we have ways to tell that we're moving, let's determine whether we are inclined (leaning) or not. While we are at it, maybe a check into our pitch would be useful. If you've ever done any woodworking or bricklaying you'd know the importance of a device called a *level*. This is a glass or plastic tube filled with a liquid almost until there is no room left for air. Notice I said almost. The key

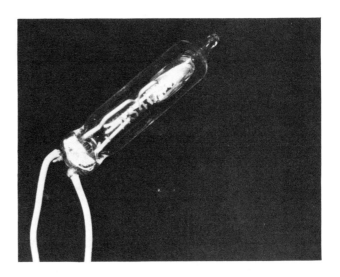

Fig. 7-4 A typical mercury switch.

to the level is this small bubble that rides just under the surface of the tube. The glass is marked on the outside with a small line to denote center. If the bubble sits directly beneath this mark with equal parts of the bubble showing to each side, the tube is level. Fig.7-2 shows a

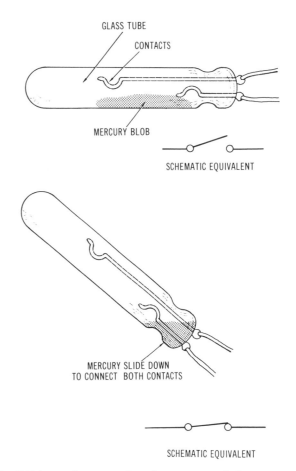

Fig. 7-5 Internal construction of a mercury switch.

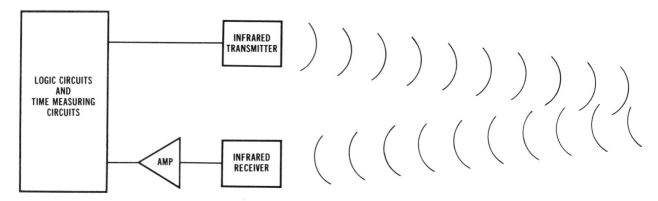

Fig. 7-6 Functional diagram of an infrared ranging system.

commercially available level with two tubes, one in each direction.

This level can help our robot determine its inclination and pitch. Let's look at converting this visual-only device to a useful sensor. Fig. 7-3 shows the approach taken. The use of the photo emitter/detector pair is becoming a habit with us. Its uses are almost without limit. Here, the area with the bubble distorts the light that normally is measured by the phototransistor. By placing three photo detectors beneath the tube, we can detect center, right, and left. Because the bubble is rather long, we are even able to get readings of right-center or left-center when both detectors sense the bubble. Yes it's crude, but it works.

A less sensitive, though useful, approach to incline sensing is the use of the mercury switch. This switch (Figs. 7-4 and 7-5) consists of a tiny glass bottle with two wire rods extending out one end to form electrical leads. A glob of the liquid metal, mercury, rolls around inside the bottle. When the bottle is held straight up the mercury forms around the two rods causing them effectively to short like the action of a switch. If you position the mercury switch bottle appropriately, you can detect *attitude*.

DIRECTION FINDING

Perhaps the only thing left to find out is what we started to talk about originally: which direction are we going and how far from the wall are we? Let's take the first under consideration.

Today, boats, planes and some cars use magnetic compass direction systems. There are automatic magnetic auto pilot systems which use devices called *magnetometers* to sense direction. These units measure the amount of lines of magnetic flux that are cut as an electromagnetic coil is moved. It is a highly analog system which requires precise electronics and hard-to-come-by magnetic components.

Other attitude sensing methods use one of two radio direction systems. The first is the LORAN C system. LORAN gets its name from an acronym of **L**ong **R**ange **A**id to **N**avigation, and it can guide you over the earth and navigate you to within 50 feet of your destination! Each point on the map has a special electronic address which is

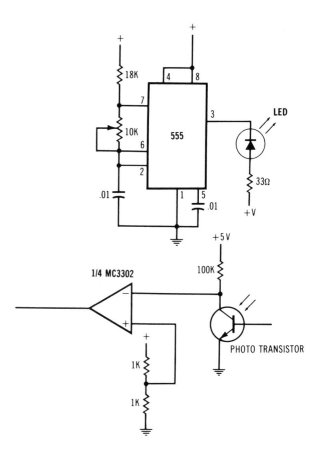

Fig. 7-7 Schematic of an optical transmitter (top) and receiver (bottom).

82

derived much like the keyswitch location scanning system described in the preceding chapter. The LORAN system, which was set up in 1974, consists of a group of low-frequency radio transmitters. These transmitters form a matrix of one master and up to four slaves.

It works this way. The master station emits a series of signals, then after a predetermined time span, a slave station does the same and on down the line. The time delay between the reception of the master signal and a slave station that you have selected determines your location. Your robot could travel the countryside and report on its position constantly. Or, perhaps, you could pre-program a course for it to follow.

The other popular system employed is called OMEGA. Like the LORAN system, it uses low-frequency radio transmitters. There are eight radio transmitters spread at equal distance that transmit a very stable frequency. By measuring the phase difference between stations and a stable reference oscillator, you're able to determine your position. The distance between transmitter lines is approximately 8 miles and resolutions down to one-quarter mile are possible.

But what about the 10 inches that must be measured between the body of the robot and the wall? Well, Omega or Loran won't help us here. Some form of local guidance system is needed. We've tried the wall-sensing rod, now we're ready for less obtrusive and destructive methods. There are two that work rather well. They are *infrared light ranging* and *ultrasonic ranging* systems. First let's investigate the use of light.

Here we go again! This time the light, however, is invisible infrared light and it is not directed straight out from its detector to a sensor. What must be done is to amplify a pulse of light so that it has sufficient strength to emit from a location, travel an appreciable distance, reflect off an object, and then return that entire distance. Of course, the energy of the light must be detectable when it arrives, therefore not just any lamp will do. It must be designed to emit a high power light pulse.

On the receiver end (Fig. 7-6), the pulse is detected and the time difference between transmit and receive is measured. This difference divided by the speed of light yields distance. Pretty uncomplicated, huh? Fig. 7-7 is a simple low-cost transmitter-receiver schematic. Later, we will learn how to connect a microprocessor to an infrared system which yields distance measurement.

Ultrasonic ranging systems work exactly like the infrared system just described except that the transducers of energy are small inaudible speakers which emit "chips" of sound. The sound energy reflects off objects and is detected much the same as with the light beam. There are a number of integrated circuits available that perform many of the transmit and receive functions. In fact, in Chapter 8 on Vision Systems, we will explore numerous examples of both ultrasonic and infrared ranging and vision circuits.

Because sensors connected with robot bodily functions rely so heavily on the design architecture of the main control units, we have only touched on some possibilities. In the following chapters, you will learn much more about sensor technology through the applications and circuits to be presented there.

Chapter 8

Vision Systems

The gift of sight is probably our most important sense. With one glimpse we can amass large amounts of data. Without sight, we soon find out how cold the world can be.

Vision, itself, is a relative thing. Do we see only with our eyes? It is said that a person has vision if he or she can predict happenings in the future, or if they can read somebody's feelings. Robots, on the other hand, are seldom fortune tellers. In fact, many robotic systems at this writing do not possess the capability to see anything.

In this chapter, we will explore vision as it relates to the capacity of a robot to see its surroundings. Basically, we will emulate the human eye. Also, you will be going a step further by providing these eyes with the capability actually to measure the distances from them to their surroundings. Let's begin with a definition of what we need from a robot vision system.

ROBOT EYES

The eyes of robots should be suited to the environment in which the machine is to operate. It is also true that the design should reflect their use. If, for instance, your robot is a rather small specialized arm that is used for inserting slides into a microscope, then small "limit-sensor eyes" should be adequate. Of course, if your robot is to walk around the house cleaning up, a full-blown tv camera and ultrasonic distance-measuring system might be required.

Notice the statement "limit-sensor eyes." This implies that those photoelectric limit sensors we have toyed with for the last three chapters are forms of vision. Actually, you could say so. For years they were called "electric

eyes" when used in security systems. Today they are taken for granted because they are so commonplace. Let's assume that you want the robot to have the capacity to distinguish light from dark, and also colors.

This application would be handy if you build a clothes-separating robot. The basic mechanism to use here is the *photocell.* Fig. 8-1 shows a photocell connected to a circuit that will detect the presence of light. The output is designed such that it snaps on when the resistance of the photocell (light-dependent resistor) allows the same voltage to be applied to the comparator as the reference. This reference voltage level can be adjusted to suit whatever light level you want to detect.

When detecting colors with a photocell, you are really only discriminating between varying intensities of light. A strong light reflection off the test material will return a portion of its brightness to the photocell depending on the color or shade of the material. Adjusting the comparator for a certain level can be done by first placing a piece of test material under the lamp and measuring the level. Adjust the reference potentiometer until the output

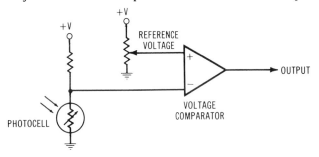

Fig. 8-1 Simple light detector.

becomes active. From this calibration level, the output reacts when a piece of material reflects the same amount of light as the test sample did.

What if you have three shades to detect? Changing the reference back and forth would present quite a problem. Consider the circuit in Fig. 8-2. Here there are four circuits identical to Fig. 8-1. The input photocell is connected to all the comparators but each one has its own reference voltage. This circuit can be adjusted to detect four separate shades. The comparators used are available four to a package so they were appropriate for this circuit layout. There is a way, however, to detect up to ten shades of color with the same amount of circuitry!

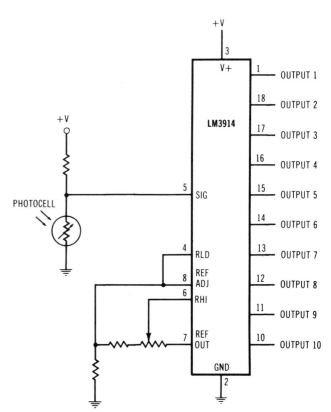

Fig. 8-3 Use of a bar graph IC in a ten-shade light-detector circuit.

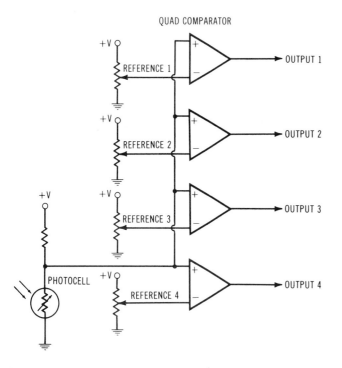

Fig. 8-2 A light-detector circuit capable of distinguishing four shades.

Fig. 8-3 shows how to connect a more recent integrated level detector circuit to our photocell "eye." You get ten individual outputs with ten separate comparators built into one chip! The National Semiconductor LM3914 Dot/Bar Display Driver can be used for this application and a number of other sensing systems. In Fig. 8-2, the photocell varies the voltage presented to the input pin of the LM3914 from approximately 5 volts to near zero. The output shown will provide an indication of where the input light level is in ten steps.

Looking at the block diagram of the LM3914 in Fig. 8-4 you can see that it basically emulates what we were trying to accomplish with Figs. 8-1 and 8-2. Fig. 8-5 shows some ways to cascade the LM3914 to obtain more resolution. You can see that this type of light detector/-discriminator is an effective robot vision system.

THE REAL THING

By now, you are probably saying, I thought this vision chapter was really going to get into some *real* eyesight, but no dice! Well, you are not totally correct. In fact, we might as well get to it and satisfy the "heavy hardware hackers" search for the real thing!

Total high-resolution vision systems primarily use two techniques. The tv camera is used with an associated video digitizer to capture one frame worth of information. Also used, today, is the CCD monolithic solid-state imager with its associated control electronics. Both methods can provide quality resolution video input.

Earlier some terms were used that may be unfamiliar to you, so why don't we start from the beginning. A tv picture image is made up of tiny spots of light. These vary in brightness to give the overall impression of shades of grey. In the case of the color tv, the spots are, in reality, three spots, but for our vision purposes we'll stick to black and white.

These light and dark spots are placed in precise locations on the screen by electromagnets. No, the spots are not metallic, they are really not separate spots (confused?). The electromagnets direct a beam of electrons that vary in intensity across the screen from left to right. As this beam retraces back to the left, it is blanked. During the retrace, it is also deflected downward verti-

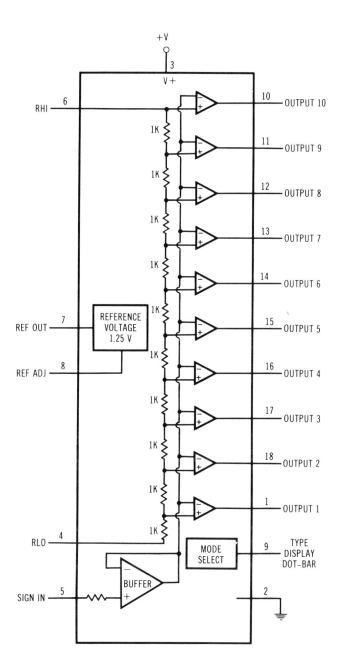

Fig. 8-4 Internal block diagram of the LM3914.

cally slightly so that it ends up sweeping across the entire screen. When the beam reaches the bottom right-hand corner of the screen, it is vertically retraced and again blanked to the upper-left or "home" position.

This scanning goes on constantly while the picture is displayed. The typical frequency of horizontal sweeps is 15.75 kHz and the vertical is retraced once every 30 Hz. One field of video dots is shown once, then the alternate field the next vertical trace. There are 525 lines of video information in the United States tv system. Two hundred and sixty-two are shown first and then the other set of lines. This process is called *interlacing*. Fig. 8-6 sums up what has just been said.

In the bottom half of the figure, you see a typical video input waveform. The negative-going pulses are the horizontal and vertical sync signals and the varying amplitude signals are the video intensity levels. Between vertical sync pulses, there is one field of data. Each video spot on the tv screen is called a *pixel*. It is the smallest definable video picture element.

These pixels have varying intensity levels. If we were to generate or represent each pixel in a computer, we would first want to determine how many intensity levels we want to allow. In standard graphics terminals, these levels range from four to two hundred and fifty-six. That would be represented by two to eight bits per pixel. This intensity information would be converted into binary weighted bits through an analog to digital converter.

VIDEO DIGITIZERS

The tv camera outputs are analog in nature. They vary from 0 to 1 volt. Standard computer or robot logic circuits tend to be digital, looking for the 0- to 4-volt signal swings with nothing in between. In order to convert the output of a camera into something a computer may recognize, we must digitize it. The video digitization process is pretty straightforward and highly time critical. Let's look at a block diagram of a typical video digitizer in Fig. 8-7.

The first stage of the digitizer is the sync separator. Here, both the vertical and horizontal sync pulses are

Fig. 8-5 Expanding the output of the circuit in Fig. 8-3 to include up to 20 shades of detection.

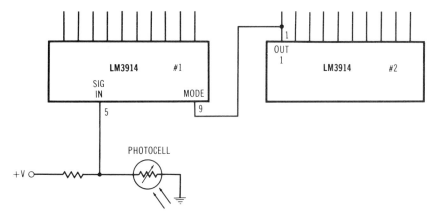

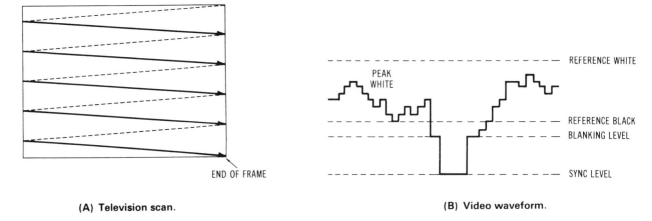

(A) Television scan.

(B) Video waveform.

Fig. 8-6 Simplified view of television scanning with standard television video waveform.

separated from the video. We need these to help determine where in the picture the pixels are to be placed. You see, the vidicon tube of the camera is scanned much the same way as the crt is in the tv. So, if we see a horizontal sync pulse, we will know it is time to jump left and down one row. Vertical sync pulses tell us that the field has either just begun or is just finishing.

Stripping sync from a video signal can be accomplished in a few ways. Figs. 8-8A and 8-8B depict two different circuits that can be used. One is a special tv integrated circuit. The other is made up simply of integrated circuits and transistors. The vertical sync pulse activates transistor Q1 effectively grounding the input to IC1a. The shorter horizontal pulses still sneak through; however, these are shunted to ground through capacitor C2. The second half of IC1 cleans up any remaining glitches and it restores the original polarity of the signal. We finish with a clean vertical sync pulse.

The vertical pulse is the more important of the two because it signals the beginning and the end of a scan. What we must do is determine how many pixels we want to represent in the image. If we want to resolve to 128 pixels horizontally and 128 vertically, we will have to divide the time between vertical sync pulses accordingly. There will be 16,384 individual picture elements in the

image array. Therefore, between the start and end vertical sync, we must place all 16,000 pixels in their proper position in the image memory. We will require 16,384 bits of memory to store a black and white 128 X 128 image.

Notice it says black and white. If you want varying levels of black or white, more memory is required. Each pixel will have to be encoded to carry the value of that intensity. Therefore, a 256 level image requires 16,384 X 8 bits/pixel or 131,072 memory locations!! Actually in most robot applications black and white will suffice.

The next step for vertical sync is to enable the pixel counter clock. When vertical sync is detected and the digitizer circuit is armed, clock pulses to increment the memory address counters are allowed to pass. Let's examine these pulses. If we assume there will be 262 lines of information being passed to us from the camera 30 times a second or every 33 milliseconds, in between the first and last vertical sync, all 16,384 pixels of information will be passed. If we divide the 33 milliseconds by the number of pixels we find the frequency of the pixel address clock. So, therefore:

$$\frac{33 \times 10^{-3}}{16,384} = 2.014 \times 10^{-6}$$

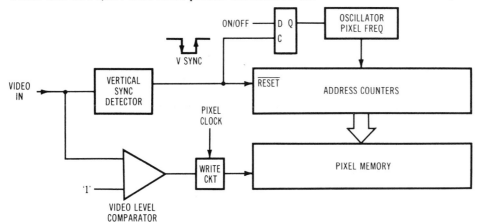

Fig. 8-7 Simple block diagram of a black and white tv digitizer.

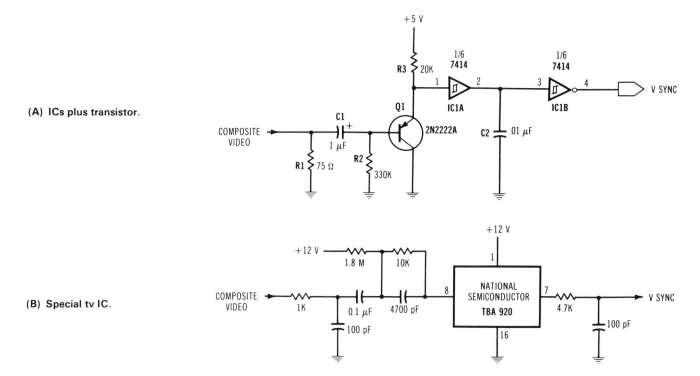

(A) ICs plus transistor.

(B) Special tv IC.

Fig. 8-8 Two simple vertical sync separator circuits.

The 2-microsecond clock assumes that there is no other use of time in the system. Actually the best way to figure the pixel clock is to divide the horizontal frequency (15.75 kHz) by the number of pixels in a line (128). This will yield a period of approximately 460 nanoseconds. This clock (looking at the block diagram), when applied to the address counters, helps place the pixel information into 16,384 locations between vertical sync pulses. The second vertical pulse shuts off the pixel clock and signals to the controller that one field has been entered. Let's see how the video information is actually digitized and stored in those memory locations.

Fig. 8-9 shows the circuitry required to convert the analog video signal into a logic level. The 2167 component is a 16K dynamic memory that requires only 5 volts to operate. Notice the use of the same comparator (lower left corner) that was used to digitize the output of the photocell earlier in this chapter. The reference voltage is set to distinguish a white level which, when true, activates the output to a logic 1 level. The pixel clock loads this into memory on its falling edge with the help of a one-shot multivibrator. The rising edge of pixel clock increments the memory address counters (CD 4024), which await the arrival of the next pixel.

This is not the only way to design a digitizer. In fact, there are more elegant approaches. If you intend to display the image on a monitor you want the digitizer to input the information into rows and columns to match your display. This is done by using the horizontal sync pulses. The occurrence of horizontal sync signals the end of one row and the beginning of another.

Well, now we have digitized a full image from a tv camera. We have over 16,000 bits of data to wade through. What do we do now? Good question. In fact, this is the toughest part of vision-system design. It takes enormous processing power with equally complex software algorithms to determine what we are seeing. In fact, there are entire books on the subject. We will not cover these algorithms here as this book is aimed at introductory levels; however, I have listed a few very readable books on the subject in the appendix.

SOLID STATE VISION

Remember it was said earlier that the other approach to video input was a thing called a CCD monolithic imager? This device is basically an integrated circuit with a clear window attached to it which allows light to fall on sensitive areas of the circuit. CCD monolithic imagers take relatively complex timing circuits and are extremely expensive. So why are they becoming so popular? Their size is the main reason as well as power usage. You can design them into the palm of a robot hand easily. How can we experiment with these devices if they cost more than the entire robot? We won't!

There is another approach to solid-state vision that is less elegant, yet extremely inexpensive. The same memory chip that you are using to store the pixel information can be converted into a sophisticated video

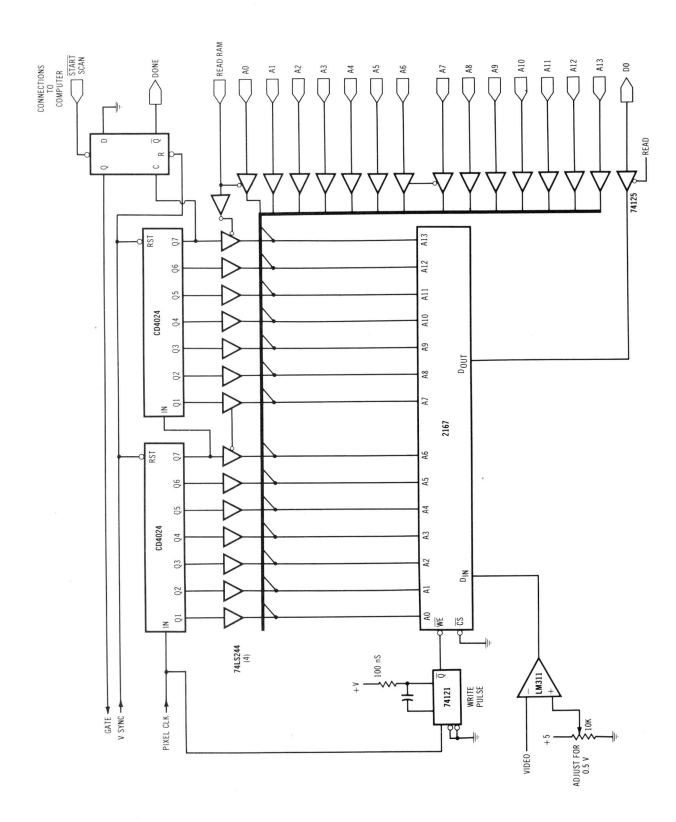

Fig. 8-9 Schematic of a **128 × 128** pixel video digitizer.

90

imager! When the protective cover is removed from a dynamic memory chip it exposes the inside electronic *die*. The cells used to hold data on this die are sensitive to light. If you write all logic ones into the chip and expose it to light, the locations getting strong light will turn to logic zeros. Therefore, if you focus an image on the chip surface using an inexpensive lens system, you should be able to distinguish light from dark areas by simply reading the contents of the chip. Another feature of this approach is that infrared light will also be detected, so if you illuminate a dark area with infrared light you can see in the dark!

Dynamic memories are ICs that store data. This information, however, is being stored internally as a charge on a tiny capacitor. As you may know, capacitors eventually bleed off their charges and the time it takes depends on their size. In this case, the capacitor is so tiny it takes a mere 2-milliseconds to lose the charge. Therefore, the charge or information is dynamic in nature and must be refreshed before the 2-millisecond time period is up. Interestingly enough, all the locations in a 16,384-bit memory chip can be refreshed by simply cycling through only 128 of them. So, every 2 milliseconds we must cycle at least 128 times. Cycles may be read operations.

Light striking the cells serves to accelerate the bleed off. Because each cell only has two states (on or off), we can detect only black or white. The key is to sharply focus the image on the die area of the chip. Fig 8-10 shows a 4096-bit RAM chip with its cover removed to expose the die. Notice how the die is partitioned into sections. This particular device is divided into four 1K portions.

We will experiment with a standard 4116 having a 16K memory circuit. These devices are relatively easy to obtain and are very inexpensive. You will, however, need to purchase the ceramic or *cerdip-type* package. The reason for this is that you will be able to remove the cover from the package in the ceramic device. To do this you should place a heated soldering iron carefully around the top edges of the device and soon the lid will slide. Carefully lift it off. There are tiny hair-like wires inside that you must not break. Cut a small piece of clear plastic the size of the lid and epoxy it in place of the cover to protect the die. You have just constructed a solid-state image sensor! Figs. 8-11, 8-12 and 8-13 detail the sequence of events just described.

The 4116 16K RAM is now manufactured by almost every semiconductor house. Here we will be using the NEC uPD 416D type from NEC Electronics Microcomputer Division. Let's look into the architecture of our image sensor now that we've gone through the trouble to disect it. A block diagram of the internal workings of the chip is shown in Fig. 8-14.

There are only 16 pins on this device which makes it ideal for placement where space is at a premium (Fig. 8-15 shows the pin designations.). The power supplies required are +5 V, -5 V and +12 V. There is one data input and one data output. The video image data will be extracted serially through the data out pin. Notice that their are seven inputs labeled A0 through A6. These are address-select pins that tell the sensor which image cell to read out or which one to set to a logic one. However, in a 16K memory, there is a need for 14 address inputs! Why? Well, it would usually be covered in the next chapter, however, it is very relevant and deserves comment here. Address lines select locations with binary coding. If there are four addresses, there will be two address lines. Each

Fig. 8-10 Photograph of a dynamic memory IC with its top removed.

Fig. 8-11 Use a soldering iron to heat the top surface of the component.

Fig. 8-12 After the cover is hot enough, remove top with a pair of pliers.

Fig. 8-13 The open-lidded device can be covered with a small piece of plastic glued into place.

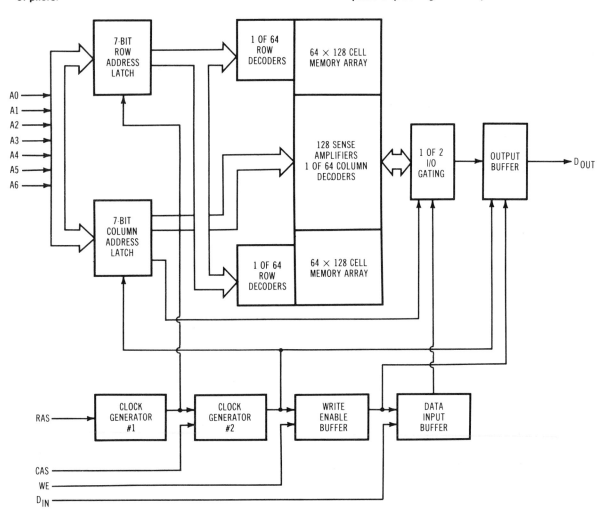

Fig. 8-14 Block diagram of the internal structure of a 16K dynamic memory.

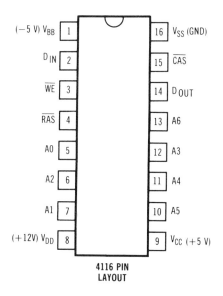

Fig. 8-15 Pin assignments of a 4116 standard 16K dynamic memory.

address line carries a value two times the previous one. So, if we go through the address lines of the 16K RAM, you can see that to reach 16,384 it takes 14 lines each of which is twice the previous line, when the first line equals a value of 1.

Thus if there are 14 lines needed and A0 through A6 are only seven, where are the other seven? In order to keep the pin count and, therefore, the package size down, the designers devised a way of electronically getting the first seven and then the next seven using two control lines called *RAS* and *CAS*. The RAS signal, when low, latches

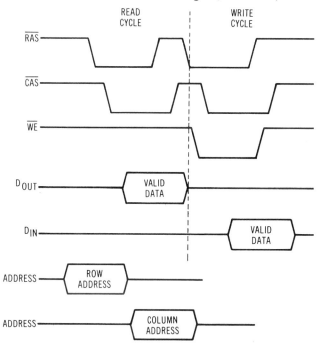

Fig. 8-16 Basic timing of the 4116 memory.

the seven row address bits into the chip, and because the RAM is arranged as a block matrix, the CAS signal latches in the seven column address bits.

If you apply the formula for finding out how many address locations there are by counting up address lines, you can see that we have an image area of 128×128 bits. A CCD imager of that size would cost several hundreds of dollars. The 16K chip will be under six dollars! Fig 8-16 details the timing relationship between the address bits and both RAS and CAS. If you don't mind the extra expense (less than $20), you can graduate to a 256×256 image area in the same size package by using a 4164 memory. This chip is 5 volts only and includes 65,536 locations! There are 8 input lines for 8 column and 8 row addresses.

Now that we know how our imager works, let's look at what it takes to get it seeing. Fig. 8-17 shows a logic circuit that can drive the image sensor and read out its contents.

Let's look at the circuit operation. On power up, the oscillator for the pixel clock starts pulsing. Each pulse will increment the address counter/multiplexer and drive the appropriate RAS and CAS signals. At first, all 16,384 locations are written into with a high logic level of 1. Then the oscillator clocks through the same locations reading them out while driving the horizontal and vertical sync signals. These operations go on indefinitely. If you want to get fancy, you can put an automatic shutter lens piece over the chip that can be activated by the signal PEEK. This effectively takes a snapshot of the image at a particular time. Fig. 8-18 shows the particulars of the cycle counter in the circuit.

Mechanically, the image sensor is placed in a painted box (preferably flat black) where only light from the image can get in. The best type of paint to use is the opaque nonreflective-type sold in photo stores. The box can be made of any material and can be as large or as small as you wish. It is not necessary to package the circuit in the same box as the RAM; however, take care to keep your lengths of wire short between the RAM; and its drivers. Noise can be picked up very easily in a robotic system especially with all those motors and electromechanical devices.

Lenses are usually a pain in the neck for an electronic experimenter to obtain. The author found a few that seem to work satisfactorily in this application, though, and they are readily available. Edmund Scientific Part Number 41,146 is a movie camera lens that works well. Most 35mm camera lenses work also although they are quite a bit more expensive. You will have to play around some to find the optimum distance between the lens and sensor. Fig. 8-19 offers some ideas for doing this. This can be done by placing a high-contrast test pattern in front of the lens at the distance you wish it to see. Adjust the lens and the spacing between lens and sensor for the sharpest image.

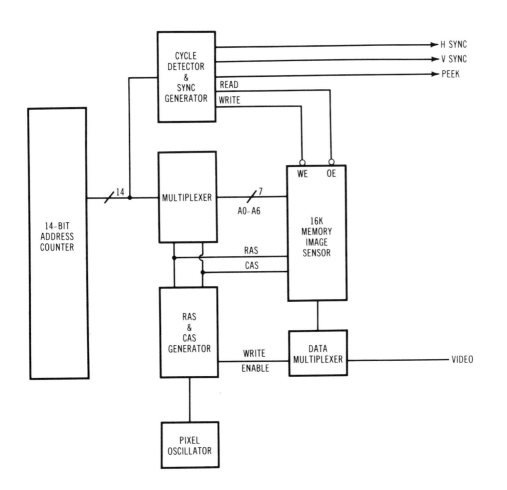

Fig. 8-17 Psuedo schematic of circuit to drive solid state image sensor.

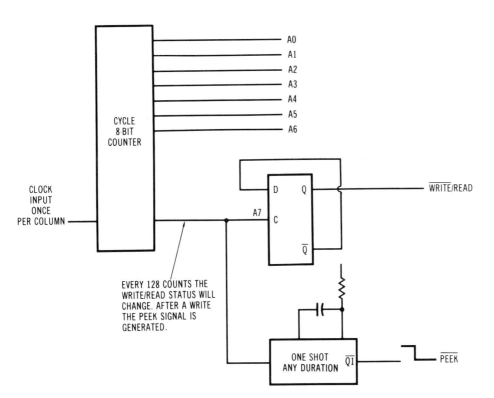

Fig. 8-18 Detail of the cycle counter.

94

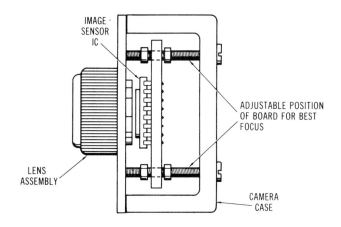

Fig. 8-19 Diagram of mechanical mounting of an image-sensor board.

How do we display the image coming out of this box? We have to do a conversion. First, the signals are coming out separately, not in the composite form of Fig. 8-6, and the video levels are 0 and 5 volts, not 0 and 1 volt. The scanner outputs are, however, exactly compatible to standard video monitors like the type sold by Ball Brothers, Inc. Their tv series of monitors takes 5-volt video levels and separate sync signals. More data for this monitor and the manufacturer's address are included in the appendix.

You will see in the next few chapters, when microprocessor control is introduced, how circuits such as the one in Fig. 8-17 can dwindle to only a few ICs. As you can see, the solid-state image scanner is relatively simple to construct. Because the sync signals are already separate, there is no need for sync separation and no need for analog comparators because the video is already TTL compatible.

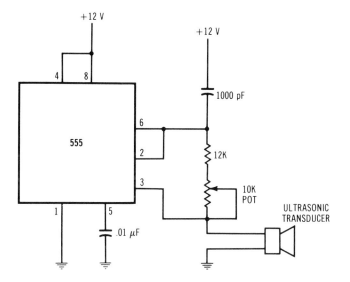

Fig. 8-20 Simple ultrasonic transmitter.

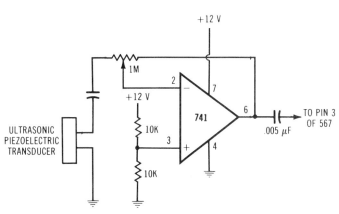

Fig. 8-22 Alternate amplifier for ultrasonic receiver.

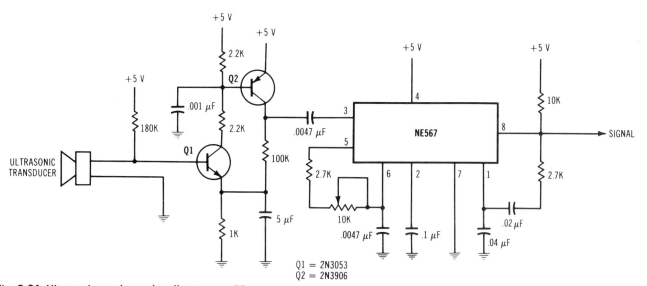

Fig. 8-21 Ultrasonic receiver using discrete amplifier.

95

JUDGING DISTANCE

We now have the ability to acquire images by a variety of methods. Our robot can see what it is gripping, where it is going and where it has been. There is possibly one more sense of vision that it might require: the ability to judge distance.

As humans, we have a crude built-in distance measuring system that makes use of the eyes and the stored knowledge of how far away a certain distance looks. We then apply this known image to the one we are encountering and *voila* . . . a rough estimate. Sure, we could apply this method to our robot system; however, that would require auto focus systems on the lenses and a complex image-analysis algorithm in the controller. There is, however, a much simpler and more economical way to obtain this judgment. In fact, this way is even more accurate.

Ultrasonics is the science of inaudible sounds. These sounds are normally up around the 40 kHz frequency range and are generally sent out in very short pulses. There are small speaker-like devices called ultrasonic ceramic transducers that are driven by conventional oscillators that can be mounted on the PCB of a distance analyzer. Let's look at a typical distance-measuring system utilizing ultrasonics. In the previous chapter, you saw a figure relating to the various functional blocks associated with producing, receiving, and analyzing an infrared distance-measuring signal. Ultrasonic ranging is very similar.

Short 40 kHz pulses of ultrasonic sound are emitted by the transducer. These sound waves leave the transducer and spread out as they travel through free air. When these waves strike an object in their path, some of the initial wave energy is deflected back toward the receiving transducer which is now acting as a microphone.

The vibrations of the reflected sound waves are very weak, compared to the transmitted energy, so they must be amplified when they are first received. After amplification, they are sent on to a discriminator circuit that stops a counter from incrementing. This counter was started when the first transmit pulse was initiated. The value in the counter relates to how long it took for the pulse to travel and return. This can give us distance by multiplying the number of counts by the speed of sound. Of course, the counts have to be in seconds or fractions of seconds.

Basically, this is all that is needed to measure distance. Let's look at some circuit implementations of both transmitter and receivers. Fig. 8-20 shows a simple 40 kHz transmitter circuit. The 555 IC is a very inexpensive 8-pin timer circuit that has been connected to work as an a-stable oscillator pulsing the transducer at a rate of 40 kHz. This frequency can be adjusted by potentiometer.

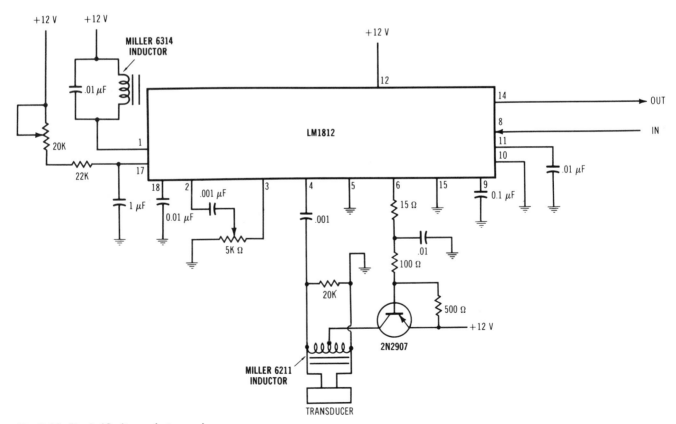

Fig. 8-23 Single IC ultrasonic transceiver.

96

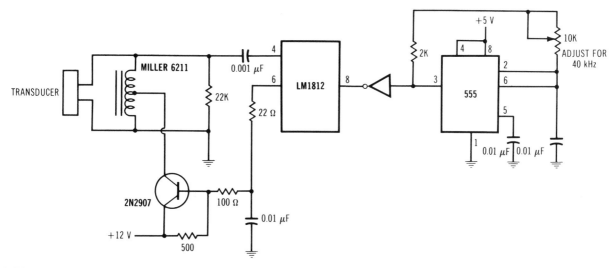

Fig. 8-24 Adding an external oscillator increases the range of the receiver section.

Using a 12-volt supply will yield a 10-volt signal swing at the transducer, which will provide ample drive. Any oscillator running at 40 kHz can be substituted for the 555. In fact, it would be possible to have a computer directly output a 40 kHz signal without any additional circuitry.

The receive portion of the system is a little more complex. Figs. 8-21 and 8-22 depict two approaches for receiving the signal. In Fig. 8-21, the received echo is amplified through a discrete transmitter amplifier, then applied to a tone decoder chip, the NE567. This IC is a phase-locked loop that contains its own oscillator (that must be adjusted to 40 kHz) and a comparator that will activate the output when it detects an incoming signal equal in frequency to itself. The circuit is very simple and inexpensive. Fig. 8-22 shows an alternative amplifier. This IC is a standard 741 that sells for well under a dollar.

Fig. 8-23, however, uses a single IC ultrasonic transceiver that will not only receive a signal when it gets an echo, but the same circuit can be used to transmit the initial pulse. Looking at the circuit you can see that transmission is initiated by a logic 1 placed on pin 8. At this time, the receiver is disabled and there will be no output from pin 14. To receive, simply ground pin 8 and watch for pin 14 to pulse to a logic 1 level. The time that has passed between transmit and receive in seconds, multiplied by 13,080 inches per second (speed of sound), gives you the distance in inches from the obstacle. The circuit in the figure has a range of 4 inches to approximately 6 feet. The addition of an external 555 oscillator IC in Fig. 8-24 will increase the range from 3 inches to 20 feet. All of the components listed on the schematic are available and at reasonable cost.

With the component count so low, you could build several of these rangers and place them at various points on the body of the robot. One mounted in the palm of a hand could serve to judge distances between it and an object. Two mounted on the front of the base and one at each corner can report any obstacles in the robot's path. There are several places these sensors could be used handily. In the next chapter, you will learn about single component computers that can be connected to these ultrasonic rangers which will give us distance in inches whenever we request it.

Fig. 8-25 Various available ultrasonic tranducers.

The device used to convert the ultrasonic pulses into sound waves is available in several shapes and sizes. Fig. 8-25 shows several types. Let's look inside these transducers. Fig. 8-26 shows the basic construction of the ceramic type manufactured by Panasonic. Notice the inclusion of the piezoelectric crystal. Remember, we briefly looked into this type device in the chapter on tactile sensing. There we were exerting physical pressure on the surface of the crystal which resulted in a voltage being produced. Here, we use it as both a receiver of pressure and a transmitter, the pressure being sound waves that are produced when a voltage excites the piezo

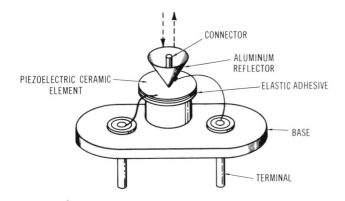

Fig. 8-26 Internal construction of the Panasonic ultrasonic transducer.

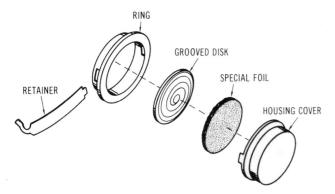

Fig. 8-27 Basic construction of the Polaroid® transducer.

Fig. 8-28 A photograph showing the Polaroid® transducer and driver board.

crystal. So, it does the opposite of sensing when a voltage is applied to it. The vibrations it produces are what we use as the ranging beam.

Polaroid Corp. has begun using ultrasonics in cameras. The information gained about the distance between it and the subject being photographed is used to focus the main lens automatically. Think of a use for the shutter

*One-Step is a registered trademark of Polaroid Corp.

Fig. 8-29 Photograph showing the complete ultrasonic ranging kit available from Polaroid®.

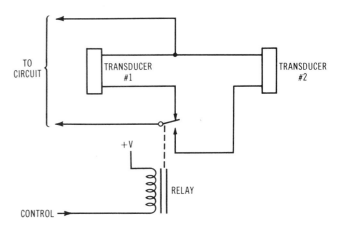

Fig. 8-30 Schematic for connecting two transducers to a ranging system board.

system employed in the Sonar One-Step®* camera used with the solid-state imager just described. The transducer they use has a larger diameter and is slimmer than the Panasonic type. Fig. 8-27 shows the construction details. Fig. 8-28 shows both the transducer and electronic package that are now available to the public in the form of an experimenter's kit.

It is called the Polaroid Ultrasonic Ranging System Designer's kit and it is available for about $150. Somewhat costly! However, it comes with a special interface that converts the received echoes directly into feet and displays the value on an LED readout. Fig. 8-29 shows what you will get for your money. They even throw in an extra transducer! This extra component can come in handy. If you need two separate areas scanned, you can do one of two things. First, you might mount the transducer on a stepper motor and physically move it to face the direction of desired ranging. A second approach is simply to mount the two transducers and switch between them. Fig. 8-30 shows a way of doing this with a small relay. Of course, it is possible to purchase more transduc-

98

ers; by expanding the switching scheme you could cover all bases with one set of electronics. This also is true of the other ultrasonic circuits we have covered.

At this time, it would benefit us if we entered into the world of computer control. You will see how simple the circuits are, and how one slight change in the computer memory can change the whole operation. Many of the hardware approaches we've made can be replaced with simple programming instructions which make it easier to change the personality of the robot at any time.

Section IV:
COMPUTER CONTROL

Chapter 9

Single Chip Intelligence

Up to this point, we have been mainly concerned with components. These are the small parts of a robot, such as the arms, legs, eyes, and sensors. We have also been working in the physical world, primarily with mechanical or electromechanical devices. Throughout, mention was made of the benefits of computer control over a certain mechanical procedure or the text eluded to that great "Master Controller" buried somewhere in the robot's brain. In this chapter, we will meet the master of control, the microcomputer. Not only will we study its ways, but we will design programs for robot control of the very mechanical components that we have just covered.

In Chapters 10 through 14, we will study the specific system examples along with their associated hardware and software designs. Before we go this deep, let's review the operation of an electronic computer for those of you who may be new to the subject.

COMPUTERS

When you decide to wash your hair with shampoo, typically you follow the directions on the side of the shampoo bottle: lather, rinse, repeat. This short list of three simple words is the solution to a complicated question of how do I get my hair washed using this shampoo. It also satisfies part of a more global problem of how do I get my hair clean.

Lather, rinse, repeat—each word implies yet a more complex breakdown where the act of lathering involves opening the bottle, pouring out a measured amount of liquid, and applying this to the hair. Each word could be called a *code word* for defining a more involved operation. The three words together form a structured way of solving a problem. Structural because it is important that each step be followed in the order it is called out.

Now that your hair is washed, let's get out of the bathroom and into computers. There are many similarities between washing your hair and the way a computer controls a robot. You see, the computer, like you, works on one operation at a time. If you tell it to test its bump sensors and move ahead if it doesn't feel anything is obstructing it, these operations will be performed in the order you stated, one by one: lather, rinse, repeat.

Computers have short words that represent more complex mundane things. They are called *op codes* (codes for operations). Although they don't, at this writing, include the three on the shampoo bottle, they do, however, have the likes of ADD, SUB, MOV, OUT, IN, and NOP. That last one looks rather strange, doesn't it? It's fairly easy to figure out the others, but this one sure doesn't sound right. The NOP stands for no operation. That's right, the computer even gets the chance to loaf occasionally.

When these op codes are put together into lists of complete instructions that describe the solution to a problem, we call it a *program*. The program on the shampoo bottle may seem very simple compared to the type used to control a robot, but as you will find out, big programs are made up of several little ones. The method you work out for accomplishing the solution in a small program is called an *algorithm*. Algorithms are nothing more than recipes.

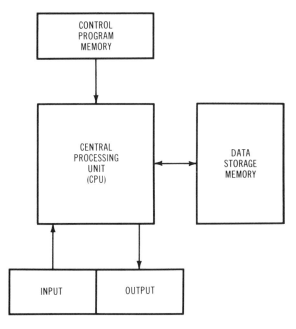

Fig. 9-1 Block diagram of a basic digital computer.

What's inside a computer? That's as good a place to start as any. Fig. 9-1 shows a block diagram of a very simple computer. The control memory shown is where the programs are located. These are broken down into many single op codes. The control memory will present them to the central processing unit in the order in which you had them written. Each new op code received at the processor is evaluated to determine what actions it is being commanded to do. You see, these op codes are instructions for the central processor. They may tell it to take some input information gained through sensors or the like, and act on it by, perhaps, outputting motor-control commands.

Notice that blocks for input and output are included. Input devices are limit switches, tactile sensors, position feedback devices, etc. The output section includes drive information to the base/legs, arm, hand, and any other directly controlled device.

On the block diagram, there is shown a separate block titled "data storage memory." In reality, both the control and data memory may be one and the same in a computer system. Some computers, however, use read only memories (ROMs) for op codes and, therefore, could not store or write data into them. In this case, some separate Random Access Memory (RAM) might be required. That is why I have included a separate block.

How big are computers? The ones we will use in this book are about as small as you can get right now. They are called single-chip microcomputers because contained within their IC package are all the functions shown in the block diagram. Some have additional functions built in such as programmable timers or analog-to-digital converters. But the greatest value these microcomputers hold for us is their size, power consumption, and ease of use.

CPU

Before programming one of these, it is very important that you understand every aspect of how they work. The most convenient place to start is with the central processing unit (CPU). Fig. 9-2 shows a typical functional block diagram of a CPU. Basically, it consists of four types of sub units:

1. Register Array
2. Arithmetic Logic Unit

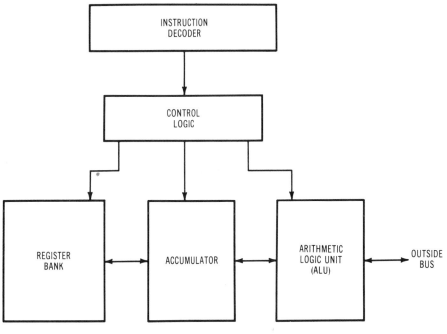

Fig. 9-2 Block diagram of a central processing unit (CPU).

3. Instruction Decoder
4. Control Circuits

The control circuits associated with the computer help to keep everything flowing smoothly.

There is an input pin on a microcomputer labeled RESET. Usually when power is first applied to the computer, there is some method of asserting a signal or voltage level to this input which will initiate a hardware reset or a start from a known point action. The control circuitry at this point will set up the address of the first instruction of control memory. This address is actually a series of output lines which connect to the memory. They address a particular location by using a binary number. Remember our discussion of the address lines in the image sensor? Each address line is binary weighted two times the previous one. Look at the binary equivalents in Chart 9-1 to familiarize yourself with this method of numbering.

The location output on the address lines of the CPU is presented to the control memory. Depending on the size of this memory, there may be thousands of these storage places. Each one has a unique address much like apartments in a large complex.

Two control outputs, one for READ, the other for WRITE, will inform the memory of the CPU's intentions. Some CPUs have one line to denote this and it is called R/W. When the line is at a 1 logic level, you will be reading memory locations, when it is at a 0, the data will be written.

Data, now that's an interesting word! It represents the information we are manipulating. Data could be the op code we are receiving from the memory, or the answer to an addition problem commanded by the op code. Data is stored and represented in the same binary manner as addresses. Each data line represents what is called a *bit* of information. If there are eight data lines, by following Chart 9-1, you can see that the information content represented may range from the number 0 to 255.

So what? If my computer is programmed in numbers, don't I just have a programmable calculator? You want this thing to talk, listen, see, and move. What will 0 to 255 do for you? Read on . . .

Computers with eight data lines are referred to as 8-bit machines. There are 4-bit, 8-bit, some 12-bit and, more recently, 16-bit microcomputers. Why the varying sizes? Information transfer. Let's assume the answer to some problem is larger than the maximum coding for the bit length machine. It may be necessary to combine two or three sets of 8-bit numbers to represent the answer. Each set of eight bits is called a *byte*. In that case, several bytes must be output, therefore, slowing down the operation of that particular instruction. After all, the computer will only output one byte at a time. Increasing the number of data lines reduces the bottle neck and, therefore, increases speed or throughput.

In these systems, the byte of data may represent many things. Take for example the limit sensors from a previous chapter. If you were to connect a number of these to a circuit that responded to a memory location address, it would be possible to "read" the state of each switch. How? Consider the diagram in Fig. 9-3. Each limit switch will essentially be connected to a unique data line. When the computer addresses the particular location that the switch address decoder responds to, the voltage levels present on the switches will be read by the CPU as a byte of data. If data line 0 is low or at 0, will the number 254 be just another number? No! You will have provided an instruction in your program that will convert the number 254 into the fact that limit switch 1 is activated. Look at Fig. 9-4. This is a flowchart of the operations necessary to read the switch port. After they are read, if the value 254 is received, some action is taken. Notice if it is not received, the computer falls back and reads again until the condition exists. This is called a *loop*. It may be a subprogram that is executed several times throughout a larger program. More about this later.

INSTRUCTION DECODER

Now that we see how op codes are fetched from memory and how they are represented in bytes, let's look at where they go once they arrive in the CPU. The Instruction Decoder does just like its name implies. Each op code represents some action to be performed. It is the function of this block to figure it out and get it done. In

Chart 9-1. Relationships of Address Locations to Address Bits

ADDRESS LINES	A15	A14	A13	A12	A11	A10	A9	A8	A7	A6	A5	A4	A3	A2	A1	A0
Weighted Value	32,768	16,384	8192	4096	2048	1024	512	256	128	64	32	16	8	4	2	1

When an address line is active, there is a Logic 1 in that position.

Example:

```
A15                                    A0
0000   0110    0111   0001  ◄── Address in binary
       /  \    / | \          |
    1024  512 64 32 16        1
```

Add the numbers together:

```
   1024
    512
     64
     32
     16
  +   1
   1649
```

Address location (declined equivalent) = 1649

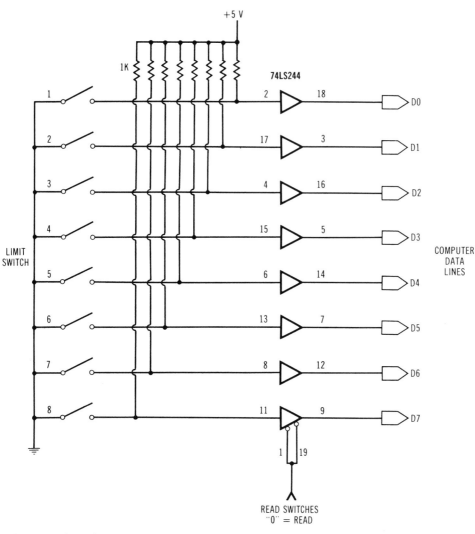

+5 V

1K

74LS244

1   2   18   D0

2   17   3   D1

3   4   16   D2

4   15   5   D3

LIMIT
SWITCH

5   6   14   D4

6   13   7   D5

7   8   12   D6

8   11   9   D7

1   19

COMPUTER
DATA
LINES

READ SWITCHES
"0" = READ

Fig. 9-3 Schematic showing the connections necessary to read 8 switches into a computer.

order to perform its duties, it will rely on the other blocks within the unit.

REGISTERS

Inside the CPU are various holding areas where single bytes of data may be temporarily stored during operations. These holding areas are called *registers*. In an 8-bit machine, these registers are normally 8 bits wide. There may be as few as two and as many as several dozen of these locations.

One register, in particular, that is common to most CPUs is the *accumulator,* or the A register. This register is used most extensively as the airlock between the inside of the CPU and the outer devices. Memory transfers usually go through the A register on their way to other destinations. The results of a computation between two numbers usually end up in this location.

The other general-purpose registers within the CPU help to eliminate the need for transfering data back and forth between the CPU and outside memory location, while performing a specific task. There are, however, at least two registers in a CPU that are somewhat dedicated in function. These are the Program Counter and the Stack Pointer.

PROGRAM COUNTER

You might assume, by the name of this register, that individual programs might be counted and stored here. Well, not really. The Program Counter contains the next binary control-memory address that will be used when retrieving an op code. Notice, we said the *next address.* Actually the contents of the Program Counter is what appears on the address outputs of the CPU. After the data requested is received by the CPU, the instruction decoder decides whether the next address is sequential or of a completely new number. In the case of a sequential decision, the Program Counter is simply incremented by adding one to its existing number.

In the case of a JMP (jump) instruction. The next following data bytes load directly into the program counter. Fig. 9-5 shows the processes that a CPU goes through

106

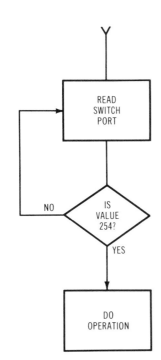

Fig. 9-4 Simple flowchart of a
read switch routine.

with the Program Counter. There are many instructions that affect the contents of this register as we will see later. Before we get into the programming aspects of the machine, there are still several hardware areas to be studied.

STACK POINTER AND INTERRUPTS

No, the CPU does not look for smoke stacks, then point to them. Although the Environmental Protection Agency might have a good use for one of those gadgets! Whenever the CPU is commanded to interrupt what it is doing, it will store away some of its registers that contain information about what it was doing at the time of the interruption. It does this because when the interruption is over, the CPU returns to where it left off.

Interrupts are useful commands. Most always they come in the form of a signal input pin called INT being toggled to its active state (usually 0). They are used in systems where the circuit causing the interrupt must have the attention of the CPU immediately, such as a collision sensor or low battery alarm. Naturally, you want the interrupt to be dedicated to your highest priority sensor. There are interrupt control ICs which allow multiple interrupt inputs that are prioritized automatically. When an interrupt is enacted, the CPU simply queries this controller to find out how important it really is.

It was briefly mentioned that during the interrupt critical CPU status information is stored for future use. Where does it go? In most cases, the CPU sets aside a portion of data memory (read or write kind) for such things. This area is called a *Stack*. The Stack Pointer is a memory address register like the Program Counter

except that it does not increment after each instruction. It is only used to point to the next available location on the Stack.

Stacks are arranged just like the name implies. The last item put on the stack will be the first one to be taken off, like a pile of books. The Stack is called a last in first out device, or a LIFO, for short. There are other times when the Stack is used during the execution of subprograms that we will investigate later.

Between the Program Counter, Stack and its pointer, and the general-purpose registers, we have most of the tools necessary to receive instructions and store their results. However, there must be some way to execute the instruction.

ALU

The Arithmetic-Logic Unit (ALU) inside the CPU performs all mathematic and logical operations requested by the op code instruction. It can add two numbers together, compare the contents of two registers, shift numbers to make them change, and a host of other operations. It is here that the processing is done. In Fig. 9-4, the decision block where it asks whether the switch value read equals 254 is performed in the ALU. The number 254 is loaded into the accumulator with a MOV (move) instruction, the switch codes are read into the ALU and both the switch value and the contents of Register A are logically compared. The ALU then produces a number (binary value) that is loaded into the CPU status word register which indicates either a match (zero condition) or not. As you study the programming aspects later, a lot of this processing will become clear.

Well, we've covered the major functional blocks of the CPU. There are other hardware type items that are associated with microcomputers, such as clocks. Each CPU is synchronized by clock pulses so that it fetches instructions and executes them in an orderly timed fashion. The

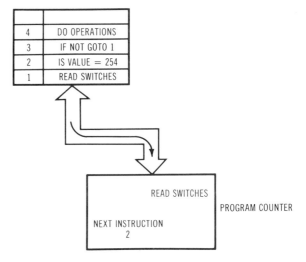

Fig. 9-5 Action and operation of the program counter.

clock frequency varies between manufacturers, but it is generally derived by connecting a crystal to the microcomputer. The frequency of this crystal determines the speed at which the operations are executed.

The intelligent machines of today have packaged an enormous amount of "thinking" power into relatively small areas. This size reduction was necessary because the demand for portable instruments has increased. The portability of intelligence is a direct result of the single chip microcomputer.

MICROCOMPUTERS

As you may or may not know, there is a difference between a microprocessor and a microcomputer. The latter contains a complete complement of program and data memory as well as input and output facilities. Most microcomputers are classified as small computers such as the Apple®, TRS-80®, ATARI®*, etc. You may even own such an animal.

The microcomputers we will study here are contained in single 40-pin IC packages. Yes, they do contain both types of memory, some I/O and in most cases a general-purpose timer for event counting, pulse-width determination or timing-delay loops. All of them operate from a single 5-volt supply with approximately a hundred milliamps. It is these compact, and low-power, attributes which allow us to construct the versatile controllers that run today's robots.

OPERATION PARTICULARS

Here we'll investigate two of the available single-chip micros. The Intel 8748 and the Motorola 68701 are easily obtained through electronics mail order houses, at reasonable cost. Each has its advantages depending on the situation you want to control. The Intel microcomputer is, by far, the least expensive and has the notoriety of being the first part to incorporate a system. The Motorola microcomputer is the most expensive but, as you will see, has the most capability. Instead of covering each separately, let's look at individual functions and identify their operations as they pertain to each part.

INTERNAL ARCHITECTURE

The functional insides of the 8748 are shown in Fig. 9-6. This is a rather simplified representation of the actual insides, however, it will suffice for this discussion. First, we see that there is 1K × 8 of program memory. This is read only memory and contains the control program for

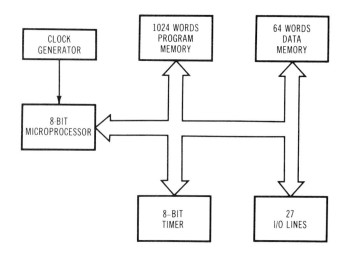

Fig. 9-6 Block diagram of the Intel 8748.

the microcomputer. In the case of the 8748, this memory is erasable and field programmable much like other EPROMs. Instructions are fetched internally from this memory, as there are no obvious data or address lines.

Fig. 9-7 shows a similarly simplified view of the functional blocks of the Motorola 68701. The erasable program memory contained in this single chip is twice that of the 8748.

Both microcomputers have erasable program memory on board in small but useful amounts. If you're used to programming a Z80 and find that you can't do much in 1K anymore, don't worry, these micro's have taken their small size into account and have instruction sets that take advantage of custom routines which allow single-byte op codes in over 70% of the set (8748). Those familiar with the 6800 family of microprocessors, or the somewhat less adept 6500 series, can take heart in knowing that the 68701 is code compatible with the 6800!

Moving on, let's look at data memory. This is where your first real disappointment will be. The 8748 gives you only 64 bytes of space. Hardly enough for a subroutine stack you say? Motorola was somewhat more generous with 128 bytes. Why the small amount of memory locations? Remember, these are I/O controllers. They are not an Apple II on a chip. When performing hardware emulation, you will find that, in many instances, you will not need even a third of the 64 available in the Intel part.

So, as far as memory goes, both the 8748 and the 68701 are alike. Sure the Motorola micro has twice the storage, but there is a comparable Intel microcomputer called the 8749 that matches it. Memory is the only attribute these

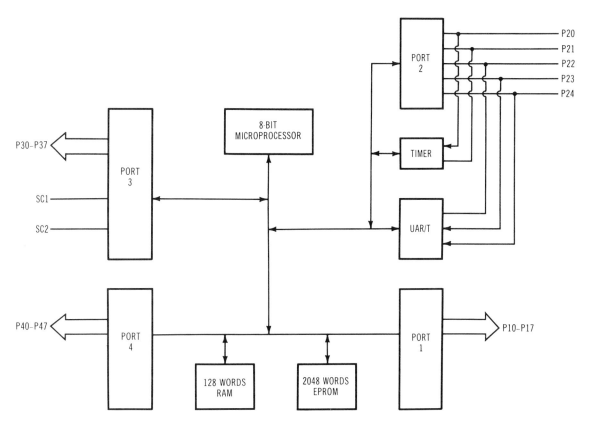

Fig. 9-7 Block diagram of the Motorola 68701.

two chips have in common. It is I/O where the 68701 shines. Looking at the block diagram, you can see that along with 28 general-purpose pins available for use as inputs or outputs, there is a full-functioning UAR/T included. This can be very handy in situations where you want to communicate serially to a host computer.

The 8748 incorporates no internal UAR/T. It does have, however, 27 input and output lines that that are very easily programmed. One should not belittle Intel for not matching Motorola's component in functionality because, you see, there is a micro that Intel makes (8751) that far surpasses the competition, but it is not widely available through experimenter outlets and is, therefore, not considered here.

Timers are very useful machines. They allow us to create a single pulse or string of pulses with little or no software intervention. We can count pulses that may present themselves to the controller and, if the period is slow enough, the counter may be used to measure its frequency. The 8748 has one 8-bit up-counter. It can be used in one of two modes: timer or event counter. The 68701 incorporates a 16-bit up-counter that allows multiple functions and a variety of uses.

NITTY-GRITTY, 8748

Well, so much for the generalities. It's time to choose a

way to go and specifically learn its inner workings. For the various robot controller designs, to be presented in the following chapters, the 8748 was chosen. Before you ask why, let me explain. You can purchase the Intel 8748 at under $15.00 (some places less that $10.00) and that's not a serious investment. Four times that price and you might get the Motorola 68701. In this day of economic uncertainties, you'd have to agree.

Let's start at the top. As I said, the 8748 contains 1024 bytes of erasable program memory. It is assumed you are familiar with EPROMs and will not go into the whys and wherefores of how they work. I will, however, explain how to program this memory. If fact, before we're through, you'll have the opportunity to actually construct an 8748 programmer/emulator that works off of anybody's home computer. Before we can get into it, there are some pins on the microcomputer that must be defined.

Fig. 9-8 shows the pinout of the 8748. Starting from pin 1, let's define the function of each.

Pin 1 T0   This is an input or output pin. You can test the state of it for either a high or low and branch to another place in the program. When used as an output, an ENT0 CLK, instruction will

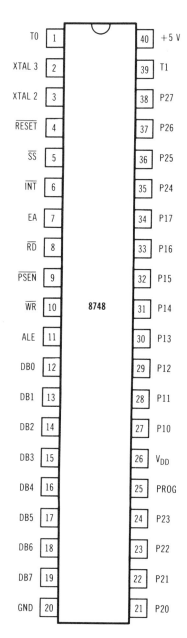

Fig. 9-8 Pinout of the 8748.

be applied to the XTAL1, pin 2, if the circuit shown in the figure is used.

Pin 4 $\overline{\text{RESET}}$ This input provides an initialization to the microcomputer. Typically it is connected to a power-on detector that would automatically invoke initialization. Fig. 9-10 shows the external particulars of making the reset input functional. When the reset is initiated, the following functions are performed:

1. The program counter is cleared (000).
2. The stack pointer is set to zero.
3. Register bank zero is selected.
4. Memory bank zero is selected.
5. The BUS outputs are floated at a high impedance state.
6. Both Port 1 and Port 2 are set to the input mode.
7. Interrupts are all disabled.
8. Timer is stopped.
9. The timer overflow flag is cleared.
10. General purpose flags F0 and F1 are cleared.
11. T0 becomes an input.

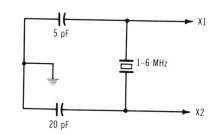

cause a clock signal, which is the crystal frequency divided by 3, to be generated from this pin. T0 is also used to select program mode when EA pin (7) is placed at programming voltage level.

Pins 2,3   These are the crystal connections.
XTAL1,2   An external crystal in the range of 1 MHz and 6 MHz may be connected across these two pins. Extra capacitance must be added to provide reliable operation. Fig. 9-9 shows typical crystal hookups. An external frequency pulse may

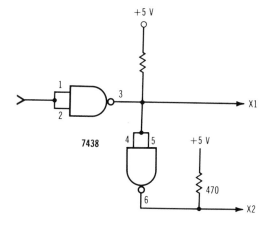

Fig. 9-9 Basic oscillator circuits for the 8748.

110

Pin 5 SS̄ No, it's not akin to the Hitler regime. It stands for single step. Remember that function which all the good front panels used to have? Well, this pin along with the ALE pin (11) and an external chip or two performs an instruction single step that is extremely useful in debugging. The circuit of Fig. 9-11 shows the circuitry necessary to implement this function.

Pin 6 ĪNT This interrupt vectors the program to program location 003. A low-level pulse initiates it. More about that later.

Pin 7 EA We already mentioned this pin in connection with programming (T0). Actually it's another of those multipurpose pins. Its title is External Access and during normal operation the pin will either be at a logic low or a high. When EA is low, all program memory fetches are taken from internal EPROM. When high, the use of an external ROM or RAM may take the place of the internal EPROM. This is useful in emulation as you will see later.

Pin 8 R̄D When accessing external memory (data) the R̄D line is used much like the Read line of any microprocessor. During program memory fetches or data memory accesses from internal functions, this pin is inactive.

Pin 9 P̄SEN When the part is configured to fetch from external program memory (EA =1) this pin acts as a combination chip enable-read line to that external memory part. The R̄D line does not respond to external program memory fetches.

Pin 10 W̄R Used in conjunction with the R̄D line on external data accesses. This pin provides write gating.

Pin 11 ALE If you are familiar with the 8085A you'll recognize this signal. When external memory is to be accessed, the Address Latch Enable (ALE) signal latches the lower eight addresses from the bus. This signal occurs once each cycle. More on external memory later.

Pins 12–19 BUS Here are eight bidirectional three-state bus lines that may be used as general-purpose I/O. If external memory is used, these lines become a combination of data bus and low order address bus (see ALE).

Pin 20 GND What can I say about ground . . . the buck stops here.

Pins 21–24 P20–P23 These are four of the eight Port 2 I/O lines. This port may be read or set. Each pin may be an input or an output. They also function as address lines when using external memory.

Pin 25 PROG This is the business pin for programming the erasable program memory. During the process, a 23-volt pulse is applied here for approximately 50 msec, which effectively copies the state of the bus lines, at that time, into the previously addressed program memory location. More about this later.

Pin 26 VDD Programming power is applied here to the potential of 25 volts. During normal operation this input should be at +5 volts.

Pins 27–34 Port 1 These are eight lines of general-purpose input or output, that are not used for any other purpose.

Pins 35–38 P24–P27 These are the upper four lines of Port 2. The lower lines are at pins 29–24. I/O expansion is accomplished through

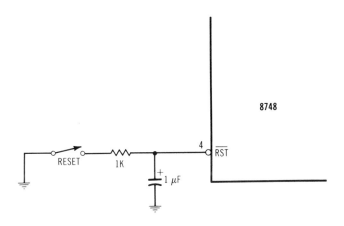

Fig. 9-10 Simple connection of capacitor and pushbutton provides 8748 with both automatic and manual reset.

111

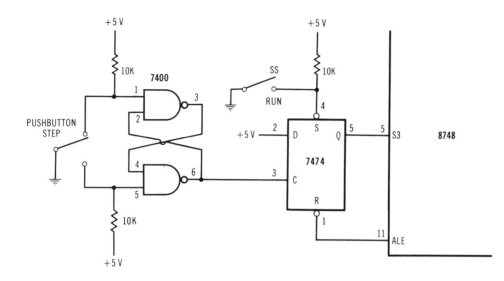

these pins and the PROG pin. More about this later.

Pin 39 T1   Remember T0? Well, T1 isn't quite as exciting; however, it does have a few functions. Besides using it as a testable input pin, T1 may be internally connected (by software) to the timer input. (Getting counting ideas?)

Pin 40 Vcc   This is where it all begins. Apply the +5 volts here.

Believe it or not, there are no other pins. Before we ventured into this chip's pinouts, we were trying to examine the programming of the erasable EPROM. Let's look at a step by step description of the program operation and try to design a circuit that allows us to accomplish it.

PROGRAMMING AND VERIFICATION

The 8748 is programmed by following the steps outlined in the exact order that they are presented:

1. Place VDD at + 5V. Make sure the oscillator is running. RESET = 0, T0 = 1, EA = 1, PROG input is open.
2. T0 = 0 (select program mode)
3. EA = 23 V
4. Apply the lower eight address inputs of the location on the Bus lines, the upper two to P20 and P21.
5. Pull RESET high (this will latch address).
6. Apply the data to be written on the BUS.
7. Place VDD at 25 V.
8. PROG pin is set to 0 volt then to +23 V for 50 ms then back to 0 volt and finally floating.
9. Bring VDD back to +5 V.
10. Select verify by pulling T0 to .5 V.
11. Read the data programmed on BUS outputs.
12. If it is okay, reset T0 to zero.
13. Bring RESET back to zero.
14. Return to step 4 for successive addresses.

Simple, yet complicated. Most of the digital programming sounds fairly easy to accomplish, but that voltage switching! Considering the range of switching, some analog transistor switches must be designed. To simplify things, working schematics of this part of the design are provided. All you need to do is build it. Fig. 9-12 shows the voltage switch. This circuit was not an original design of the author. It was included in a recent article in *Digital Design Magazine*, July 1982, titled "*A Simple Programmer for the 8748*," by Terry Hinshaw. Only the voltage switch from this article was used and the programmer design was improved.

The circuit is quite simple, as you can see. The 7406 inverters have open collector outputs suitable for driving the transistors shown. The VDD circuit selects between +5 volts (PC4 = 1) and +25 volts. Similarly, the EA circuit switches from +5 volts (PC5 = 1) to +23 volts (approximate after the diode and transistor). If the microcomputer you are programming is an 8748H, this voltage must by 18 volts. This is also true of the VDD input. This potential may be accomplished by allowing the +25 volts to drop through a 7.0 V zener diode or provide an 18.7 volt input. The PROG pin, as you might have guessed, is somewhat more complex. Here we must provide zero volts (PC6 = 1, PC7 = 0), then swing to +23 V (+18 V for 8748H) which is PC6 = 0, PC7 = 1 for 50 msec then back to zero, then ultimately to a float (PC6 = 1, PC7 = 1). With the required circuit already designed for us, let's proceed. Thank you, Mr Hinshaw.

You have undoubtedly noticed by now that there is a strange device number in the left half of Fig. 9-12. That is

112

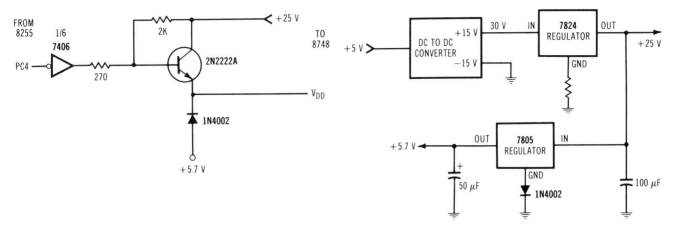

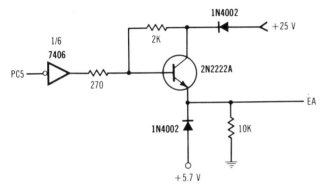

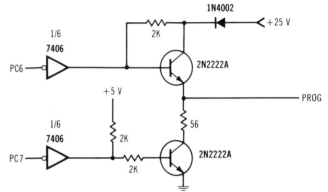

Fig. 9-12 Voltage switching circuits for 8748 programmer.

the key to super simple programmer design. The 8255, for the uninitiated, is a programmable I/O chip. We connect this to a home computer and let software manipulate the outputs in the sequence necessary for correct programming. To be more specific, there are three 8-bit I/O ports on the 8255. Port A is used as a data/address bus. Port B functions as a control register of sorts and Port C gets all the high voltage action.

Looking back at the sequence of operations, we can deduce that the state of the 8255 outputs at initialization are:

Port A	(BUS)	= To effect a high impedance, set this port to the input mode and keep the others as outputs.
Port B7	($\overline{WR}$)	= 1 (write strobe to RAM), more later.
B6	(AS)	= 0 (address strobe to RAM), more later.
B5	(RAM)	= 1 (select for emulator RAM), more later.
B4	($\overline{RD}$)	= 1 (read strobe for RAM), more later.
B3	($\overline{SS}$)	= 0 (single-step control), more later.

Port C7	(VP2)	= 1 (PROG voltage selector.)
C6	(VP1)	= 1 C5 (EA) = 1 EA control +5 V
C4	(VDD)	= VDD control +5 V
C3	(RESET)	= 0 (directly controls 8748 reset)
C2	(T0)	= 1 (directly controls 8748 T0)
C1	(A9)	= X (don't care) upper address bit A9
C0	(A8)	= x (don't care) upper address bit A8

After seeing this, Fig. 9-13 will dispel any confusion you may have about how the 8255 fits into the circuit. For the time being, ignore the middle RAM related circuitry. This is used for emulation and will be thoroughly explained later. In fact, we have to leave this programmer for a while because the BASIC program that is written to control it allows for emulation as well. Before you emulate you should know what you're doing, so we'll have to get into the actual operation of this thing we call an 8748.

MEMORY UTILIZATION

It's time for you to see what this 8748 looks like. If you haven't come across it before (Fig. 9-14), it bears a strange resemblance to an overfed EPROM. That window in the

113

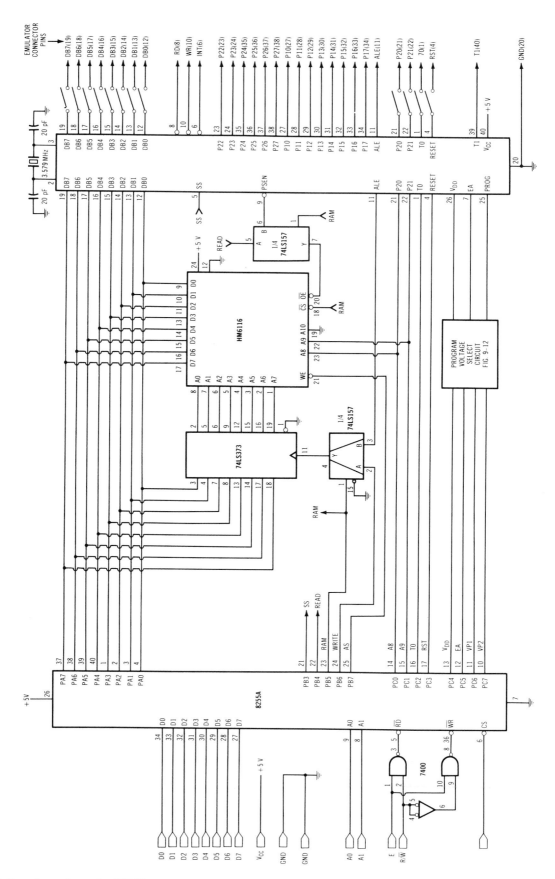

Fig. 9-13 Complete schematic of 8748 programmer/emulator.

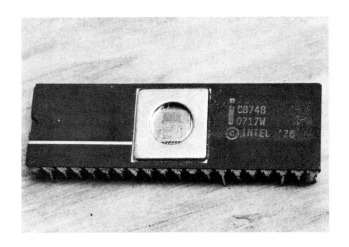

Fig. 9-14 Photograph of 8748.

center of the package allows the ultraviolet light to enter and flood the chip for erasure. Moving closer we see the data memory (if you can't see it, just take my word for it . . . it's there).

Fig. 9-15 shows the breakdown of what those 64 data memory locations are used for. Starting from zero, there are eight general-purpose registers,(Bank 0) R0 through R7. These may be written to, read from, incremented, decremented and used for just about anything your heart desires. Following these, there is an area set aside as a subroutine stack. There are enough locations here for eight subroutines to be nested simultaneously. Each time that you initiate a CALL instruction, the current program address is pushed onto this stack, very much like the larger microprocessors.

Well, we've identified 24 locations so far. The next eight support an optional second register bank (Bank 1). At any time in the program, a SEL RB1 instruction will do an immediate switcheroo. All the instructions pertaining to the first bank can be used with the second because the R numbers are identical. Just make sure you remember which bank you're in.

Finally, there are thirty-two 8-bit memory locations that are not used by any specific instruction. These may be used as you wish. In fact, let's examine the instructions available for moving in and out of this internal memory. All data moves pass through the accumulator. The following instructions work on this data memory:

MOV	A, @R0	ADD A, @R0
MOV	A, @R1	ADD A, @R1
MOV	A, @R0	ADDC A, @R0
MOV	@R1, A	ADDC A, @R1
MOV	@R0, #data	ANL A, @R0
MOV	@R1, #data	ANL A, @R1
XCH	A, @R0	ORL A, @R0
XCH	A, @R1	ORL A, @R1
XCHD	A, @R0	XRL A, @R0
XCHD	A, @R1	XRL A, @R1

Quite a list isn't it? Now let's see what this foreign language really means. The column on the left involves straight moves to and from. You'll notice that each instruction is repeated once for each of R0 and R1. Some explanation is necessary here.

Whenever you address external memory in the 8748, be it data or program memory, you do so using either register 0 or register 1 as a pointer. Therefore, the first instruction in the left column allows the contents of the data memory location pointed to by R0 to be moved into the accumulator. The same is true about the second, except R1 is the pointer. The second group provides for just the opposite. The contents of the accumulator is stored in a location pointed to by one of these registers.

The third group allows you to set any memory location directly with the data word of your choice. This word is the second part of the instruction. You see this constitutes our very first two-byte instruction. The others, so far, are one byte only. Here, the second byte contains the immediate data. After these instructions comes a very useful command. The XCH op code allows the accumulator and the addressed memory location to swap places instantaneously with one byte of instruction. The last, XCHD,

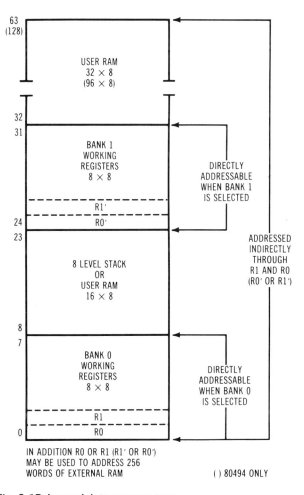

Fig. 9-15 Internal data memory map.

115

transfers only the lower four bits (nibble) of each. This is very useful when working with four-bit BCD data.

That does it for the left. Is it beginning to become clear that the 1024 program locations may be plenty? As you can see, there are many very useful instructions that occupy only one byte of program space. Still not convinced? Let's go on.

The right column of instructions provides the ability to perform arithmetic and logical functions on the contents of data memory. The first set will add the contents of the addressed location to the data present in the accumulator. The result is left in the accumulator and the data memory location contents are unchanged. The next set does the same with the inclusion of the carry bit information that may have been left from a previous operation.

The logical functions of AND, OR and Exclusive OR are accommodated throughout the next three sets. In all cases, the result of the logical operation is left in the accumulator. All of the instructions in the right column are one byte in length.

Remember there are three types of memory that the 8748 can handle. They are Data Memory, Program Memory, and External Data Memory. The designers of this microcomputer certainly did not forget them, as illustrated in the following instructions arranged just so these may be fully utilized:

MOVX A, @R0 MOVX @R0, A MOVP A, @A
MOVX A, @R1 MOVX @R1, A MOVP3 A, @A

This time let's start with the far right column. Instruction MOVP allows the contents of a program memory location to be transferred into the accumulator. Oddly enough, this instruction uses the contents of that very same accumulator to address that location. Notice, also, that the program memory internal to the micro is over 1000 locations deep, and the accumulator may only address up to 256!

In this machine, program memory is divided into pages. Each page is—you guessed it—256 locations deep. So, when you use an instruction like MOVP in a program, only the 256 locations available in the current operation page are allowed to transfer. This sometimes presents a serious limit. After all, what would we use an instruction like this for anyway?

Have you ever used a microprocessor to encode a keyboard? If you read the chapter on tactile sensing, you will, no doubt, remember the algorithm shown, where a touch pad or keyboard key press is detected, the number derived from a series of wild and wonderful readings pointed to a location in a table of key values. Use this instruction to point to that table, and build the table in program memory.

External fetches outside the chip can get hairy. The BUS pins act as a combination address/data bus. First, the 8 bits of address pointer data from either R0 or R1 are placed out on the BUS pins. Then, the ALE signal rises and falls. On this falling edge of ALE, you want to latch this address. To do this will depend on the memory device you use externally. Some chips allow you to connect to a multiplexed bus and have internal address latches. Others don't, like the ones commonly used for ROM or RAM storage. In this case, an external latch IC must be used. Fig. 9-16 shows the particulars of connecting the external memory. Notice in the figure, if you are connecting external program memory (as we will do for emulation), that EA must be pulled high and that PSEN is used as an output enable. Notice, also, that port lines P20 and P21 will now act as address lines A8 and A9, respectively.

Whenever you try to interface an external memory device to any single-chip microcomputer, you sacrifice I/O lines. In this case, there is also a possibility of expanding the Program Memory Off chip to 4096 bytes. An actual barrier is encountered as you attempt to leave the 2K point. To traverse higher requires that a SEL MB1 instruction be exercised. This will effectively allow another 2K. Of course, you must remember that only 1K is resident on the chip. When accessing these higher locations, port pins P22 and P23 become address lines A10 and A11. So, it is a good idea not to utilize these four pins as important I/O lines if you ever decide to emulate or use external memory.

The other instruction dealing with program memory moving is MOVP3. Remember, it was said that getting table data within the same or current page is limiting? Well, this instruction allows you to access anything in Page 3 (last 256 locations of internal memory) at any time. This says that you put your data tables high up in memory where they won't interfere with programs. Well, that's one problem solved.

Now let's turn to the left set of instructions. The columns of instructions here represent the capability to store and retrieve data from an external memory device. It is assumed that this device is RAM; however, any IC which can be addressed like memory may be substituted. Let me explain. Remember the fact that the Motorola 68701 had an onboard UAR/T? Well, it is a relatively easy thing to hook an industry standard, couple of dollar, UAR/T onto the 8748. Fig. 9-17 shows you the connections to allow the use of an 8251A UAR/T. To show the versatility of the 8748, some interesting interfacing is included.

Have you ever had to add a UAR/T to a system? Sure these devices come in small (relatively speaking) packages now and require little software maintenance to keep them going. But what about the bit-rate clocks you've had to provide? Suddenly, the single IC circuit becomes several devices. If you opt for one of those single-chip

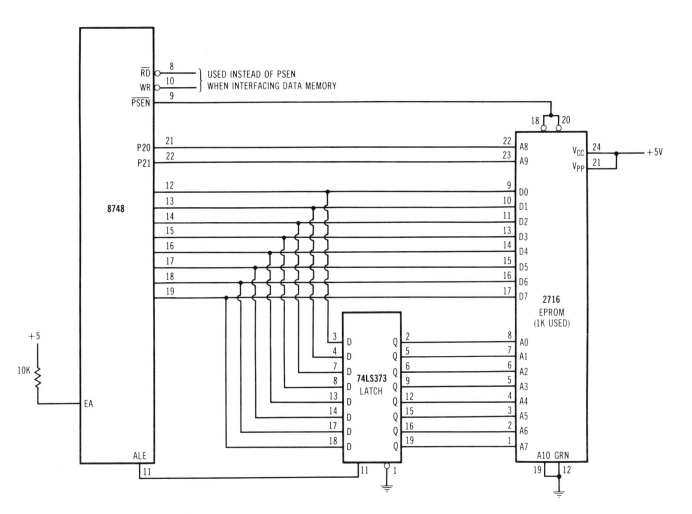

Fig. 9-16 Connections necessary to implement external program memory.

baud-rate generators, you may as well buy another 8748 for the price these devices demand, and don't forget the extra crystal. That sets you back another three or four dollars. Discouraged? Don't be. Remember you have a dedicated I/O controller here.

The designers have thought of this problem and have provided some relief by allowing the crystal frequency clock divided by fifteen to output from the ALE line. If you set up your UAR/T to accept a frequency 16 times that needed for a certain bit rate, you can select a crystal to run both the 8748 and the UAR/T. The example in the Fig. 9-17 transmits and receives at 9600 baud given the frequency of crystal that the author chose.

Another problematical input of the 8251A is the CLK line. This pin demands a clock frequency at least 4.5 times greater than the bit rate. The TO output (ENTO CLK), which is the crystal frequency divided by three, clock was enabled to provide this. It works fine.

You might notice that there is no address latch present in Fig. 9-17. No, there is none on board the UAR/T. How then are the internal registers addressed? Well, you can ignore the address information coming from either R0 or

R1. That's right. You have control over what goes in or out of the chip by the RD and WR lines. Use a port line to select the UAR/T, and to address (via C/D) internal register locations. Because this is the only device present outside the 8748, you really don't need to care what happens to the pointer data.

So, in retrospect, memory manipulations with the 8748 are not only simple, but very useful. All of the instructions except the immediate data move are contained in one-byte chunks.

ACCUMULATOR INSTRUCTIONS

Remember we found that all data moves go through the accumulator? Well, let's see just what operation can be done with this register. The following is a list of accumulator instructions:

INC A	CPL A
DEC A	SWAP A
CLR A	DA A

These are the accumulator instructions that *only* utilize

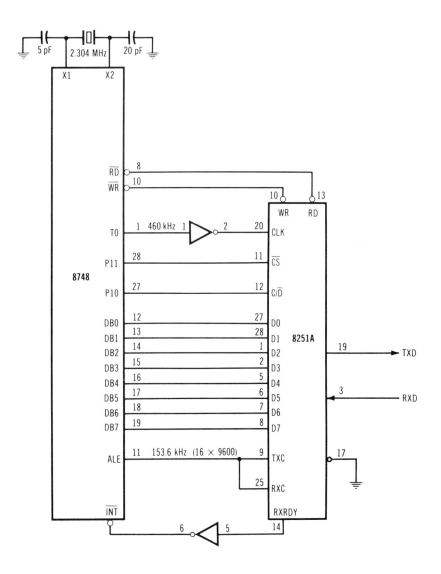

Fig. 9-17 Schematic showing connections of 8251A UAR/T.

the accumulator. Register and logical operations involving the accumulator will be covered separately. Basically, the list includes some of the more simple instructions in the 8748 repertoire. INC A will add +1 to the value presently resident there. If the previous value was FF (all ones), an INC will reset the accumulator to zero. Upon doing this, however, the carry flag (not yet described) will assume a value of 1.

DEC will do the opposite. Every time it is involved, the value in the accumulator will decrease by one. Instruction CLR resets the accumulator to all zeros. And CPL complements each bit. If the value FF is stored into A before CPL is exercised, the value 00 results. This instruction comes in handy if you have to invert data that is coming from a port or when you have to output data to a port that is connected through open collector drivers. The CPL instruction assures the correct signal polarity output.

SWAP is an interesting instruction. Have you ever been working with the lower four bits of a register, and

then wanted to move them up to the high order four bits? This type of operation is done frequently when building an address from hex keypad entry. The SWAP instruction performs an actual transfer of high order nibble (D7, D6, D5, D4) for low order. The result you see in the accumulator looks like this:

Before	D7	D6	D5	D4		D3	D2	D1	D0
	1	0	1	1		1	1	1	0
After	D7	D6	D5	D4		D3	D2	D1	D0
	1	1	1	0		1	0	1	1

Working with 4-bit values brings to mind a lot of BCD applications. Doing arithmetic in BCD can be cumbersome without some help from the microprocessor. The DA instruction provides this help in the form of the ability to readjust the BCD value in the accumulator after performing an addition between two BCD numbers.

118

The instruction adjusts the result of the addition (now left in the accumulator) into two BCD digits. This is done in the following sequence:

1. Check bits 0 through 3 for a value greater than 9. If the value is not that high, go to Step 2. If the contents is greater than 9 or the auxiliary carry bit is 1 (to be covered later), then increment the accumulator by 6.
2. Check bits 4 through 7 for a value greater than 9. If the value is not that high, then proceed to the next instruction. If the value is greater than 9 or, if the carry bit (to be covered later) is a 1, then the value in the four upper bits is incremented by 6. If an overflow occurs, the carry bit is set.

Aren't you glad you don't have to do all that in separate programming statements? The DA single-byte instruction does it all. In fact, all the accumulator instructions we've just covered are one-byte-only types.

PROGRAM STATUS WORD

During our discussions recently, the carry bit and auxiliary carry flag have come up. I guess it's time to discuss the processor's way of checking status when doing arithmetic or logical operations. The Program Status Word (PSW) should be a relatively familiar entity to those of you with a background in other microprocessors. It is here that the Carry Flag, Auxiliary Carry, etc., reside. Let's look at the structure of the PSW location in the 8748. Fig. 9-18 describes the PSW.

As you can see in the figure, the first three bits act as a sort of pointer to the stack memory area. If you recall, it was mentioned that there are eight levels of subroutine nesting that may be handled by the stack. These locations reside just above the first register bank in Data Memory. These three bits point to which two-byte location is next in line for storing a return address. To see exactly how this is performed, let's digress a moment into the areas that use the stack: CALL instructions and INTerrupts.

INTERRUPTION OF INSTRUCTION SEQUENCE

Commonly used routines or groups of instructions may be written once and used many times through the use of the CALL instruction. In larger microprocessors, this equates to a "JUMP to subroutine". There are eight versions of the CALL instructions.

CALL (page 0)	CALL (page 4)
CALL (page 1)	CALL (page 5)
CALL (page 2)	CALL (page 6)
CALL (page 3)	CALL (page 7)

Each CALL instruction has a unique hex op code. They allow you to jump to a subroutine located anywhere in program memory, as long as you specify the page where the routine begins. Remember, the 8748 works with 256-byte chunks of memory at a time. The first 1024 locations (pages 0-3) are located on-chip. The other thousand may be accessed as external program memory. If you select memory bank 1 (SEL MB1 instruction) you get another 2K of external program space. It should be cautioned, however, that the CALL instruction and any other page-oriented instruction will function in that relative page regardless of which bank is selected. Page 0 of bank 1 is in locations 2048-2303 of external program memory.

The CALL instruction consists of two bytes. The first, of course, is the op code. One of the eight-page related codes is used here. The second byte is the location of the subroutine (address) within that page. When the processor encounters a CALL, the first thing it does is store the present value of the Program Counter and the upper four bits (carry, aux carry, F0 and bank) onto the stack. As it is possible to address up to 4K (internal + external banks 0 and 1) of program memory, there is a need for twelve address bits. The actual placement of this information on the stack is outlined in Fig. 9-19.

After the stack is loaded, the low order eight bits of the Program Counter are reloaded from the second byte of the

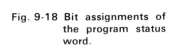

Fig. 9-18 Bit assignments of the program status word.

PROGRAM STATUS WORD
(PSW)

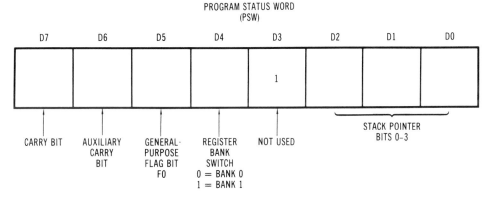

D7	D6	D5	D4	D3	D2	D1	D0
				1			

CARRY BIT — AUXILIARY CARRY BIT — GENERAL-PURPOSE FLAG BIT F0 — REGISTER BANK SWITCH 0 = BANK 0 1 = BANK 1 — NOT USED — STACK POINTER BITS 0–3

CALL instruction. The upper (A8, A9, A10) bits are adjusted according to the bank of the CALL and execution is resumed at that new location. Normal instruction processing continues until a return from subroutine (RET) instruction is encountered.

There are two return instructions. RET and RETR will both enable you to retreat to the original calling point, but they don't return you exactly the same way. The RET instruction will decrement the Stack Pointer (PSW bits 0-3) to point to where you stored the directions for home. The Program Counter will then get its previous set of clothes (a-dress?) and resume processing at home. Notice that it left behind the upper four bits of the PSW! This instruction may be used in cases where the status of the PSW bits are either not used or are unimportant to that particular point in the program. The next CALL instruction will clobber those bits that are left, so be sure you don't need to know what their state was when you left.

For those of you who tend to be extra cautious all the time, there is a return that includes restoring the PSW to its initial state. The RETR instruction resumes processing at home and restores the PSW. Why not be a little brave sometimes, use RET occasionally. The Surgeon General has not determined it to be unhealthy! On that note, why don't you take a break here. Get up, walk around. This stuff can be pretty dry.

Well, so far we've seen how the accumulator may be accessed directly. We've investigated the stack and the use of subroutines. There is another case where the 8748 program execution may be interrupted. The INT input pin causes an immediate interrupt. This is a hardware function that is involved whenever a low level is detected on the INT pin. When it occurs, both the Program Counter and the upper four PSW bits are saved on the stack. Hardware inside the processor then loads the address value 003 into the Program Counter and execution is picked up there. Normally you would put a JMP (jump) instruction in location 003 which catapults you into a general-purpose interrupt routine. We will cover jumps a little later. After executing the interrupt service routine, you can re-enter your program right where you left off by performing an RETR instruction. So, keep in mind when you're programming to carve out some space around location 003. In fact, take a look right now at Fig. 9-20. It shows the layout of the program memory. Indicated in the figure are the reset and interrupt locations. The timer interrupt shown there will be covered later.

There may be times that you might not want to be interrupted. In fact, it is a good idea not to be while you are processing an interrupt request. The 8748 provides the ability to disable or enable the operation of the $\overline{INT}$ line through the use of two instructions: EN I and DIS I provide the means.

PSW (CONT'D)

Getting back to where we left off, let's investigate the remainder of the program status word. Bit 4 (D3) is not used, and when it is read, a logic 1 appears in this place. The next bit location to the left is an indication of which register bank is currently being utilized. When you do either a SEL RB0 or a SEL RB1 instruction, it is this bit that is affected.

D5 is a general-purpose readable and writable flag. It is called F0. In fact, elsewhere within the microcomputer is another flag bit called F1. These can be used whenever you need someplace to mark the fact that something has occurred. For instance, if your program determined that you are in a certain mode (like transmit in a radio controller), this bit may be used to mark and store that fact. Any time you need to know what mode you're in, just read the flag bit. There are a number of instructions that manipulate or utilize both flags.

CLR	F0	JF0
CLR	F1	JF1
CPR	F0	
CPR	F1	

The first set (CLR) does just what it implies. The contents of flags 0 and 1 are zero after each are executed. The next set will assume the contents is the exact opposite of what it was previous to the instruction (CPL). The column on the right is our first encounter with conditional branching. JF0 means that if the contents of F0 is "1", then jump to a certain address. The value of the place

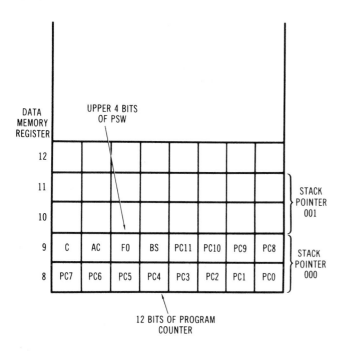

DATA MEMORY REGISTER

UPPER 4 BITS OF PSW

12								
11								
10								
9	C	AC	F0	BS	PC11	PC10	PC9	PC8
8	PC7	PC6	PC5	PC4	PC3	PC2	PC1	PC0

STACK POINTER 001

STACK POINTER 000

12 BITS OF PROGRAM COUNTER

Fig. 9-19 Diagram showing how addresses are placed on the internal stack.

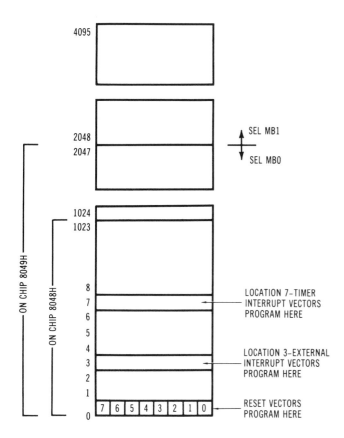

4095

2048
2047

SEL MB1

SEL MB0

1024
1023

ON CHIP 8049H

ON CHIP 8048H

8
7
6
5
4
3
2
1
0

LOCATION 7-TIMER
INTERRUPT VECTORS
PROGRAM HERE

LOCATION 3-EXTERNAL
INTERRUPT VECTORS
PROGRAM HERE

| 7 | 6 | 5 | 4 | 3 | 2 | 1 | 0 |

RESET VECTORS
PROGRAM HERE

Fig. 9-20 Internal and external program memory map.

to go is contained in the following byte. You may traverse 256 places or within one page. As you can see, both flags may be set, cleared, and tested. What more could you want?

Bit 6 of the PSW and bit 7 are carry flags. The first one (AC), the auxiliary carry, is active following the DA instruction (decimal adjust) we talked about earlier. When an overflow occurs between BCD digits, this flag goes positive. The other carry bit is used to indicate that the accumulator has overflowed (goes from FF to 00) during the previous instruction. This is helpful when doing addition in that it indicates when a carry-over operation must be performed.

It is possible at any time to change the entire contents of the PSW by simply moving the data resident in the accumulator directly into it. The MOV PSW,A provides this. Conversely, the contents of the PSW may be moved into the accumulator by executing a MOV A,PSW instruction.

ARITHMETIC AND LOGIC FUNCTIONS

That about covers the PSW. Those carry flags do bring up another group of instructions, however. The following list describes the range of arithmetic and logic operations that come with the controller.

ADD   A,Rr   ORL   A,Rr
ADD   A,#data   ORL   A,#data
ADDC   A,Rr   XRL   A,Rr
ADDC   A,#data   XRL   A,#data
ANL   A,Rr
ANL   A,#data

Notice that each operation has two methods of getting the immediate data to operate on the accumulator. The first ADD A,Rr adds the contents of A with the contents of the register specified (0-7), the result is left in the accumulator. The next does the same except it tests the carry flag to see if the previous operation overflowed.

The 8748 has the capability of performing logical ANDs, ORs and Exclusive ORs on its data. The next three sets illustrate the operations as they exist in the chip. Either the data immediately following or the specified register provides the other operand.

Arithmetic with computers can be performed a number of ways. It is possible to multiply the contents of a register or accumulator by simply shifting the bits one position to the left. If you were to write an algorithm to perform this shift using MOVE, AND, and OR instructions, it would be relatively complex. The 8748 allows you to perform shifts, either left or right, with the use of one-byte op codes.

RL   A   RR   A
RLC   A   RRC   A

These codes pertain to the shift instructions. The left column shifts the contents of the accumulator left one bit. At that time, a zero is placed into bit 0. The next one will shift left into the carry flag. Bit 7 replaces the previous information in the flag which will be placed in bit 0 (a vicious circle). The column on the right shifts everything to the right.

REGISTER OPERATIONS

Throughout these discussions, both register banks that are resident on-chip have been mentioned briefly. You have seen bank selection instructions, registers used as immediate data, and registers used as address pointers. There is a section of instructions dedicated specifically to these registers. Let's look at them.

MOV   A, Rr   INC   Rr
MOV   Rr,A   DEC   Rr
MOV   A,#data   INC   @R0
MOV   Rr,#data   INC   @R1
XCH   A,Rr   DJNZ Rr,addr

The first two instructions on the left allow you to traffic data between any register and the accumulator.

Both of these and the last one in the column move between the two places. Of course, XCH will change both locations where the MOVes only affect the destination, be it register or accumulator. The MOV A,#data and MOV Rr,#data are two-byte instructions that allow you initially to set a value into either. The second byte contains the data to be transferred. The column on the right allows you to add one or subtract one from any register. By the way, these instructions that specify an Rr are only one byte in length. Each register has its associated op code. So, the INC Rr instruction is really eight separate ones! The same applies for any register-based instruction.

The INC @R0 and INC @R1 instructions really pertain to manipulating internal data memory and should have been covered earlier. My apologies for this. They must have gotten inadvertently swept under the rug. However, they are useful. Any location in data memory pointed to by either R0 or R1 may have its contents incremented.

Last, but certainly not least, is the DJNZ instruction. This operation is worth its weight in gold. With it you can decrement the contents of a specified register and test it to see if it has become zero. If the test proves negative, it will jump you to the address specified in the following byte. It does all this in one instruction! Very useful in counting delays or counting anything. You will find that the register array included on-chip can be very helpful. In many instances, you may not even need to use the data memory storage area. These registers are extremely useful in that you can use them for not only data storage but for pointing to other locations during jump operations.

BRANCHES, JUMPS, AND GENERAL LEAPFROGGING

You have seen, by now, that there are many opportunities within the instruction set to catapult yourself to another location. Typically this kind of leapfrogging occurs whenever a decision block is encountered. Within the 8748, there are a number of specific conditions that may be tested and a Jump performed as a result. The general JMP instruction has been covered, as have the JF0, JF1 and DJNZ commands. The list that follows outlines the rest of them.

JMPP @A	JT0,addr	JBN,addr
JC,addr	JNT0,addr	JTF,addr
JNC,addr	JT1,addr	
JZ,addr	JNT1,addr	
JNZ,addr	JN1,addr	

Quite a list isn't it? Let's start on the left. The first is a complex table-oriented jump much like the MOVP,@A instruction. Here the contents of the program memory location pointed to by the number in the accumulator replaces the low order eight bits of the Program Counter. Effectively, it jumps you anywhere within the current page. This instruction may come in handy if you are running a machine that is receiving codes from an external terminal. Each incoming code catapults you into specific command handlers at varying places within program memory.

The next four test the state of the carry flag or test whether the contents of the accumulator is zero and take appropriate action. Moving into the middle column, we see that these provide the opportunity to test the state of the T0 and T1 input pins of the chip. Of course, if you are to use T0 as an input, you cannot perform the ENT0 CLK instruction. You will find that these input pins come in handy for receiving serial data or for counting applications.

Another instruction that can be used for serial information is the JNI command. This one jumps to the specified address whenever the interrupt line is low. Now that may be confusing. Let me explain. Remember we found that you can disable interrupts? Well, when they are disabled you can use this line as a general-purpose input line through this test instruction. Where does the serial data come in? Let's look at an example of receiving data (Fig. 9-21).

As you can see in the figure, the initial low-going pulses of the start bit trigger an interrupt. At this time, your service routine should provide the ability to disable further interrupts and start looking at (polling) the INT line with the JNI instruction. Using the internal timer, you should be able to count bit times and successfully receive the serial data word. Of course, it would be necessary to know, in advance, what bit rate the data will be clocking in at. The value that you set in the timer would

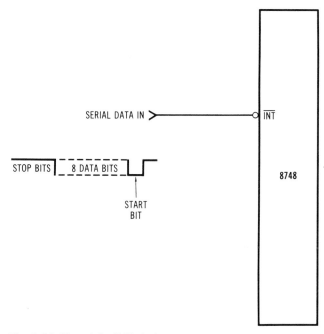

Fig. 9-21 Use of the INT pin for reception of serial data.

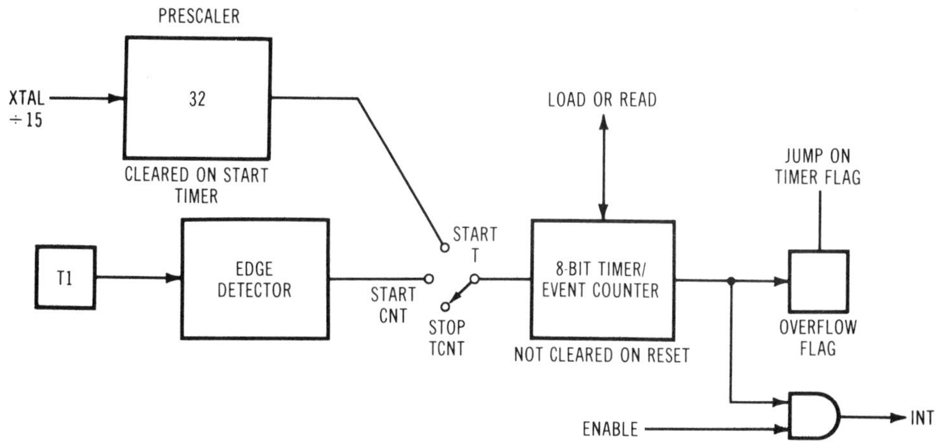

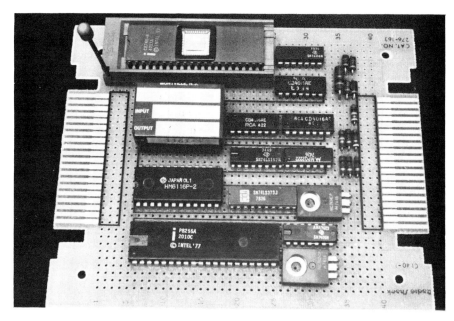

Fig. 9-22 Internal connection of the timer-counter during various mode operations.

Fig. 9-23 Photograph of complete 8748 programmer/emulator.

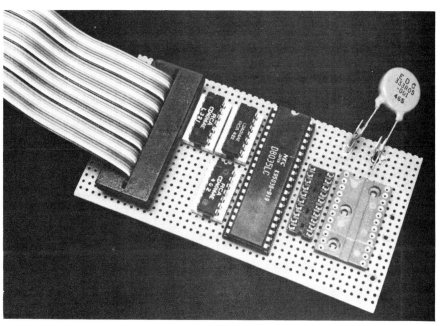

Fig. 9-24 Photograph of a simple 8748 emulator.

be one bit time. If the $\overline{INT}$ line remains low for one complete bit time then the data bit is a zero. Moving through the word, after the eighth bit has been received you start looking for high stop bits. When the complete word is finished processing, simply enable interrupts to catch another transmission.

The column on the right shows only two more jump instructions. In actuality, the first JBN is a general name for eight separate jumps. Each bit of the accumulator may be tested for a logic '1' level using this instruction. Simply substituting the numbers 0 through 7 into the n

spot will call out the bit you wish to test. This instruction is particularly useful in I/O processing where you are looking for the state of a certain bit out of a field of eight to change.

The last jump has to do with the internal timer. Until now, this piece of hardware has not been covered. There are eight instructions that pertain to it and there is no time like the present.

TIMER

Included within the 8748 is a general-purpose 8-bit

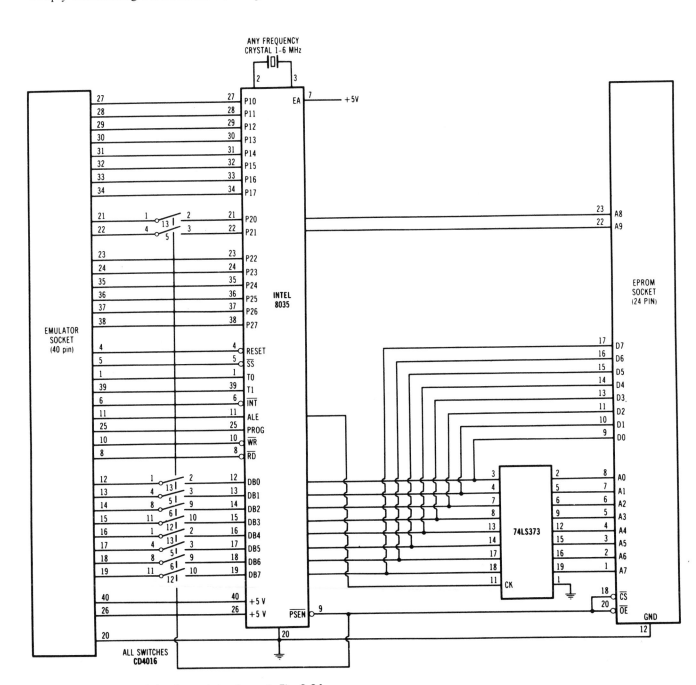

Fig. 9-25 Schematic of simple emulator shown in Fig. 9-24.

```
1 '          8748 DEVELOPMENT SYSTEM
2 '
3 '
5 CLEAR 5000
10 CLS:PRINT"ONE MOMENT PLEASE": DIM CODE(1024)
15 FOR X = 0 TO 1023: CODE(X) = 0: NEXT X
20 CLS:PRINT "MCS-48 DEVELOPMENT SYSTEM"
30 OUT=128:IN=144:BUS=49152:VOLTS=247
40 P2=49153:P3=49154:CTL=49155:STATUS=176
50 GOSUB 200
60 PRINT: PRINT "SELECT FROM THE FOLLOWING"
70 PRINT: PRINT "1) PROGRAM 8748"
80 PRINT "2) READ 8748"
90 PRINT "3) EMULATE 8748"
100 INPUT A
110 ON A GOTO 1000, 2000, 3000
120 GOTO 10
200 POKE(CTL),IN
210 POKE(P3),VOLTS
220 POKE(P2),STATUS
230 RETURN
500 HI=0: LO=0: POKE(CTL),OUT
505 L=X
510 IF L=> 512 THEN HI=HI= 2: L = L - 512
520 IF L=> 256 THEN HI=HI OR 1: L = L - 256
530 LO=L: HI=HI OR VOLTS
540 POKE(BUS),LO
550 POKE(P3), HI
560 RETURN
1000 CLS: PRINT "8748 PROGRAMMER"
1005 GOSUB 1010
1007 GOTO 1240
1010 PRINT: PRINT "PROGRAM IS IN:"
1020 PRINT "1) SYSTEM RAM"
1030 PRINT "2) CASSETTE FILE"
1040 PRINT "3) TO BE ENTERED BY KEYBOARD"
1050 INPUT A: IF A > 3 THEN GOTO 1000
1060 IF A = 3 THEN GOTO 1150
1070 IF A = 1 THEN GOTO 1235
1080 IF A = 2 THEN INPUT "FILE NAME ="; A$
1090 OPEN "I", -1, A$
1100 FOR X = 0 TO 1023
1110 IF EOF(-1) THEN GOTO 1240
1120 INPUT #-1, CODE(1024)
1130 NEXT X
1140 GOTO 1240
1150 CLS
1160 INPUT "ENTER START ADDRESS"; A
1170 INPUT "ENTER END ADDRESS"; B
1180 CLS: FOR X = A TO B
1190 PRINT X;"=";
1195 INPUT C$
1200 IF C$ = " " THEN GOTO 1235
1210 IF C$ = "R" THEN X = X - 1: GOTO 1190
1220 CODE(X) = VAL(C$)
1230 NEXT X
1235 RETURN
1240 PRINT "INSERT 8748 INTO SOCKET"
1250 PRINT"PRESS <ENTER> TO PROGRAM"
```

Listing 9-1 8748 Development System

```
1260 INPUT A
1270 CLS:PRINT"PROGRAMMING LOCATION
1280 FOR X = 0 TO 1023
1300 VOLTS = VOLTS AND 251
1310 POKE(P3), VOLTS
1320 VOLTS = VOLTS AND 223
1330 POKE(P3), VOLTS
1340 GOSUB 500
1350 VOLTS = VOLTS OR 8
1360 POKE(P3), VOLTS
1370 POKE(BUS), CODE(X)
1380 VOLTS = VOLTS AND 239
1390 POKE(P3), VOLTS
1400 VOLTS = VOLTS AND 191
1410 POKE(P3), VOLTS
1420 VOLTS = VOLTS OR 64
1430 VOLTS = VOLTS AND 127
1440 POKE(PE), VOLTS
1450 FOR T = 1 TO 5: NEXT T
1460 VOLTS = VOLTS AND 191
1470 VOLTS = VOLTS OR 128
1480 POKE(P3), VOLTS
1490 VOLTS = VOLTS OR 64
1500 POKE(P3), VOLTS
1510 VOLTS = VOLTS OR 16
1520 POKE(P3), VOLTS
1530 POKE(CTL), IN
1540 VOLTS = VOLTS OR 4
1550 POKE(P3), VOLTS
1560 VFY=  PEEK(BUS)
1570 IF VFY <> CODE(X) THEN PRINT "PROBLEM AT LOCATION"; X: GOTO 1240
1580 PRINT@21,X:NEXT X
1590 GOSUB 200
1600 PRINT "PROGRAMMING COMPLETE"
1610 PRINT "YOU MAY REMOVE DEVICE"
1620 PRINT "PRESS <ENTER> FO MENU"
1630 INPUT A: GOTO 20
2000 CLS
2010 PRINT "INSERT 8748 INTO SOCKET"
2020 PRINT "PRESS <ENTER> TO READ"
2030 INPUT A
2040 CLS
2045 PRINT"READING LOCATION"
2050 FOR X = 0 TO 1023
2060 VOLTS = VOLTS AND 223
2070 POKE(P3), VOLTS
2080 GOSUB 500
2090 VOLTS = VOLTS OR 8
2100 POKE(P3), VOLTS
2110 POKE(CTL), IN
2120 CODE(X) = PEEK(BUS)
2130 VOLTS = VOLTS AND 247
2140 POKE(P3), VOLTS
2150 PRINT@17,X:NEXT X
2155 GOSUB 200
2157 FOR X = 0 TO 1023
2160 IF C <> 0 THEN GOTO 2170
2162 NEXT X
2165 PRINT "PART IS ERASED"
```

Listing 9-1—cont. 8748 Development System

```
2168 GOTO 2350
2170 PRINT "READING COMPLETE"
2180 PRINT: PRINT "PRESS <1> FOR MENU"
2190 PRINT "PRESS <2> TO EXAMINE MEMORY"
2200 PRINT "PRESS <3> TO ENTER PROGRAM MODE"
2210 INPUT A
2220 ON A GOTO 20, 2230, 1240
2230 CLS: PRINT "EXAMINE MEMORY"
2240 PRINT: PRINT "ENTER START ADDRESS"
2250 INPUT A: CLS
2260 FOR X = A TO 1023
2270 PRINT X "="; CODE(X)
2280 A$=INKEY$:IF A$="" THEN 2280
2290 IF A$ = " " THEN GOTO 2330
2300 IF A$ = "R" THEN X = X - 1: GOTO 2270
2310 IF A$ = "Q" THEN GOTO 20
2320 CODE(X) = VAL(A$)
2330 NEXT X
2340 PRINT "END OF MEMORY"
2350 PRINT "PRESS <ENTER> FOR MENU"
2360 INPUT A
2370 GOTO 20
3000 CLS
3010 PRINT "8748 EMULATOR"
3020 PRINT "INSERT 8035 INTO SOCKET"
3030 PRINT "PRESS <ENTER> TO BEGIN"
3040 INPUT A
3050 CLS
3055 GOSUB 1010
3059 CLS:PRINT"LOADING EMULATION RAM"
3060 FOR X = 0 TO 1023
3070 GOSUB 500
3080 STATUS = STATUS AND 223
3090 POKE(P2), STATUS
3100 STATUS = STATUS OR 64
3110 POKE(P2), STATUS
3120 STATUS = STATUS AND 191
3130 POKE(P2), STATUS
3140 POKE(BUS), CODE(X)
3150 STATUS = STATUS AND 127
3160 POKE(P2), STATUS
3170 STATUS = STATUS OR 128
3180 POKE(P2), STATUS
3190 STATUS = STATUS OR 32
3200 POKE(P2), STATUS
3210 PRINT@22,X:NEXT X
3220 CLS: PRINT "EMULATOR"
3230 PRINT: PRINT "1) TO BEGIN RUNNING"
3240 PRINT "2) TO STOP"
3250 PRINT "3) TO RETURN TO MENU"
3260 INPUT A
3270 IF A = 1 THEN VOLTS = VOLTS OR 8: POKE(P3), VOLTS: PRINT: PRINT
     "PROGRAM RUNNING": GOTO 3230
3280 IF A = 2 THEN VOLTS = VOLTS AND 247: POKE(P3), VOLTS: PRINT: PRINT
     "PROGRAM STOPPED": GOTO 3230
3290 IF A = 3 THEN GOTO 20
3300 GOTO 3220
```

Listing 9-1—cont. 8748 Development System

counter that may be operated under program control. Counters come in handy when long time delays must be utilized. The processor need only set up the counter value, connect some constant frequency clock to it and go off doing other things while it is busy counting the time away. Think of it as the timer built into some ovens. If you had to sit in front of the oven all day waiting for the roast to be cooked, you'd get nothing else done.

This particular counter only counts up. That is, every clock pulse increments the value contained in it. When it overflows (FF to 00), there is a flag associated within the hardware that gets set. It is this flag that the JTF instruction tests. You also have the option of allowing an interrupt to occur upon overflow. When this is enabled, through the use of the EN TCNTI instruction, the Program Counter vectors you to location 007 in program memory. The same rules apply to this interrupt as in the general-purpose external one. It is disabled by performing a DIS TCNTI instruction.

In reality, there are two modes of operation for the counter. The first, and most used, is the timer mode. This is where a known time-base clock is applied to increment the value. The time base is derived from the master clock oscillator. Fig 9-22 shows the internal connections of the two modes.

In the timer mode, as you can see, a STRT T instruction connects the counter to the master clock (actually the crystal frequency divided by 15) through a divide by 32 prescaler. Initial values may be entered into the counter through the MOV T,A instruction. Conversely, the contents of the timer may be read at any time through the MOV A,T. When using the counter mode, the multipurpose T1 input becomes the clock source. This allows you to count events that may happen and interrupt when enough of them have occurred.

The only other instructions not covered so far deal with I/O. These will be covered quite thoroughly in Chapter 11 where we design and construct our first micro-computer-based robot controller.

PROGRAM EMULATION

Fig. 9-23 shows a picture of the complete programmer/emulator. Emulation is performed through the use of an 8035 device. This is basically an 8748 without the internal ROM. External program memory is connected as described previously. A drawing of a stand-alone emulator without the programmer is shown in Fig. 9-24, the schematic is detailed in Fig. 9-25.

You can insert either an EPROM or other 1K memory device into the program memory socket The author built a 1K ROM emulator that plugs into the socket. With it, the data can be changed via keyboard commands. The programmer/emulator, however, has this programmable feature built in. At this time, look at the program in Listing 9-1. This is the BASIC program that operates the board. The plan was to add enough remarks so that it is self-documenting.

Throughout the next few chapters, we will be getting deeper into the programming and use of the 8748. It is hoped that you found this chapter to be a useful introduction to small-size intelligence.

Chapter 10

Motion Control

The subject of controlled motion came up a few chapters ago, and some ideas were presented as to how to go about detecting direction and controlling momentum. All those suggestions alluded to some form of computer counting position marks on a drive gear and energizing motors. Let's look at a very good example of this principle.

Inside your local department store, located among the action toys, is a product of Milton Bradley Electronics Division called Big Trak. This is a programmable tank about 13 inches long. It is quite sturdy and can execute a prestored series of motion commands. These commands are entered via a small keypad located on the rear of the unit (see Fig. 10-1). You can enter up to 16 commands of "forward," "stop," "turn," "reverse," etc. When you press the "go" button, the tank executes the instructions in the order that you entered them. Sound familiar?

Yes, there is a microcomputer inside this toy, and it is of the single-chip variety. We haven't covered this particular device yet, though. It is made by Texas Instruments and is called a TMS 1000. There is not an erasable field programmable version though so you won't be able to reprogram it, nor will you be able to obtain one to play with. These devices are only available in large quantity and the control program is factory-wired when it is built. We can, however, look at the circuitry around the chip and explore the inside structure of the TMS 1000.

In the center of Big Trak is an electronics board that controls the tank. The large 28-pin IC is the microcomputer, the smaller 16-pin component is a 75494 hex digit driver. What's that? It is meant to drive LED readouts, but there are no LEDs in Big Trak. The outputs are capable of high current drive, however, so they are used simply as I/O drive circuits. It is this chip that pulses the light on the front of the unit during a "fire" command, and it drives the speaker for various sound effects. There really isn't much else on the board.

Fig. 10-1 Photograph of Big Trak control keypad.

Fig. 10-2 shows the complete schematic of this control board. Notice the transistor drive circuits that are connected to the motors. There are two motors in the base arranged like the one described in Chapter 3. The keypad is connected to I/O lines that scan it for a keypress. Internally, keypresses are stored in the microcomputer's data memory. All this runs on four D-cell batteries and one 9-volt cell.

Let's examine the TMS 1000 to get a better feeling for how Big Trak performs. Fig. 10-3 is the block diagram of the chip. You should notice that this is a 4-bit machine. The ALU and all registers are 4 bits wide. There is an accumulator, instruction decoder, 999 byte (8-bit) control program memory, 64-byte (4-bit) data memory and

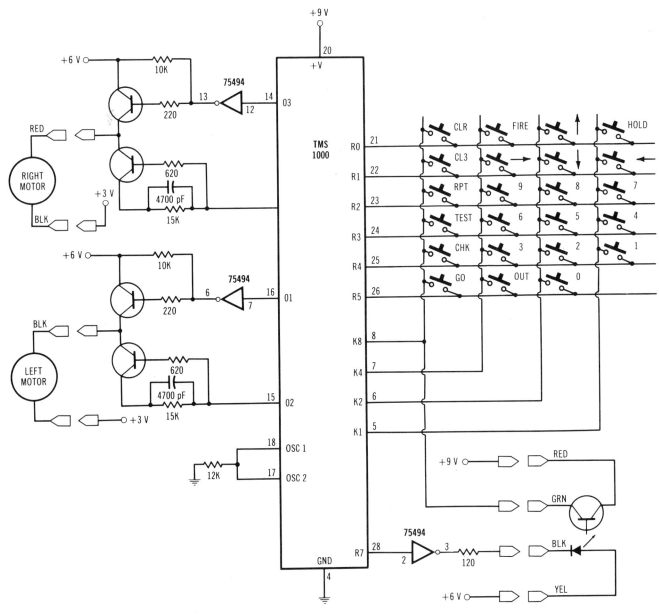

Fig. 10-2 Schematic of Big Trak control board.

various general-purpose registers and I/O facilities.

Looking at the schematic, we see that the keypad is connected similar to an X-Y matrix. Four of the keyboard lines enter the K1, K2, K4, and K8 inputs of the microcomputer. These lines constitute a data-input port. The processor, under program control, selectively turns on one of the R outputs (also connected to the keypad) then reads the K input port. During normal operation, the K lines read all zeros. When a key is pressed, the corresponding R line is connected to a K line, causing it to be a logic 1. The processor, when reading a change in state of the K lines, goes into a normal keyscan look up of the value received.

The motor-driver circuits are controlled by the actions of outputs 01, 02, 03 and 04. Two of these are connected

directly to transistor drivers and the other two are inverted through the 75494. Looking back at Chapter 4 will give you a good idea of what the microcomputer is doing with the driver transistors. Remember these output lines assume a high (1) or low (0) on program command.

Sound is generated during motion to emulate the roar of a tank as well as the pulsating burp of the phasor cannon during a "fire" command. These noises come out of several outputs on the chip and are wire-or'd to produce the necessary levels. The 75494 buffers their signals and drives the speaker through a 17-ohm limiting resistor.

Wheel position is sensed by a photoelectric detector (described in detail in Chapter 5) and read through the K8 input line when the output of R7 is enabled. This is a good example of multiplexing pins between duties to reduce

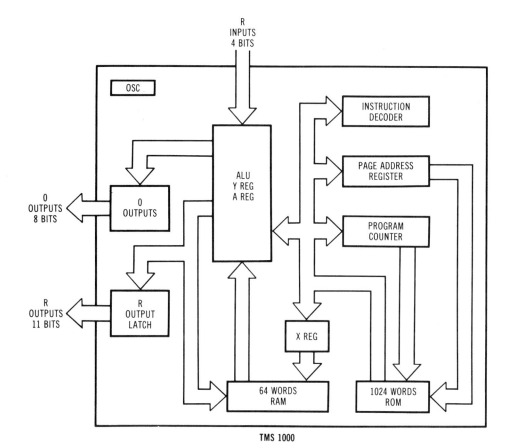

Fig. 10-3 Block diagram of TMS1000.

R INPUTS 4 BITS

OSC

INSTRUCTION DECODER

PAGE ADDRESS REGISTER

PROGRAM COUNTER

ALU Y REG A REG

0 OUTPUTS 8 BITS

0 OUTPUTS

R OUTPUTS 11 BITS

R OUTPUT LATCH

X REG

64 WORDS RAM

1024 WORDS ROM

TMS 1000

hardware. Big Trak detects motion in the forward or reverse direction by lengths of the body. That is, if you give it a "Forward 1" command, it moves ahead approximately 13 inches. It cannot resolve to a finer position than that in those directions. However while turning, the resolution it can determine is to a much greater degree.

Let's examine all the commands that this tank will perform, and while you are reading, think of how useful this subassembly could be if you were to integrate it into your robot.

The Forward command is signified by an arrow pointing toward the front of Big Trak. After pushing this button, you may enter the number of lengths you

wish it to travel from 1–99. Imagine, 99 works out to be 108 feet!!

The Reverse button, being an opposite arrow to the Forward one, works the same as the latter.

Right or Left turns are accomplished by pushing the buttons pointing in their respective directions. The units entered after the command, however, are much more detailed than before. Fig. 10-4 shows the units and their direction. For instance, if you were to turn right 15, this would translate to a turn of approximately 90 degrees.

With these basic motion commands, a lot of roving can be accomplished. There are, however, several other auxiliary instructions.

The Hold button acts as a wait command that accepts units of 1–99. Each unit represents 0.1 second. It is believed that the microcomputer will sit and increment a register to perform this command. It is useful between motion commands, because it gives the tank the capability to lose momentum from the previous step so that it does not interfere with the next.

The Fire button pulses the phasor lamp up to 99 times.

Repeat allows you to jump back a specified number of instructions and execute them again. This effectively expands the limit on storage as long as you can use the

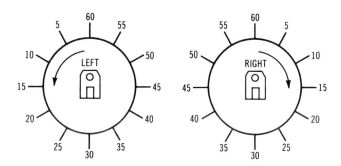

Fig. 10-4 Compass point direction codes for use with the RIGHT and LEFT commands.

same instructions. This command can only be used once, however.

Big Trak is sold with one accessory, at this writing. It is a motorized dump-truck trailer that connects to the tank through a 1/4-inch phone jack on the top of the unit. Big Trak controls the dumper by a special command called OUT. When you push this button, there are no units expected. The OUT signal from pin 11 of the 75494 turns on for approximately 4 seconds, then turns off.

The TEST command is used for initial checkout and can only be pressed immediately after power is applied to the tank. It is probably used in manufacturing to assure proper operation of the package. After you press this button, the tank immediately moves forward two lengths, fires three times, waits a few seconds, then reverses two lengths.

It's a good check out to see if the batteries are strong.

The CLR button erases the memory used to store program steps. It should be pressed before entering a new program.

CLS erases the step you last programmed or entered much like the button on your calculator.

CHK allows you to test an instruction before it is entered into memory. If you are unsure that a "forward 9" will not crash into the wall, you simply press CHK after the command and it will perform the step immediately.

GO executes the entire 16-command memory from first entry to last.

It should be noted that the IN key was not physically connected inside the unit the author purchased. I believe this is to be a future enhancement.

Well, now that we know how and what Big Trak does, can we somehow connect it into our systems and utilize its built-in motion programming? You bet!

INTERFACING BIG TRAK

Since we can't get into the program memory of the TMS 1000 to change it so that it will look for commands from another computer we will have to emulate the human interface. The easiest point of entry into this circuit is through the keyboard interface. We can emulate the contact closing action of the keypad using electronic circuits connected to an external computer. The block diagram in Fig. 10-5 is for a device that can be used whenever you are emulating the closing of mechanical contacts with a low-level signal. Don't try to emulate the power switch to your tv with this one!

The CD4051 is what is called an analog switch. In fact, there are eight of them in the package. Also included is a digital decoder so that only three binary inputs may select one of the eight switches to close. Connecting two of these devices, as shown in Fig. 10-6, will perform all the actions

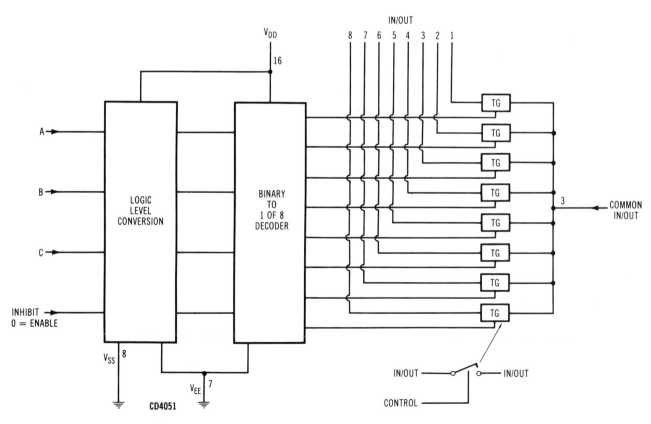

Fig. 10-5 Block diagram of CD4051 analog multiplexer.

132

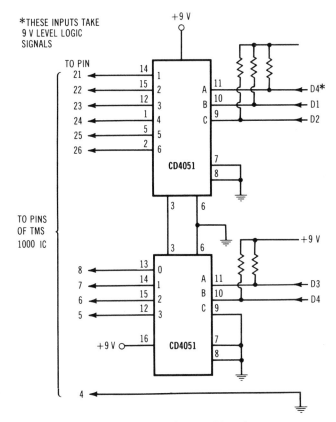

*THESE INPUTS TAKE 9 V LEVEL LOGIC SIGNALS

Fig. 10-6 Schematic of external-control interface.

of the manual input keypad. You don't even have to disconnect the original pad; it could be used for local input. With five data lines, you can call up any button command. Table 10-1 lists the buttons and their 5-bit code equivalents.

Let's assume that you have a home computer which you can program in BASIC. This may be the same unit that you were using to figure torque in previous chapters.

Table 10-1 Command Codes for External Interface

Command	Code					Decimal Equivalent
	D4	D3	D2	D1	D0	
Forward	1	0	0	0	1	17
Reverse	1	0	0	1	0	18
Right	0	1	0	1	0	10
Left	1	1	0	1	0	26
Clear	0	0	0	0	1	01
Hold	1	1	0	0	1	25
Repeat	0	0	0	1	1	03
Fire	0	1	0	0	1	09
Out	0	1	1	1	0	14
Go	0	0	1	1	0	06
0	1	0	1	1	0	22
1	1	1	1	0	1	29
2	1	0	1	0	1	21
3	0	1	1	0	1	13
4	1	1	1	0	0	28
5	1	0	1	0	0	20
6	0	1	1	0	0	12
7	1	1	0	1	1	27
8	1	0	0	1	1	19
9	0	1	0	1	1	11

There is one restriction though. To connect this external keypad interface to your computer, it will have to be capable of producing a parallel output. That is, if you do a POKE to a certain address or an OUT to a desired port, the data specified with those commands will be available as TTL levels that you can physically connect via cable to the Big Trak interface. As mentioned before in the robot experimentation, a Radio Shack TRS-80 Color Computer was used. If this happens to be the same as your machine, you're in luck. Fig. 10-7 is the schematic of a parallel output port for the color computer. Fig. 10-8 shows the board. If you are using a standard computer system, chances are good there is a board available.

Back to the main stream. I have designed a program in BASIC that allows you to enter commands by computer into Big Trak. This program is shown in Listing 10-1 and allows you to send entire programs to the tank with a single keypress. The listing is self-explanatory in operation, and should be relatively easy to adapt to other brands of home computers.

One thing you will find annoying, though, as you use the Big Trak with a personal computer is the cord. That cord has got to go! It seems that it gets tangled up every way you turn. After all, wasn't this book supposed to be about microprocessor-controlled robots? Then let's build a small-board microcomputer that can interface to the Big Trak in much the same way the larger personal computer does.

LOCAL CONTROL

Looking back at the schematic of the external interface in Fig. 10-6, we see that it is necessary to provide at least five parallel outputs. We could accomplish this with any of the single-chip processors we have covered so far. But it would be nice if some other computer could communicate with this local controller. After all, we are only constructing an intelligent motion platform, not the entire robot controller. If you haven't yet gotten into machine language programming (op codes), you might find yourself wishing for a single-chip device that executes BASIC like the personal computer.

You're in luck. There are two such devices available at this writing. Zilog Corp. makes a preprogrammed Z8 single-chip with what is called Tiny BASIC, and National Semiconductor has introduced a preprogrammed 8070 with Tiny BASIC. Both devices are simply programmed versions of their standard high-volume microcomputers. In Chapter 9, I zeroed in on one particular chip, but that does not represent the multitude of other products available.

For the Big Trak controller, the Z8 Tiny Basic device was chosen. The full product identification is the Z8671 Single Chip BASIC Interpreter. Zilog's address, etc., is listed in the appendix. Let's investigate this chip.

133

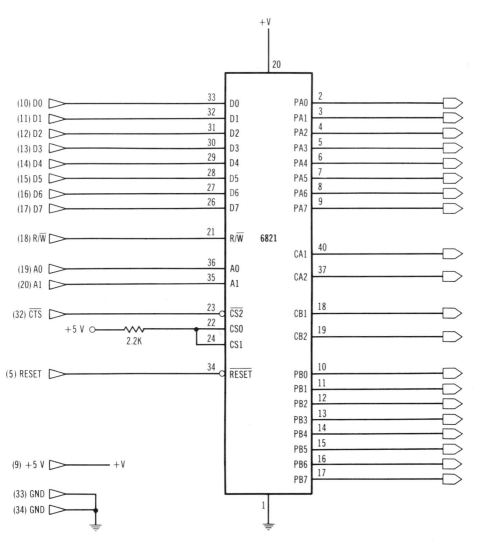

Fig. 10-7 Circuit for simple
parallel interface to
TRS-80 Color Com-
puter.

Fig. 10-9 shows a block diagram of the internal workings of the Z8. The program memory, in the case of the Z8671, is preloaded with op codes that perform Tiny BASIC operations. Most of the data memory is used in the interpretation process; however, there is a small

Fig. 10-8 Photograph of parallel interface.

amount left over for a simple program or two. If you only use the internal memory for storage, then all the port lines are available as user parallel outputs. The serial converter is used to input the program, however, more on that later.

The Z8 itself looks very much like an 8748 from the outside. A crystal must be attached between X1 and X2 with the same sort of capacitance added for stability. It is a 5-volt–only part and requires the same type of reset external capacitor. When external memory is used (as we will attempt), the lower seven address bits are output on the pins of Port 1 (Bus port of 8748) and a signal called AS, or address strobe, locks them into an external latch (see Fig. 10-10). This same device will now either present data or receive data. Read-Write control lines are added and a few of the Port 0 lines constitute higher order address lines. When using an external memory device, the port pins that are still free are those of Port 2 (all eight) and of Port 3 (just six). The external memory we will add to the Z8671 is for program storage. It turns out that by adding only two other ICs to the Z8671 we get 4K bytes of storage and the ability to select communications baud rates of the serial input port. Fig. 10-11 shows the entire

```
10 CLEAR 500
20 DIM A$(16): POKE 49152, 0
30 V = 1
35 GOSUB 500
40 FOR X = 1 TO 16
50 A$(X) = ""
60 NEXT X
70 CLS
80 PRINT "BIG TRAK COMMANDER"
90 FOR X = 1 TO 16
100 PRINT: PRINT "ENTER COMMAND"; X
110 INPUT C$
120 IF C$ = "GO" THEN GOTO 600
130 IF C$ = "CLR" THEN GOTO 30
140 A$(X) = C$
150 NEXT X
160 PRINT: PRINT "COMMAND BUFFER FULL"
170 PRINT: PRINT "ENTER EITHER A GO OR CLR COMMAND"
180 INPUT C$
190 IF C$="GO" THEN 600
195 IF C$="CLR" THEN GOTO 30
200 GOTO 160
400 GOSUB 500
410 GOTO 740
500 POKE 49152, V
510 FOR T = 1 TO 5
520 NEXT T
530 POKE 49152, 0
540 RETURN
600 FOR Y = 1 TO X
610 Z = 1
620 C$ = MID$(A$(Y), Z, 1)
630 IF C$=" " OR C$="" THEN Z=Z-1:GOTO 650
640 Z=Z+1:GOTO 620
650 C$ = LEFT$(A$(Y), Z)
660 IF C$ = "FORWARD" THEN V = 17: GOTO 400
670 IF C$ = "REVERSE" THEN V = 18: GOTO 400
680 IF C$ = "LEFT" THEN V = 26: GOTO 400
690 IF C$ = "RIGHT" THEN V = 10: GOTO 400
700 IF C$ = "FIRE" THEN V = 9: GOTO 400
710 IF C$ = "REPEAT" THEN V = 3: GOTO 400
720 IF C$ = "HOLD" THEN V = 25: GOTO 400
730 IF C$ = "OUT" THEN V = 14: GOTO 400
740 Z = Z + 2
750 C$ = MID$(A$(Y), Z, 1)
760 V = VAL(C$)
770 GOSUB 500
780 Z = Z + 1
790 C$ = MID$(A$(Y), Z, 1)
800 IF C$ = " " OR C$="" THEN GOTO 830
810 V = VAL(C$)
820 GOSUB 500
830 NEXT Y
840 PRINT: PRINT "COMMANDS TRASMITTED"
850 PRINT: PRINT "PRESS <ENTER> TO GO"
860 INPUT A
870 V = 6
880 GOSUB 500
890 GOTO 80
```

Listing 10-1 Big Trak Commander.

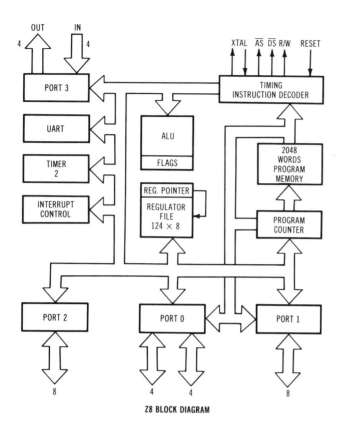

Z8 BLOCK DIAGRAM

Fig. 10-9 Block diagram of the Zilog Z8 microcomputer.

Big Trak local-control computer. Fig. 10-12 is a photograph of the board as it was constructed. Using perf board with stick-on etch patterns called EZ-Circuit by Bishop Graphics Inc. (ordering information in the appendix), it was constructed in one evening. The strange shape of the board conforms nicely to the area in which it mounts on the existing Big Trak control board. Fig. 10-13 shows the ribbon cable connector used to interface with the Big Trak electronics. A mating connector mounted on the Z8 local controller (Fig. 10-14) fits into the one of Big Trak, then the Z8 board is bolted down to secure the connection.

In my construction, it was decided to put the voltage-level converters (7407s) on the Z8 board. The analog switches need 9-volt logic levels and the 7407 buffers, being open-collector outputs, perform the necessary conversion from TTL.

ADDING PROGRAM STORAGE

The external memory chip used in this controller is another Zilog family member. It is internally arranged as 4K × 8 bits of storage with internal address latching capability. It comes as a 28-pin device and eliminates the need for external components. It is called the Z6132 and is available from the same source as the Z8671. Fig. 10-15 shows the internal block diagram of the Z6132. Actually,

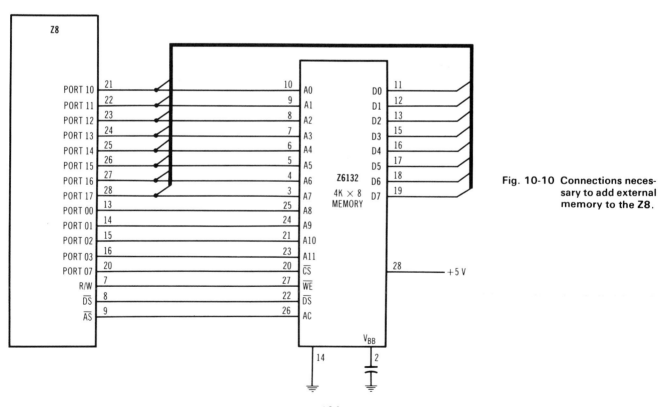

Fig. 10-10 Connections necessary to add external memory to the Z8.

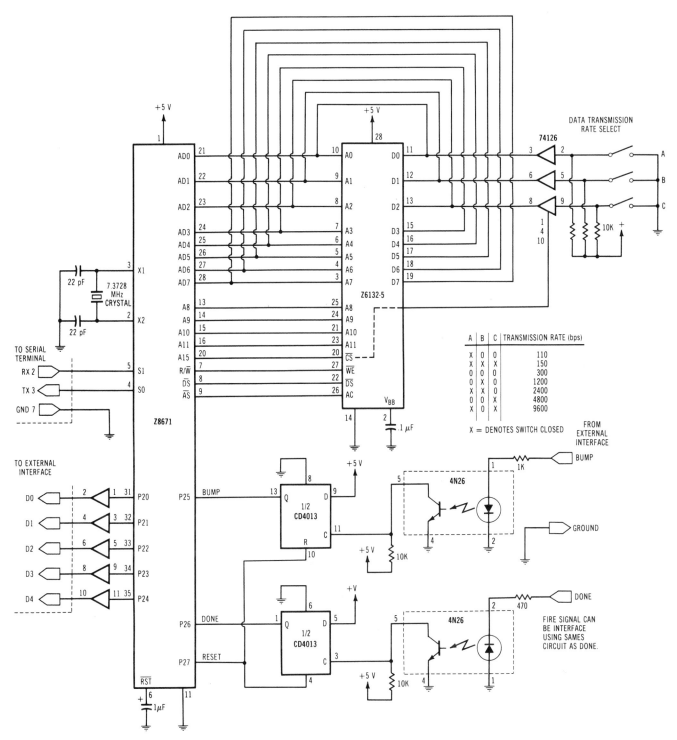

Fig. 10-11 Schematic of local-control computer.

this micro includes 4K $\times$ 8 bits of dynamic memory. Just like the type we used in the image sensor. Except all the refresh control circuitry is built in. There is a busy line to tell outside devices, that may be requesting a memory cycle, that it is in the process of refreshing. The control lines for the part have been designed to interface beautifully with the Z8671.

SERIAL I/O

Before we go into the 74126 that is directing the baud-rate selection circuitry, let's digress a moment to talk about serial communication. If you have a mechanical or electrical background, you might not have become acquainted with this type of I/O. If you already know it,

137

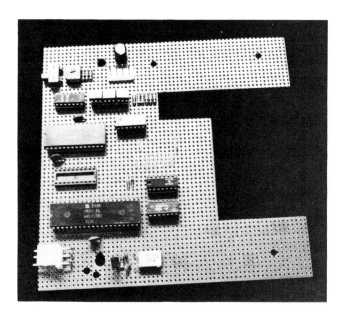

Fig. 10-12 Photograph showing local-control board.

Fig. 10-14 External-control interface wired directly on top of existing ICs on Big Trak control board. The connector shown mates with the one in Fig. 10-13.

simply skip this portion of the text. There might be a few, however, who are unsure; if so, communicating with the Z8671 will never be fully understood and, therefore, the serial link that is so important to the operation of the chips will also be lost. So here goes.

The Z8671 will communicate with an external computer, terminal, or other device capable of serial asynchronous communication. This type of signaling has become a standard. Characters to be presented to an external device are first converted from their parallel nature to a serial bit stream by shifting out the bits one by one (see Fig. 10-16). In order for a receiving device to know when a transmission is about to happen, a low-level pulse called a *start bit* is produced. Then, following the same bit

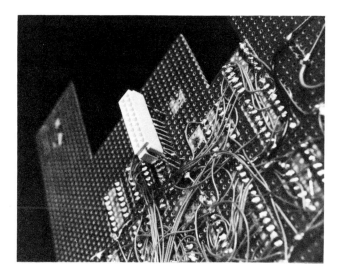

Fig. 10-13 Underside view of local-control board showing interface connector.

timing as the start pulse, all eight character bits are sent one after the other, least significant bit first (Bit 1). When the last of the character bits are finished, there may be an optional bit called *parity* sent. This is an error-checking bit. If you choose to work with even parity, this extra bit will be a "1" if the total amount of character bits is odd, because the function of the parity bit is to even out the amount of ones (at least in this case). If odd parity is used, the parity bit will assure the transmission of an odd number of ones. It is also possible to select that no parity be sent. In fact, the Z8671 does not transmit parity. Finally, the last bit transmission from the device is a thing called a *stop bit*. The Z8671 actually sends two stop bits out between characters. These will signal the receiving terminal that the character has ended. A stop bit is a "1" which is the normal resting state of the serial line out of the Z8671. So, as you can see, stop bits are actually pretimed gaps between transmissions.

Baud rate is the speed at which the character is being sent. Actually, bits-per-second applies more correctly to this communication. The old teletypewriters "speak" at 110 bits per second, but it is possible to find many alphanumeric terminals that work at 9600 bits per second. The Z8671 has the capability to transmit and receive at seven baud-rate settings. They are listed along with the switch settings necessary to achieve that rate on the main schematic. The Z8671, on power up, will read location FFFD or 65,533, if you like decimal, to get the baud-rate code. On the schematic, you will see that whenever the Z8671 accesses memory higher than 32,768, A15 will go to a logic "1" which will activate the baud-rate switch gates. In this application, we never expect to access memory that high in the address range unless it is for the switch code. Fig. 10-17 summarizes the format of these serial transmissions which the Z8671 will transmit and receive.

138

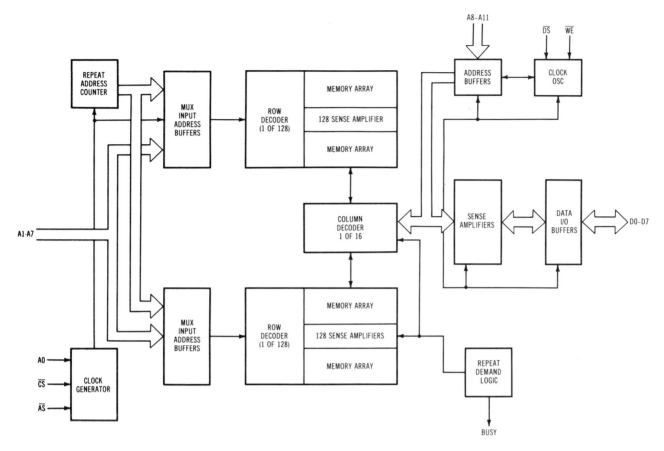

Fig. 10-15 Block diagram of Zilog Z6132 memory.

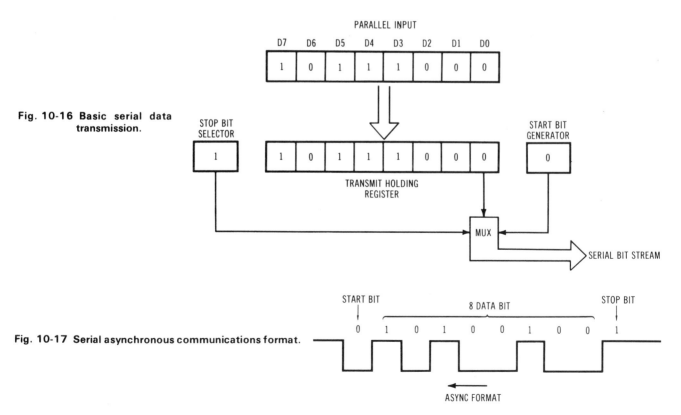

Fig. 10-16 Basic serial data transmission.

Fig. 10-17 Serial asynchronous communications format.

139

BACK TO BASICS

When you first apply power to the local controller, the Z8671 sends you a prompt character of ":". This signifies that the memory has been initialized, and the editor is ready to accept program information. After each line of program is entered, the prompt will appear signaling that everything is all right. If you should enter a strange command or do something out of the ordinary, it will return with an error code that will look like the following:

!ERROR CODE AT LINE NUMBER

The words error code and line number will be replaced by the appropriate values. There are numerous possible error codes that you may encounter. So, it will be hard to enter the wrong information.

The nice thing about this BASIC is that it allows easy examination of memory addresses, I/O ports or registers much like assembly language. It is not character intensive in that each command does not consist of many English words. This would tend to increase is memory usage. It also allows numbers to be represented in either decimal or hexadecimal. There are fourteen BASIC statements that are allowed:

GO@	INPUT/IN	PRINT	STOP
GOSUB	LET	REM	USR
GOTO	LIST	RETURN	
IF/THEN	NEW	RUN	

Basic mathematical operators of +, -, *, / are allowed and integers in the range of -32768 to +32768 may be used. However, unsigned integers representing 0 to 65536 may be entered when referring to memory addresses. Line numbers may be in the range of 1 to 32768.

Variables are called by letters A through Z and may be used as they are in any variety of BASIC. There is one logical operator available, that is AND. It may be used to mask, turn off or isolate bits. You can perform a logical OR by complementing AND, which is by subtracting each element in the statement from a minus one:

$$- 1 - AND (- 1 - A, - 1 - B)$$

Memory addresses or register names may be called out by an expression with the "@" symbol:

$$LET @2 = 149$$

will place the value 149 into register 2. The reverse may be accomplished:

$$A = @2$$

This will place the value of register 2 into variable A.

The reason that register 2 is shown is that in the Z8671 registers 2 and 3 are actually Ports 2 and 3. So, if we want to send a CLR button code to the Big Trak electronics, we simply put that code into register 2 via an assignment statement. To Read inputs from Big Trak just do as described with A = @2. Why read inputs from Big Trak? Let's look at a potentially serious drawback to the Big Trak intelligent motion system.

COLLISION DETECTOR

Before we go any further, I want you to perform the following experiment, but make sure the unit is 2 feet from a wall:

Program into Big Trak:

CSB

↑

9

9

GO

Ever spin your wheels thinking you were going places while you were really standing still? Well, that's what your so-called intelligent platform is doing right now! Sure, you wouldn't consciously send it into a wall, but what if it is under automatic control and the vision system you built saw 3 feet and erroneously reported 30 feet? You want some way to tell the TMS 1000 within Big Trak to quit.

Unfortunately, this microcomputer is programmed to ignore the keypad during program execution. Now there are two methods that can be used to force it to stop. One is to pull the reset line to the chip pin 9, but not knowing whether this would effect an orderly shut down, the other way was chosen. I simply cut off 9-volt power to the chip. This is done with tiny microswitches of the kind we investigated in Chapter 5.

Collision detection bumpers (Fig. 10-18) were made of lightweight wood that is strong enough to survive a collision. The microswitches are activated by shafts of wood dowel material that are spring loaded and attached to the bumper. Pressure on the bumper activates the switch which interrupts power (see the schematic in Fig. 10-19) because the switch is wired for a normally closed circuit. When a collision occurs, Big Trak loses power to the motors, and the spring tends to push it away from the wall, which will again apply power to the board. After the collision, Big Trak sits idly by awaiting instructions, because its memory has been erased.

This is all well and good, but how does the Z8671 know that something is wrong? We will have to include a circuit that detects the presence of the 9 volts applied to the TMS

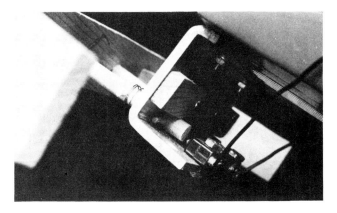

Fig. 10-18 Close up of Big Trak bump sensor.

Fig. 10-19 Schematic of bump-sensing system.

Fig. 10-20 Circuit for interfacing bump sensor to local-control computer.

Fig. 10-21 Interface to FIRE output that provides TTL level pulse.

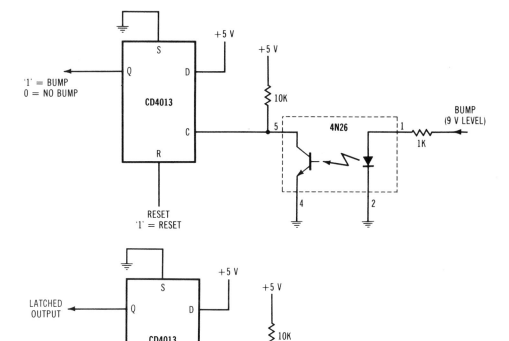

1000. The circuit shown in Fig. 10-20 performs this nicely. The device used here is an optical coupler that is very much like the gear-position detector used in the motor compartment except there is no interruptible gap between the emitter and detector. It is used as a way of detecting the presence of a voltage without physically connecting to it. We can use one of these circuits, also, to convert the pulsing flash of the fire lamp into useful TTL control pulses. Fig. 10-21 shows the connections necessary for that operation.

Now, if we run the TTL signal called BUMP into one of the unused Port 2 pins, it is possible to test for this condition. It would be wise to put this test in just after any "GO" command is issued. You might have it jump to a reverse routine on encountering a collision.

One more problem. How do we know when Big Trak has finished its program? We need some sort of "done" signal which tells us that it will accept new program information. I used the OUT instruction as a signal that it is almost done.

What you can do is make sure that "OUT" is the last instruction entered before the "GO." This will pulse the output pin 11 of the 75494, when it is performed. I connected this output to an optical-coupler circuit like the one in Fig. 10-21. When you detect this signal, it is clear that the last instruction has ended, but you have to wait for the short time that the Big Trak sound output finishes. This takes an additional few seconds, so build a wait loop after the "done" detection. All these detections are latched by flip-flops. It is necessary to toggle the reset line, Port 2 bit 7, between detections. This can be done in the following manner:

$$@2 = 96$$

$$@2 = 224$$

The eighth bit will go low, then high while not affecting the other control bits. You should send a zero to the Big Trak interface when no button is being commanded, and immediately after a button command.

POWERING THE SYSTEM

Big Trak uses four D-cell batteries to run the motors as they cause the greatest drain. This voltage is broken up into +6 V and +3 V supplies. The 6-volt supply also powers the 75494. A smaller 9-volt battery is required to run the TMS 1000. The Z8671 requires 5 volts, as does the memory. I decided to provide a separate power-supply system for the local controller because of noise spikes

present on the Big Trak controller. Fig. 10-22 shows the schematic of the power system implemented with the local controller.

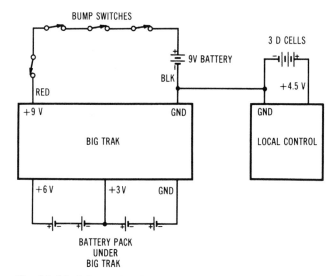

Fig. 10-22 Schematic of motion platform power system.

More information on the Z8671 can be obtained by contacting Zilog or any of their sales offices. Actually, the National Semiconductor INS8073 BASIC controller would work equally as well in this application. What I've tried to show is how a simple toy can be converted into a sophisticated intelligent machine with the incorporation of single-chip control electronics. Next we will look at a way for controlling the operations of a hand-arm system.

Chapter 11

Manipulator
Control

Using microprocessors to control the actions of a robot manipulator can prove to be very effective. Local control of an entire arm subsystem or even just the hand will greatly off-load much of the mundane mechanical operations from the main controller, leaving it to perform more demanding work, such as pattern analysis or path navigation.

Unfortunately, there are no two manipulators alike. Some may consist of a shoulder, elbow, wrist, and hand; while others may only include the shoulder and hand parts. To define a general-purpose manipulator controller, we must first decide which types of mechanisms, be they electromechanical or electronic, we wish to include in the system. This, along with a definition of the actions we want the controller to perform, will give us a start toward a working design.

This chapter will be presented differently from the rest of the book. Here you will be led through the design of a robot subsystem controller. The order in which the design is accomplished is synonymous with how products are created in actual industrial engineering departments. For those of you who are engineers, this should look familiar. If you are not a part of the regular electronics community, welcome to the functional specification portion of design!

FUNCTIONAL SPECIFICATION

The actual design phase of the controller will go smoothly because we will be defining its operations here. This is where every command, and every reaction the machine is to do, is spelled out in painstaking detail. Let's decide what we need.

Because any particular manipulator may have a number of controllable mechanisms, let's pick numbers that might fit most applications. Our controller, therefore, will have the ability to do the following: (refer to the block diagram in Fig. 11-1).

1. Control eight motors that provide forward or reverse motion.
2. Detect motion and position of all motors.
3. Have the capability to drive the motors at two speeds.
4. Detect the closure of eight separate limit switches.
5. Control of eight general-purpose outputs.

Initially, these specifications may seem aggressive for a first project in manipulator control, but as you will see, we will be able to accomplish the design without too much difficulty. For those of you who felt there should have been more meat in the section on the Intel 8748 processor, your patience is now rewarded. This controller is based on the 8748.

OPERATIONS

Let's break down each mechanism and explain how and what is to be performed.

1. Control eight motors that provide forward and reverse motion.

The controller provides the capability to address each of eight separate motors and commands them to operate

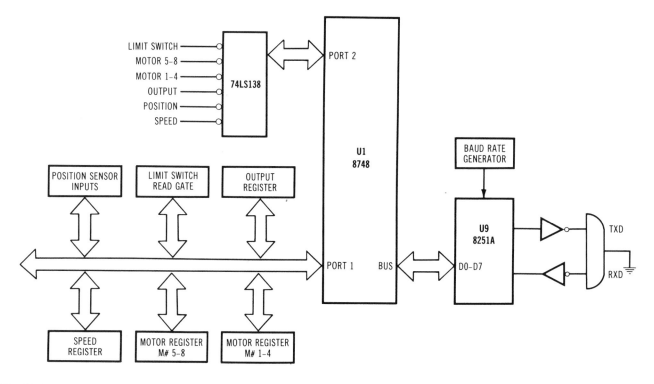

Fig. 11-1 Block diagram of manipulator controller.

either in one direction or another. This is done by using a separate electronic switch for forward and another for reverse. The two switches must never be on at the same time. This prevents the possibility of damage to the controller power source.

Each motor will have the capability to report its motion and position to the controller through an optical position-sensing system, like those described in Chapter 8. The position disk, when moving, will interrupt the path of the optical beam which sends count pulses to the controller. When commanding a particular motor to move, you must also provide an *amount of movement* number which corresponds to the number of count pulses required to reach that particular position. The controller will supervise without operator intervention, the serveilance of position. It will also, upon reaching the desired location, automatically stop the motor.

2. Detection of motion and position.

This was addressed partially in No. 1, but it needs some further explanation here. The controller must provide circuitry to interface with optical-position sensors. These may be simply a phototransistor whose collector will present a logic 0 when the position beam is detected. Each logic value change decrements a holding register in which the initial count value is placed. If, for instance, you wish a motor to advance 127 places (which is the maximum per motion instruction), this number is stored in the holding register for that motor. The motor is started and from that point on, changing states detected on the associated position sensor phototransistor of that motor will de-

crease the value of the holding register by one. When the register equals zero, the controller stops the motor.

3. Capability to drive the motors at two speeds.

There are times when you may want the manipulator to move very precisely in space. At other times, fast motion from place to place is necessary. The same speed of operation cannot suffice in both situations. Therefore, it is desirable to provide two speeds of operation. One fast speed and one slow is a good compromise. It is possible to provide several ranges of operating speed, but the complexity of the controller increases and the result may not be worth the added expense.

4. Detect the closure of eight separate limit switches.

We talked about limit switches in Chapter 5 where we found that they provide us feedback when a manipulator has reached its physical end point. They also are used to report on gross position, as in the case where a limit switch is activated by an object moving along a conveyor system. These sensors need not be mounted directly on the manipulator. They could be simple pushbutton inputs to the controller signaling for some manual operation, such as start or stop.

This motor controller must automatically read the status of all eight of these switches. In the event that one changes state (defined as logic 1 = open, logic 0 = closed), the controller should let us know in the form of a message indicating the sensor number that has changed. It also should have the ability to read, on demand, the state of any of the eight limit switches. The program controlling the manipulator could use the information from these switches for various control tasks, such as signalling when an operation is finished and another can begin.

Also, the controller should provide automatic speed reduction upon demand when the limit switch associated with a motor is activated. In this mode, fast, yet precise, motion is attained by allowing the motor to race toward a destination, then slowing when it gets close to its position (signalled by the closing of a limit switch).

5. Control of eight general-purpose outputs.

Last but not least, the controller must have the ability to do other things besides control the joints of a manipulator. The eight outputs are for just what they are named: *general purpose*. You might want to control the motion of a conveyor or some sort of controllable work surface that is being used in conjunction with the manipulator. If there is none, you could control an electronic vision system mounted on the manipulator. A combination of output and limit-switch input—one output for shutter control, another for lighting—can be used in an auto-focus system for the vision lens. There is nothing that says a limit switch has to be mechanical. It could be the output of an auto-focus sensor, such as those used in slide projectors. As long as it presents a logic zero when activated, the output could enable the auto-focus motor to drive the lens. The applications are limitless and by now you probably have several of your own.

Well, we've launched an interesting design effort. However, there is another important aspect of this system to define: the method of communication to and from the controller and the language or *protocol* used in this dialogue. It was mentioned before that certain messages must be passed between the controller and master computer. In robot systems, the master computer may be the brain. In stand-alone manufacturing robot systems, this brain may be simply a large computer placed in a central location in the plant. In both cases, we refer to this overpowering being as the *host*.

Host communications to and from controllers can take many forms. It will be easier for us, however, if we keep the number of physical connections between the two units to a minimum. After all, we are a robot system and there should be some consideration given toward the overall weight of such a system. Two-way serial communication as described in Chapter 10 can provide us with ample capability to share information, while keeping the wiring to a minimum. If we design to an industry standard such as the RS232C, we gain the advantage of using standard terminals and components in the design phase.

COMMANDS

With the communication medium established, let's decide what the two units are going to say to each other. Looking back at the five requirements outlined previously, we can derive the following eight commands:

1. MOVE x, ± y
2. MOVES x, ± y
3. MOVER x, ± y
4. STOP x
5. X (abort)
6. READ s
7. CHECK x
8. OUT z, on/off

These commands should be further explained:

1. Move x, ± y

This message from the host commands the controller to operate motor x (1 through 8) until y (number of position holes) is reached. The + or − indicates direction in forward or reverse, respectively. The speed assumed for motion is the normal fast speed. Plus may be omitted. The number of position holes can be from 1 to 128.

2. MOVES x, ± y

Doing basically the same operation as done in No. 1, this command, however, tells the controller to move at the slower speed.

3. MOVER x, ± y

This is the first of the complex commands. The R stands for Ramp in that the controller operates motor x toward position y in the + or − direction until limit switch of the same number has activated, then the speed of motion will be decreased for the remaining duration of the move.

4. STOP x

The stop command is used to cease motion in any of the eight motors as defined by x. Stopping a motor does not zero out its position-holding register and does not effect other motors or sensors.

5. X (abort)

On the remote possibility that the manipulator is going to do physical damage to itself or other things, or if it just isn't operating properly, the X command immediately stops all motors and general purpose outputs. The controller, after performing these tasks then does a reset and initializes itself.

6. READ s

The read command allows the host to receive the status of the limit switch addressed by s (1 through 8).

7. CHECK x

Although it is the controller's job automatically to sense the position of each motor while it is operating, it may be convenient for the host to know its position also. The CHECK command reports the remaining distance to a destination in counts that are present in the holding register of the addressed motor x.

8. OUT z, on/off

The general-purpose outputs may be operated using this command. Specifying the output number z (1 through 8) and the condition (on or off), sets each appropriately. The ON state results in a logic zero being present on the output line, and the opposite (logic one) for an OFF state.

Well, there you have it. Each command is entered by its associated word and the appropriate variable data being sent to the controller over the RS232C serial link. The command words are comprised of a string of ASCII codes. These codes are also an industry standard. Each letter of the alphabet, all numbers 0 through 9, and punctuation marks have their own unique code number. The ASCII code is reprinted in Table 11-1 for those of you who are not familiar with it. The command word, MOVE, comes across the serial link as the following series of numbers: 77, 79, 56, 45. After each command word, you may insert spaces or commas. The controller disregards all but necessary information such as that of the motor number (x). In between variables, commas or spaces may be inserted and the end of a MOVE command is signified by a carriage return (CR). All other commands are self-terminating.

Table 11-1. Device Select Codes

P20	P21	P22	Device
0	0	0	None
1	0	0	Limit Switches
0	1	0	Motors 1-4
1	1	0	Motors 5-8
0	0	1	Output
1	0	1	Position Sensors
0	1	1	Speed Register
1	1	1	Nothing

RESPONSES

We've defined the messages that are sent to the controller, but we have not yet established the responses to them. Let's do that now. Looking at the commands, we see that only two of them require a formal informational response. The two that do are the READ s and CHECK x commands. It might prove useful, however, to respond in some way to every command that is received after it is performed. In this way, the host gets a positive reaction to each command that can be used to signal that the controller is doing well and is ready for another command. We also talked about the necessity of a response message that is generated when the controller senses a change in state of the limit switches.

Taking the previous discussions further, we derive the following responses to commands:

1. ACK code (decimal 06) is sent whenever a command is received and it has been executed.
2. BEL code (decimal 07) is sent when the state of the limit switch group has changed. This code is followed by the number of the switch.
3. SYN code (decimal 22) is sent before each of the values expected in either the READ or CHECK command. The READ response returns with "C" for closed (state 0) or "O" for open (logic 1). CHECK responds with the number of counts left in the holding register for the particular motor.

In all cases, the last code transmitted to the host in the response is the ACK (code 06) signifying that the code has been received and executed. In summary:

Command	Response
MOVE x, ± y (CR)	ACK
MOVES x, ± y (CR)	ACK
MOVER x, ± y (CR)	ACK
STOP x	ACK
X	ACK
READ s	SYN
	"C" or "O"
	ACK
CHECK x (CR)	SYN
	x,x,x — value in BCD
	ACK
OUT z, on/off (CR)	ACK

When we first power up the controller, it clears all holding registers, disables all general-purpose outputs, and enables itself to receive commands. This action is called *initialization* and is performed in response to a power up reset generated on the controller. This same reset routine can be repeated during operation by issuing an X command. This is a good place to finish the definition phase of the project, and as it turns out an excellent entrance into the design phase.

HARDWARE DESIGN

Controlling a complete manipulator is not always the most efficient of methods. You may want to design a simple hand controller, then oné for the wrist, etc. This type of design will tend to keep circuitry at a minimum and the board size small. The controller presented here is not extremely small in size; however, it will fit in the base structure of most manipulators.

As I mentioned earlier, the design is based on the Intel 8748 single-chip microcontroller. Let's proceed with the design of the board, taking time out to learn more about this processor chip as we need it. The best place to start is on power up. Remember we said that an initialization routine must be performed at that time. The 8748 has provision for an external reset input. If we connect this line to a push-button that is pulled up to +5 volts through a resistor, we can force the processor to stop everything and start executing its program from the beginning. Well, this is all right, but it would be more helpful if this reset were performed automatically when power is first applied. Intel has anticipated this need and has designed the reset input such that if you connect a capacitor from its input to ground (Fig. 11-2), the line remains at a logic zero for a short time after power is applied. This short time is determined by the size of the capacitor selected. It was found that a 10 microfarad capacitor provides a long clean reset on power up.

Before describing what happens next, there are several other circuit connections that must be made to allow the processor even to get this far. The first of course is +5 -volt power and ground. The allowable power range for the VCC input pin 40 is +4.5 volts to +5.5 volts. In a robot system where batteries may be used, the +5-volt supply is best regulated by a device called a three-terminal regulator. Fig. 11-3 shows a commonly available regulator device for providing +5 volts to controller circuits. The same voltage is applied to the VDD input, pin 26. During normal operation, this is just another supply pin, yet, when you are programming the erasable ROM inside the 8748, the voltage on this pin must be +24 to +26 volts. This is what is applied by the programmer circuit described in Chapter 9. The ground or negative side of the battery supply is connected to the VSS, pin 20.

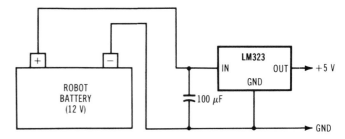

Fig. 11-3 Voltage regulator provides 5-volt power from a 12-volt battery.

There is one more pin that must be connected. Remember in the discussion of the 8748, it was mentioned that there are devices which can be purchased having no internal control memory? Well, if this is so you connect the External Access (EA, pin 7) to +5 volts, also. However, we will utilize the on-chip memory in this design so the EA line is grounded, telling the processor to get all instructions from inside.

The device will not get any instructions or do anything else for that matter if there is no master clock-crystal connected. For this project, a 6.00 MHz frequency clock was chosen that is connected between pins 2 and 3 along with its associated balancing capacitors. The complete initial connections are shown in Fig. 11-4.

RESET

Back to the capacitor where it is connected to the reset line. It has finally charged up enough to bring the processor out of the reset condition. The Program Counter is forced to a zero state, along with the Stack Pointer. The first set of registers are selected (Bank 7) and the memory band selected is also zero. The BUS output lines are turned off to a high-impedance state (as if disconnected from the circuit) and Ports 1 and 2 become inputs (their outputs look as though they are high).

Also, at this time, external and internal counter interrupt requests are disabled and the 8-bit counter/timer (internal to the 8748) is stopped. There are two general-purpose register bits available for keeping notes on certain operations that are called *flag bits* F0 and F1. These are both cleared to zero. Basically, the processor "cleans house" on a reset. It sets itself up to begin performing its master's commands. That master, of course, is you!

Before we begin writing an initialization program for the manipulator controller, let's design the rest of the hardware. So we'll have to leave the 8748 chomping at the bit and eager to start.

MOTOR CONTROL

In Chapter 4, we went over much of the motor control circuits. We covered both unidirectional and bidirectional designs. Here in this chapter, you will see another

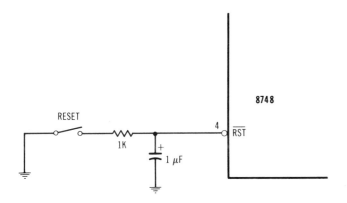

Fig. 11-2 Reset circuit for the 8748.

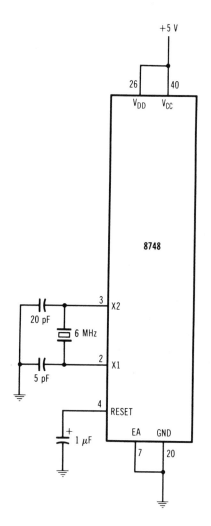

technique to control the operation of a bidirectional motor. Fig. 11-5 shows two separate approaches that you can use in the design of the controller. The first (Fig. 11-5A) uses two relays. One relay is connected to +12 volts, the other is connected to −12 volts. The motor is connected between both of the relays and ground. Depending on which relay is energized, the motor turns forward or reverse. Note that if both relays are activated, the +12 volts is directly connected to the −12 volts. You will want to avoid this condition. Two schemes have been devised to prevent this and I will present them soon.

Fig. 11-5B shows the same circuit using solid-state transistors as the switching elements. The same electrical dangers exist in this circuit, and it has no real advantage over the relay design except possibly the space saved on the board, although you can purchase some very small relays. This brings up a major point. Be sure to calculate the amount of power that these devices will be switching. You may need a rather large relay if you intend to switch a large motor.

Back to protection, Fig. 11-6 shows a way, using a double-pole relay, that effectively eliminates the possibility of providing a voltage path from both relays at once. Another way is to make certain in the program that you don't send out the enable bits to both relays.

Let's look at how we can control the motors using the 8748. Fig. 11-1 shows how to connect the Port 1 output lines to act as a data bus. Notice that the motor forward and reverse latches, speed latches, the position-counter inputs, the limit switch inputs, and the general-purpose outputs all feed into, or out of, this bus. Each controllable entity is selected by the processor before communicating with it. This selection is performed by using a 3-bit code

Fig. 11-4 Basic connections of 8748.

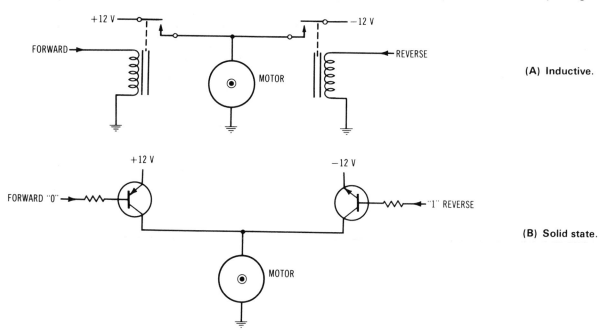

(A) Inductive.

(B) Solid state.

Fig. 11-5 Two simple bidirectional motor-control circuits.

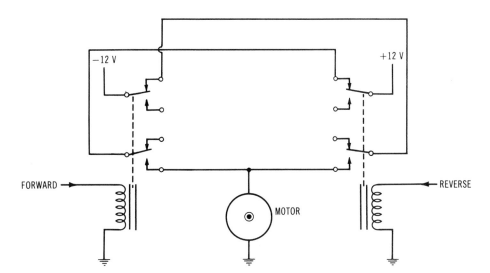

Fig. 11-6 Motor-control circuit devised such that simultaneous powering of the motor from both sources is impossible.

that enables one of eight devices. In this design, there are only six implemented; there is ample room for expansion.

The device selection takes place through the use of the 74LS138, a three-line to eight-line demultiplexer. Three bits of Port 2 are used as inputs to the demultiplexer and the code of the selected device is placed on them. Data is then moved into or out of each section through the Port 1 lines.

Going back to the motor control, we see in Fig. 11-7 the actual design of the motor register. Each device controls four motors in a forward or reverse motion. The reason for keeping both forward and reverse in the same register is to protect against momentary short circuits when both controls are energized, if the protecting circuit shown in Fig. 11-6 is not used. If the forward controls were in separate devices from the reverse controls, there would be a very short time period where the processor is between

registers after having enabled forward and is in the process of disabling reverse. The 8748 loads numbers to its port lines in 8-bit chunks, so having the two controls side by side prevents the processor from addressing the motor twice.

On each of the controlled motors, there should be a position feedback device. It doesn't really matter what type of device it is, as long as it provides a pulsing logic zero, periodically, which represents a distance that the motor has traveled. To read this input device, the processor sends the code 101 (decimal 5) to the address selector. After it is selected, an 8-bit wide 74LS244 input gate opens up to the Port 1 bus. Now, the processor can read the state of all eight feedback devices. Fig. 11-8 shows that the position sensors are connected similarly to the limit-switch inputs. Both are read in the same way, selected, however, by different address codes.

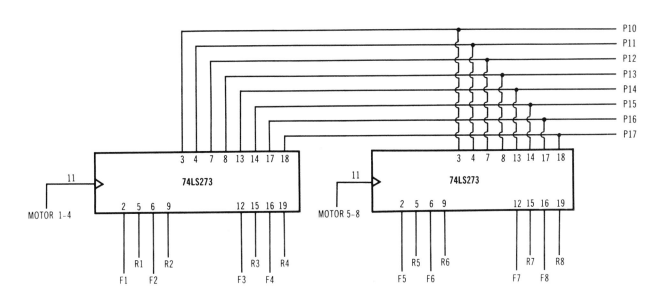

Fig. 11-7 Motor-control registers (outputs labeled F are forward controls, R denotes reverse).

149

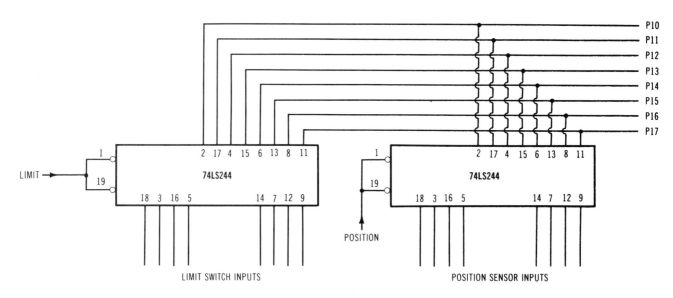

Fig. 11-8 Input Read circuitry for limit-switch and position-sensor inputs.

In conjunction with the motor-control circuits, there is the speed-control latch. The outputs of each of its eight bits goes to a circuit that selects either of two speeds for the motor. Fig. 11-9 shows the register and two motor circuits connected. The other outputs are connected similarly but not shown for reason of clarity. Speed is controlled through the use of pulse-width modulation, as described in Chapter 4. The slower the pulses to the motor, the slower the speed. One oscillator is used for the entire eight motors. The frequency of pulses out of this oscillator is divided in half by the 74LS74, which provides pulses for the slower speed.

Each motor is connected through appropriate gating to either the slow- or fast-speed pulses. The speed-control register selects which one gets what pulses. It is loaded off the Port 1 bus in the same way that the motor-control registers are.

Last but not least is the general-purpose output register which is also eight bits wide. Loading this register is done similarly to the motor and speed registers. Table 11-1 summarizes the address codes associated with each device.

Putting all this information together shows us that we have completed the control portion of our manipulator

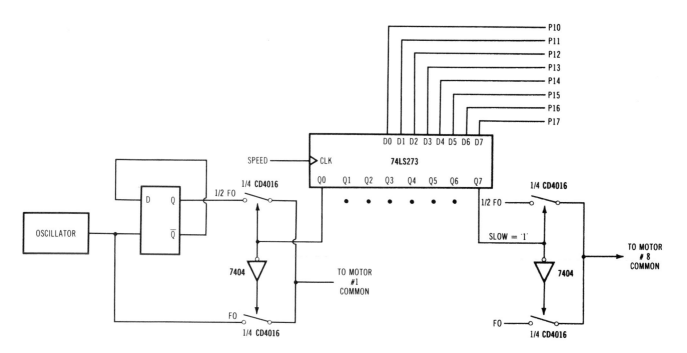

Fig. 11-9 Speed-control register circuit.

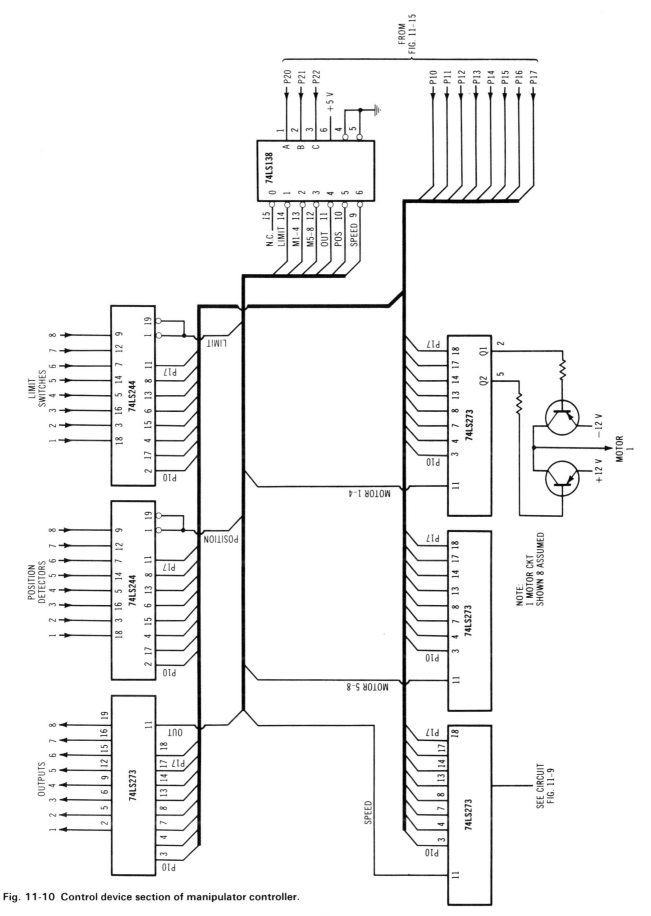

Fig. 11-10 Control device section of manipulator controller.

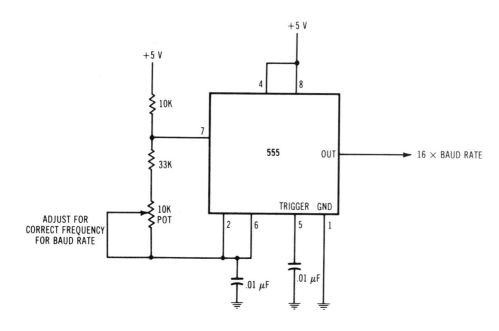

Fig. 11-11 Simple IC timer based baud-rate generator.

controller. Fig. 11-10 shows all the connections completed thus far. Now the area that requires our concentration is how to talk to the host.

COMMUNICATIONS SECTION

Serial ASCII asynchronous communications between host computers and peripheral devices (like the controller) have been built for years. Because of this fact,

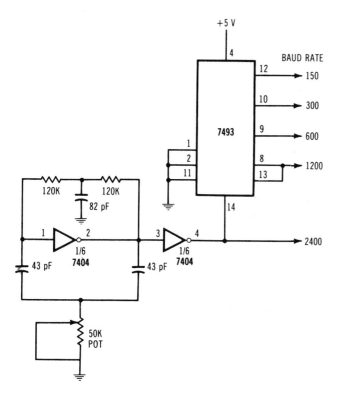

Fig. 11-12 Multiple output baud-rate generator.

there are a number of integrated-circuit devices that accomplish it all for us. The IC chosen for the controller is one manufactured by Intel. It is called the 8251A and it contains everything you need to talk to the host except a communications reference-clock generator.

The reference generator sets the rate at which each word will travel the serial link. In the previous chapter, the Z8 microcontroller included this circuit, and all that was required was for you to tell it, via switches, the rate you wanted.

Well, here we have to provide it separately. Three circuits that vary in complexity are presented in Figs. 11-11 through 11-13.

The first of these circuits (Fig. 11-11) utilizes a 555 timer circuit connected as an oscillator that is variable by changing the resistance of the potentiometer. Generally, this circuit operates around one communications rate. The figure design is for 9600 bits per second which is a standard speed. However, if you require the capability to interface to different hosts at different speeds, then the circuit in Fig. 11-12 can do the job. It allows switchable rates and is fairly low in cost. The IC in Fig. 11-13 does it all. This device is called a *baud-rate generator*, and it provides 1 of 16 standard communications frequencies! This baud-rate generator is the one I've chosen to use.

Connecting the clock to the 8251A is easy. Simply tie the transmit clock and receive clock lines together and insert the FO output of the baud-rate generator. That is if you intend to talk and listen at the same rate. It is possible to utilize the 8251A in a mode where they would be different, but this is seldom done in these applications. There is, however, another clock input the 8251A. This input is labeled CLK and must be at least 4.5 times greater than the speed of the highest communications rate you intend to use. In some applications, this may be

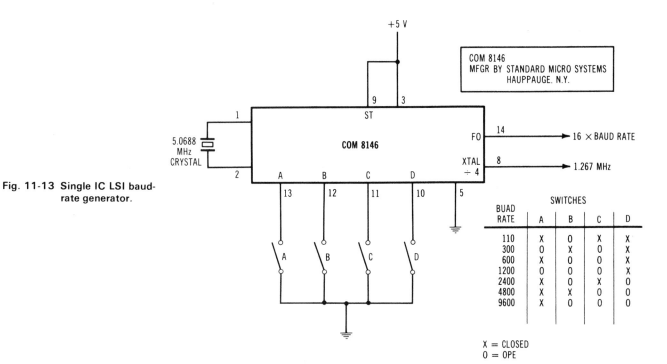

Fig. 11-13 Single IC LSI baud-
rate generator.

BUAD RATE	SWITCHES			
	A	B	C	D
110	X	0	X	X
300	0	X	0	X
600	X	0	0	X
1200	0	0	0	X
2400	X	0	X	0
4800	X	X	0	0
9600	X	0	0	0

X = CLOSED
0 = OPE

difficult to provide except that the baud-rate generator chosen has an output especially for such emergencies. Fig. 11-14 shows all the connections necessary between the baud-rate device and the 8251A.

The 8251A is a serial receiver/transmitter. Internally, it has a control register, status register, transmit data register, and a receive register. Selection between control/status and data is accomplished using a single pin labeled appropriately C/D. When this line is at a logic 1, the data presented on the bus pins D0 through D7 is either control information from the 8748, or status information being presented to the 8748. If the input is at a logic zero, receiver data may be passed to the processor or data may be placed in the transmit register for output by the processor. Transfers to and from the processor are controlled by write and read control inputs. These lines are connected directly to the RD and WR outputs of the 8748. The data lines of the 8251A are connected to the BUS port of the 8748. External memory instructions allow the 8748 to communicate with the 8251A directly over the BUS port. We will go into this more deeply in the software section. Fig. 11-15 shows the connections between the 8748 and the 8251A. Joining Figs. 11-15 and 11-10 together renders the entire manipulator-controller schematic.

SOFTWARE DESIGN

Remember we left the 8748 hanging in mid air after reset, while we played with hardware? Well, here is where we pick it up again. The first thing the controller must do is perform the initialization of all devices including itself.

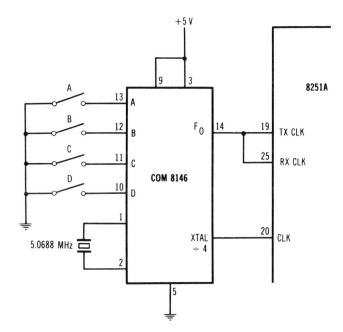

Fig. 11-14 Connections between baud-rate generator and UAR/T.

So, we start the software design effort for the controller by writing the initialize routine. Fig. 11-16 illustrates the flow of operations that must be performed. Let's examine each operation separately.

The first action performed is to go through and clear all registers. Where are they and which one does what? Before we can go much further, it is obvious that some definition must be established here, also. What must be decided on is called a *data base*. I have established the following:

Bank 0	Bank 1
R0 — Motor 1	R0 — Last Position
R1 — Motor 2	R1 — Last Limit
R2 — Motor 3	R2 — Run Register
R3 — Motor 4	R3 — Ramp Register
R4 — Motor 5	R4 — General Purpose
R5 — Motor 6	R5 — General Purpose
R6 — Motor 7	R6 — General Purpose
R7 — Motor 8	R7 — General Purpose

The registers in Bank 0 are used when the initial count for motor movement is loaded. They are also the registers that are decremented each time a position sensor changes state in its associated detector. The 8748 must first clear or load with all zeros these eight motor registers upon initialization. Up to this point we have not examined any of the instruction codes of the 8748.

It is necessary now that we start learning while we write the program. The register-clearing function in the flow-chart is called from a general-use subprogram named

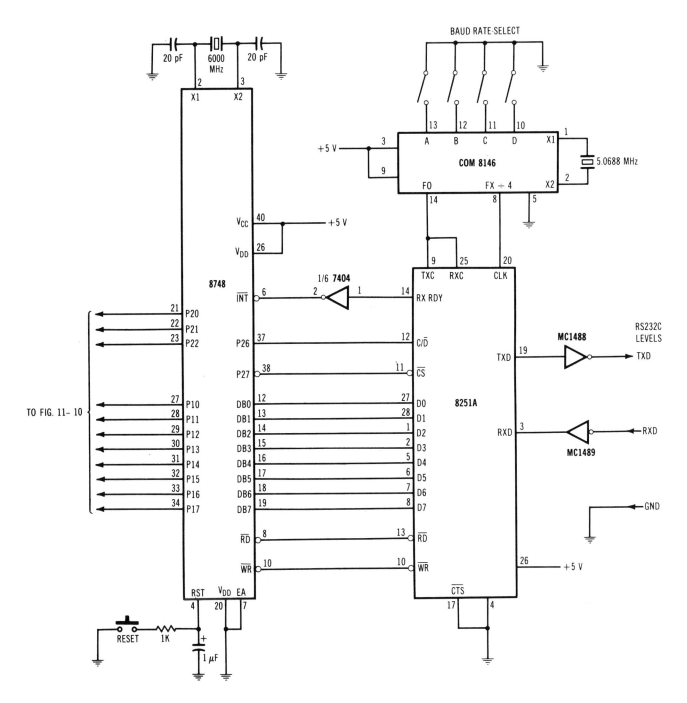

Fig. 11-15 Communications section of manipulator controller.

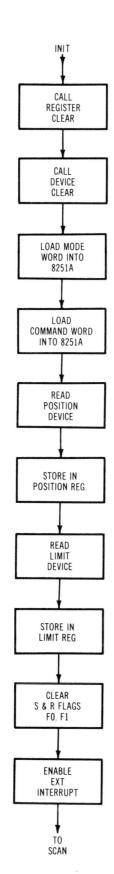

INIT

CALL
REGISTER
CLEAR

CALL
DEVICE
CLEAR

LOAD MODE
WORD INTO
8251A

LOAD
COMMAND WORD
INTO 8251A

READ
POSITION
DEVICE

STORE IN
POSITION REG.

READ
LIMIT
DEVICE

STORE IN
LIMIT REG

CLEAR
S & R FLAGS
F0, F1

ENABLE
EXT
INTERRUPT

TO
SCAN

Fig. 11-16 Flowchart of Initialization routine.

REGCLR. Later on, we'll go into subroutines, but now, look at the machine language equivalent of it shown in Fig. 11-17.

The CLR A instruction makes the contents of the accumulator equal zero. Remember we found that most data manipulations go through the accumulator, so in

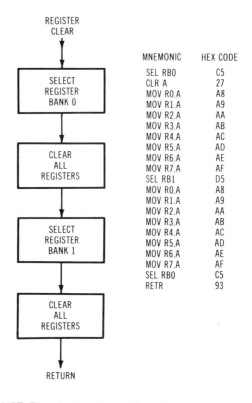

REGISTER
CLEAR

SELECT
REGISTER
BANK 0

CLEAR
ALL
REGISTERS

SELECT
REGISTER
BANK 1

CLEAR
ALL
REGISTERS

RETURN

MNEMONIC	HEX CODE
SEL RB0	C5
CLR A	27
MOV R0,A	A8
MOV R1,A	A9
MOV R2,A	AA
MOV R3,A	AB
MOV R4,A	AC
MOV R5,A	AD
MOV R6,A	AE
MOV R7,A	AF
SEL RB1	D5
MOV R0,A	A8
MOV R1,A	A9
MOV R2,A	AA
MOV R3,A	AB
MOV R4,A	AC
MOV R5,A	AD
MOV R6,A	AE
MOV R7,A	AF
SEL RB0	C5
RETR	93

Fig. 11-17 Flowchart and assembly code representation of Register Clear subroutine.

this machine, we take what is in the accumulator (0) and place it into each of the eight motor registers. That is exactly what the MOV RX,A instruction accomplishes. In machine language coding, you will notice that the value or place to the right of the comma is placed into the variable to the left. Therefore, the value of zero from A ends up in each of the motor registers R0 through R7. That is easy, right? The same operations are performed on register Bank 1. Let's look back at the flowchart in Fig. 11-18.

It is now time to shut off the motors or make sure they are all off. Remember that there are two 8-bit registers associated with them. Moving data from the accumulator out to the motor-control registers is not as easy to do as it was to the internal registers. Let me explain why. The 74LS273 latch devices require a control-line input that tells them when to grab data from the P1 Bus.

Notice in the schematics (Figs. 11-10 and 11-15) that all the register and gate devices share the bus; therefore, it is convenient to implement the address selector tied to Port 2 lines 0, 1, and 2. It should be obvious that in order to

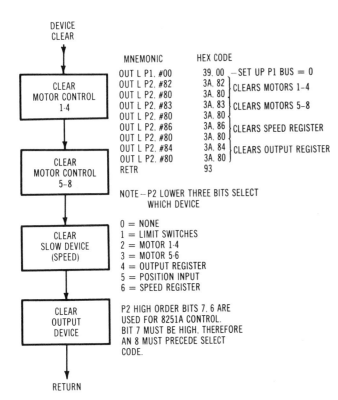

MNEMONIC	HEX CODE	
OUT L P1, #00	39. 00	—SET UP P1 BUS = 0
OUT L P2, #82	3A. 82	} CLEARS MOTORS 1-4
OUT L P2, #80	3A. 80	
OUT L P2, #83	3A. 83	} CLEARS MOTORS 5-8
OUT L P2, #80	3A. 80	
OUT L P2, #86	3A. 86	} CLEARS SPEED REGISTER
OUT L P2, #80	3A. 80	
OUT L P2, #84	3A. 84	} CLEARS OUTPUT REGISTER
OUT L P2, #80	3A. 80	
RETR	93	

NOTE—P2 LOWER THREE BITS SELECT WHICH DEVICE

0 = NONE
1 = LIMIT SWITCHES
2 = MOTOR 1-4
3 = MOTOR 5-6
4 = OUTPUT REGISTER
5 = POSITION INPUT
6 = SPEED REGISTER

P2 HIGH ORDER BITS 7, 6 ARE USED FOR 8251A CONTROL. BIT 7 MUST BE HIGH. THEREFORE AN 8 MUST PRECEDE SELECT CODE.

Fig. 11-18 Flow and code of Device Clear subroutine.

direct the transfer of data to a certain device on the bus, that its address must be set up first.

PORT OPERATIONS

Now comes the tricky part. Port 2 is used for many things, and it must be changed by the accumulator all at once. So how do we place the motor-control register address out on these lines without affecting the other Port 2 lines? There are two instructions called ANL P2 and ORL P2 that are used for just that purpose. They perform the logical operations of AND and OR on the port data bits presently there with the addresses you wish to add or subtract.

Let me show you an example:

ANL P2,A(0)
Port 2 contents BEFORE = 11100111.
Port 2 operations DURING = 00000000 = A contents
Port 2 contents AFTER = 00000000

The ANL instruction took the value stored in A, which was zero, and logically ANDed it with the bit pattern presently in the Port 2 output register. The result cleared all output bits, because for a logical AND to produce a 1 both values must be a 1. Let's take this a bit further and realize that placing a zero anywhere during the ANL instruction clears the corresponding bit. It should be

noted, here, that when bit patterns are shown it is assumed that the least significant bit (D0) is on the right.

The ORL instruction works the opposite of the ANL instruction. It can be used to insert a 1 into the bit pattern. Look at the following example:

ORL P2,A(4)
Port 2 contents BEFORE = 11000011
Port 2 contents DURING = 00000100 = A contents
Port 2 contents AFTER = 11000111

Notice that the third bit position now includes a one. These two instructions will be used extensively when we operate on the ports. The strobe line I was referring to that latches data into the motor control register needs to toggle from 1 to 0 then back to 1 during operation. This is done the following way:

ORL P2,A(08)
ANL P2,A(F7)
ORL P2,A(08)

In this example, hexadecimal coding was used when referring to values in the accumulator. If you are not familiar with hex code, Table 11-2 is provided to help you convert numbers from the familiar decimal to hex and back. So, let's return to our program. Clearing devices is also accomplished with a subroutine. The coding shown in Fig. 11-18 spells out the particulars of device data strobing. Basically the device is selected, then a low pulse is asserted on the strobe output of Port 2.

If you are confused about the use of the pound sign (#), this merely indicates that the following data is to be used in the instruction instead of register or accumulator data.

Table 11-2. Hexadecimal Encoding

NUMBER	VALUE WEIGHT			
	8	4	2	1
	HEX CODE			
0	0	0	0	0
1	0	0	0	1
2	0	0	1	0
3	0	0	1	1
4	0	1	0	0
5	0	1	0	1
6	0	1	1	0
7	0	1	1	1
8	1	0	0	0
9	1	0	0	1
A	1	0	1	0
B	1	0	1	1
C	1	1	0	0
D	1	1	0	1
E	1	1	1	0
F	1	1	1	1

Example:
Hex Value **3C**
Binary Equivalent **0011 1100**

Basically, we have left the zero in the accumulator that was initially put in there.

Go through the listing in Fig. 11-18 and note that we perform the same type of "ritual" for the other motor-control register. Then the general-purpose output register is massaged in the same way. We finish with clearing the speed-control register.

There is only one thing left to perform. We must read the initial condition of the position feedback sensors to determine from where to start counting. This is accomplished by selecting the address (101) and doing an IN A,P1 instruction. We now have it in the accumulator, and there it cannot stay. If you'll notice, we've used up the initial eight general-purpose registers of the 8748, so it is time to switch into the second bank of seven. This is done by performing a SEL RB1 instruction. It figuratively opens the door to eight more rooms. However, you must remember that to go back and access the motor registers, that door must be closed by doing a SEL RB0 instruction.

Now that we are using register Bank 1, we have eight more data storage places. Let's store the current state of the position sensors in R0. Then we must get the current state of the eight limit switches and store them in R1. We should switch back to register Bank 0 now.

INITIALIZING THE 8251A

This concludes the initialization of the inputs and outputs. There is another device in the system that requires setup: the 8251A. Without initializing this device, there is no communication with the host. The 8251A has two registers internally that must be set up to enable operation. The first is the *mode register* (see Fig. 11-19A). It is accessed by placing a zero on bit 7 of Port 2 and simply performing a move to external memory from the accumulator. The 1 in bit 6 selects the control section of the device and the data we send in sets up the mode of operation of the 8251A.

Looking at Fig.11-19 you can see that some of the parameters mentioned in Chapter 10 dealing with serial communications are selected through this register. From left to right we find the first two (D7 and D8) which specify the number of stop bits to insert. I have arbitrarily picked 2. Then comes the parity information. The choice was for no parity. The number of data bits we will receive and transmit is eight and the baud-rate generator chosen works with a factor of 16. Combining all these we come up with a mode word of CE.

The command register is next. It is accessed directly

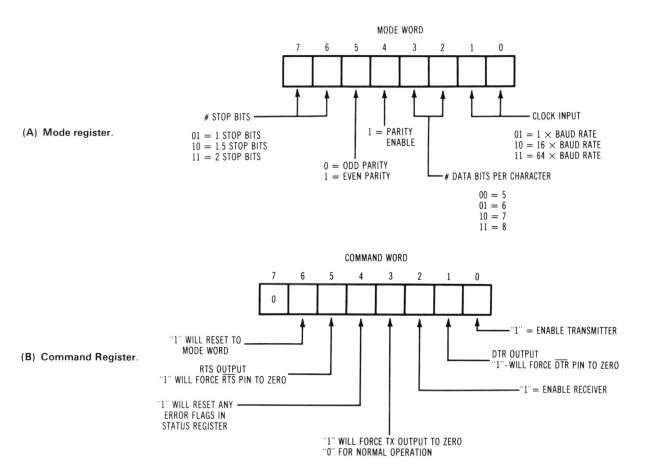

(A) Mode register.

(B) Command Register.

Fig. 11-19 Bit assignments of the 8251A Mode and Command word registers.

157

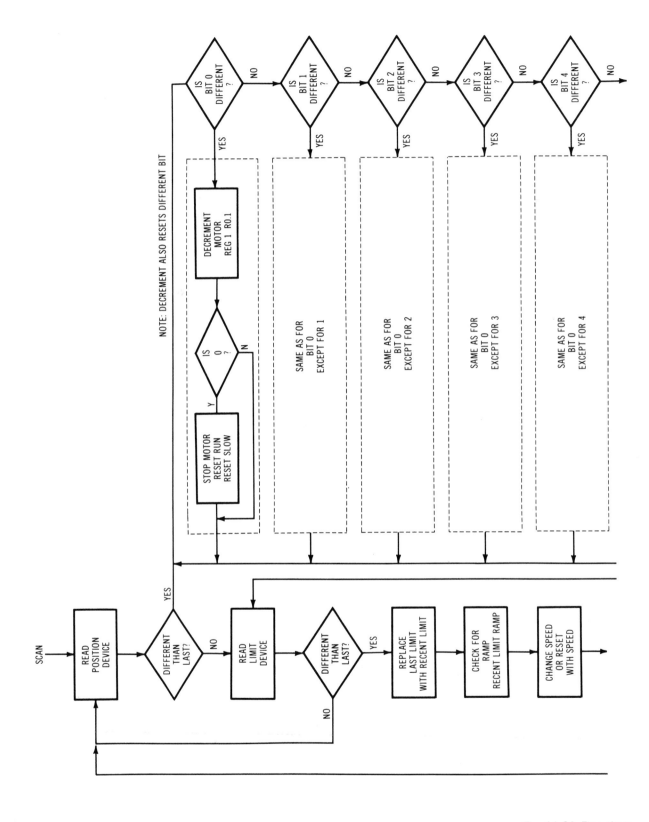

NOTE: DECREMENT ALSO RESETS DIFFERENT BIT

Fig. 11-20 Flowchart

158

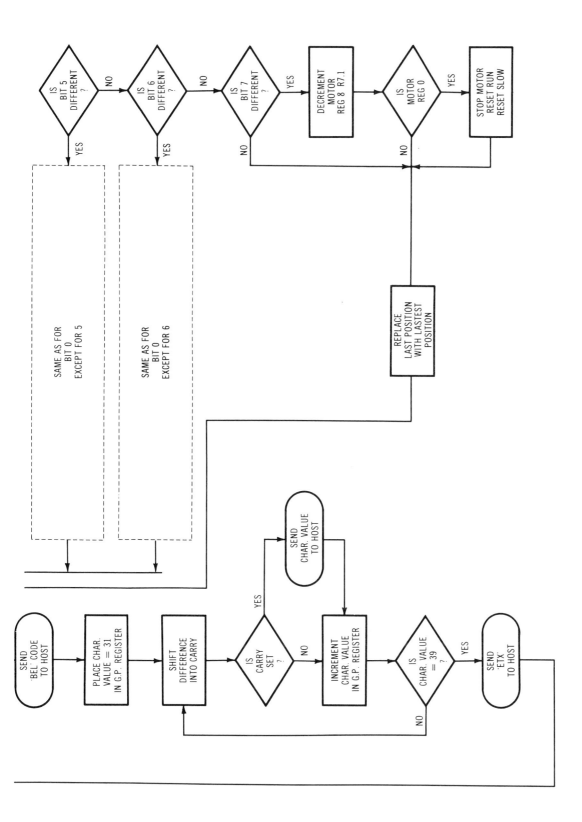

of Scan routine.

after you place the mode word. The parameters of a command word are in Fig. 11-19B. The only bits to be concerned with are bits D0 and D2. They control the enabling of the receiver and transmitter. Some programmers prefer to change these bits constantly during operation, but I just enable both of them at the beginning of the program. The command word will be 05.

That is it for the 8251A. The last instruction to be executed in the initialization routine is to enable the interrupts. What interrupts? Well, if you take a closer look again at the schematic in Fig. 11-15, you will see that the receiver ready output line of the 8251A is connected through an inverter to the 8748 interrupt line. This causes an interrupt to the program whenever a character is received from the host. The transmitter ready line is connected to the T1 input pin of the 8748 and is tested to see if it is all right to transmit a character to the host. You will see both in action later.

This entire initialization routine, that took us forever to go through, takes the 8748 only a fraction of a second. The actual code starts at address 010 of the program memory. When reset clears the Program Counter, it picks up its first instruction at location 000. A Jump instruction is placed there that catapults it to the initialization routine at address 010.

Let's review. So far we have reset the 8748, cleared its motor registers, and initialized both the motor-control registers and the speed-select registers. The general-purpose outputs are off and we have a copy of the initial condition of the limit switches and position sensors. We are also now open for business to the host.

The 8748 instructions we've become familiar with are the following:

CLR A	OUT A
MOV R0,A	IN A
ORL P2,A	SEL RB1
ORL P2,# data	SEL RB0
ANL P2,A	MOV X @ R1,A
ANL P2,# data	EN I
MOV A,# data	

Not bad for a start!

And just a start it is. There are several more routines to cover in this controller. The next is the SCAN routine. This is where the computer automatically checks the position sensors for change as well as the state of the limit switches. Fig. 11-20 shows the flowchart of operations to be performed in this section. This program is larger than the initialization routine. Also, there are portions of code that we have not encountered yet.

Examining the flowchart we see that the first operation is to read the state of the position sensors. This is done with the same code we used before when we obtained their initial state. Then it must be determined if they have changed from the last sample. This is done by a method

called *comparison*, using Exclusive OR logic. In an Exclusive OR situation, two inputs produce a logic 1 if they are different, yet they cause the output to become a zero if they are the same. So, performing an XOR,A,R0 compares the last reading (now residing in register Bank 1!) with the one just taken. The result remains in the accumulator.

Realize that the operation just performed destroys the reading just taken on the sensors. This is why preceding that code we must store away the reading just taken for safe keeping. You may use any of the four general purpose registers.

At this point, a decision must be made. If the remaining value left in A is not zero, then there must have been a change. Now we get into a wild and wonderful program loop. Pay very close attention or you'll become lost.

The byte of information contained in the accumulator coming into this loop has a '1' bit pertaining to each position sensor that has changed state since the last reading. This loop must identify these sensors and determine which motor they represent. Then they must decide if the motor in question is, indeed, running. If it is, then its associated motor register is decremented by 1. The resulting value is checked to see if it has reached zero. If per chance it has, then that motor is stopped by resetting the motor-control device bit and both the RUN bits and SLOW (speed select) bits for that motor are also cleared.

The way the loop works, it feeds itself. The first bit is processed, and when it is through it is necessary for it to clear its associated *difference* bit. That way the second time through it will not once again process the same motor. When all bits are finished processing, the loop empties out to go through the remainder of the SCAN routine.

With the position sensors out of the way, the controller can now process the limit switches. The device attached to them is read and a similar test for differences, like that used with the position sensors, is performed. If no change is found, the program simply goes back to the position sensors again.

When a change is found in the limit switches, several things must happen and a few might happen. The first and foremost task is to memorize this latest status. This is done simply by replacing the old with the new. Then let's see if any of the changed switches were involved in a RAMP-type motor instruction. You remember this is where the motor travels at normal speed until the limit switch of the same number (as the motor) has changed state. From that point until it is stopped, the motor travels at half speed.

Checking for this condition is performed on all eight positions of the limit sensors at once, by comparing the changed status logic 1 levels to a register called appropriately the "RAMP Register". A corresponding logic 1 in

160

that register bit position, when the two are ANDed together, results in a logic 1 being set in all bit positions requiring a speed change. This speed change value is then ORed to the existing information resident in the slow device. It is called a slow device not because it executes like a turtle, but because a logic 1 level in any bit position indicates a slow-speed selection for the corresponding motor.

With that out of the way, we can now proceed to tell the host that the limit switches have changed. First, we must resurrect the difference information (easy if you kept a copy in a general-purpose register). We take this byte and shift it one bit at a time into the processor's carry bit location. Here it can be tested for a logic 1 or 0. With each shift, I incremented an ASCII value in a register. This kept track of which position (hence which switch) was being tested. When a logic 1 is found, indicating a change, the ASCII code in that register is sent to the host. Starting with a code of 30 (0) and incrementing once per shift yields the proper code per switch value. The end of the byte is signalled when you have shifted past code 38. Notice that, before the shifting began, the host was signalled with the Bell code. In some terminals, this actually rings a bell or activates a beeper. The familiar ACK message code is sent last, then it is on to the position sensors again. Ever wonder why this routine is called SCAN?

RECEPTION OF COMMANDS

If the scanning process goes on forever, looping and looping, how do we ever get out to do other things? Remember the last action that we performed during initialization? This is where those interrupts come in. Now you know why they call them interrupts. The processor actually stops the SCAN routine, does something else for a while, then starts again right where it left off.

What caused this interruption anyway? The 8251A, if you recall, is connected to the INT input through an inverter. This input expects to see a logic 0 for activation. The 8251A, on receipt of a character from the host, sets its receiver-ready pin to a logic 1. The inverter converts this to signal the interrupt and the rest is automatic. The 8748 stores away the Program Counter location of where it was in the stack. It then vectors itself to location 003 where it picks up the next instruction. I designed it to execute a Jump instruction there to go to the address of the interrupt routine.

This routine is actually called a *command handler*, for it is here that the "mutterings" of the host are interpreted and carried out. Fig. 11-21 shows the flowchart pertaining to this routine. Remember, that entering this routine means there is a character waiting in the receiver data register of the 8251A. Let's get it and determine which command it is.

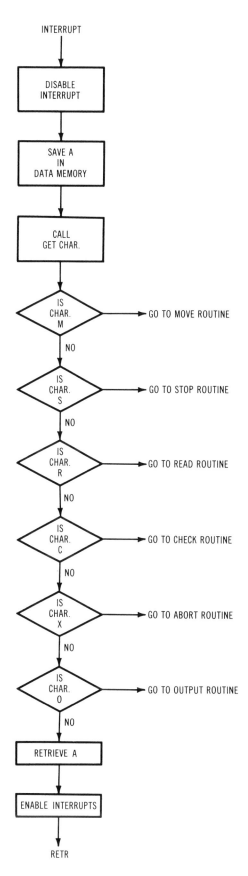

Fig. 11-21 Flowchart of Interrupt command handler.

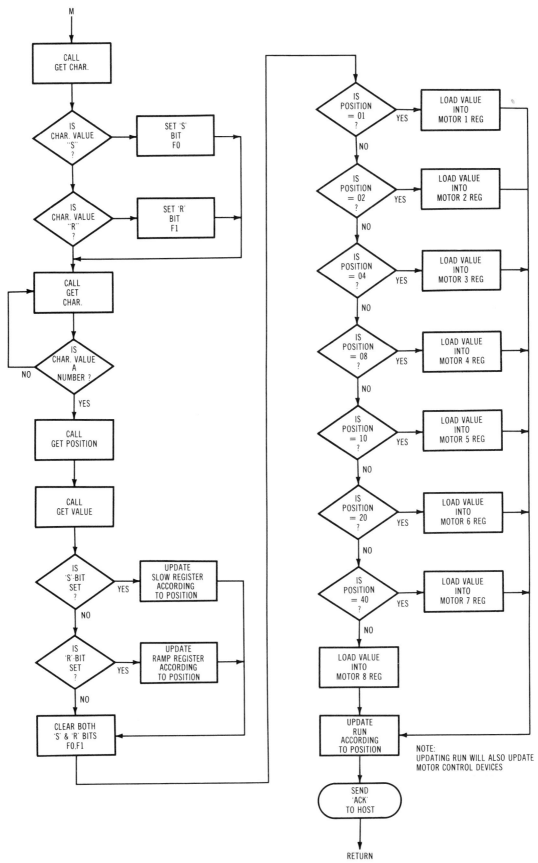

Fig. 11-22 Move command flowchart.

162

You will note that outside of the MOVE commands, the first letter of each command word is unique. It is this character (the one now in the data register) that determines the command operation. The flowchart shows how it is retrieved and subsequently tested for each command category, but what is this? The interrupts have been disabled? Does this mean that no more inputs from the host will be processed?

No. This means simply that we do not want to be interrupted right now during this phase of the program. If we need character input, we must look for it manually. This operation is called *polling*. Let's pump out one of those command words to the MOVE subprogram to see how this type of character input is done. (Refer to Fig. 11-22.)

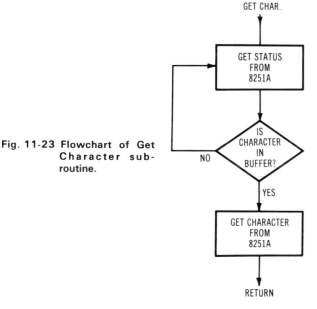

Fig. 11-23 Flowchart of Get Character subroutine.

GET CHAR.

GET STATUS FROM 8251A

IS CHARACTER IN BUFFER?

NO

YES

GET CHARACTER FROM 8251A

RETURN

MOVE COMMAND

There is another CALL request. This is a signal to the 8748 to temporarily jump to a routine that just gets a character. This program is located elsewhere and has a defined set of input parameters and output parameters so that it may be called whenever character input without causing an interrupt is needed. Look at Fig. 11-23. Here you see that the status register of the 8251A must be read to determine if there is a character pending. The receiver ready output pin status is readable through this register. Fig 11-24 shows the bit assignment the status register of the 8251A. If there is a character, it is read into the accumulator. This reading status and data from the 8251A requires some talk about hardware and how it is implemented on the controller. The C/D line, as mentioned before, must be set to the proper position (either control-logic 1 or data-logic 0) before performing a MOVE external memory into the 8748. Normally during a MOVX instruction, the 8748 outputs an address code on its eight bus lines momentarily before receiving or transmitting data.

This address information comes from either register 0 or register 1 (you specify which). In my code, shown in Table 11-3, R0 was arbitrarily specified. The circuit, as it is designed in the controller, does not use this address, so it discards it. Unfortunately this instruction is needed because it will activate the READ or WRITE control lines during the proper time to transfer data between the 8748 and the 8251A. The code in Table 11-3 gives you a good understanding of how to communicate with the 8251A.

Well, what do we want from this next character? It should be the motor number that we wish to move; however, the host may have decided to separate the "M" and the number by a comma or a space. In fact, the entire

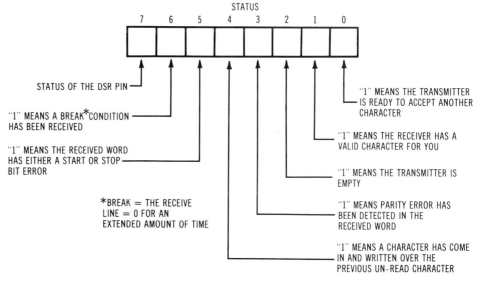

STATUS

7 6 5 4 3 2 1 0

STATUS OF THE DSR PIN

"1" MEANS A BREAK*CONDITION HAS BEEN RECEIVED

Fig. 11-24 Bit assignments of 8251A Status register.

"1" MEANS THE RECEIVED WORD HAS EITHER A START OR STOP BIT ERROR

*BREAK = THE RECEIVE LINE = 0 FOR AN EXTENDED AMOUNT OF TIME

"1" MEANS THE TRANSMITTER IS READY TO ACCEPT ANOTHER CHARACTER

"1" MEANS THE RECEIVER HAS A VALID CHARACTER FOR YOU

"1" MEANS THE TRANSMITTER IS EMPTY

"1" MEANS PARITY ERROR HAS BEEN DETECTED IN THE RECEIVED WORD

"1" MEANS A CHARACTER HAS COME IN AND WRITTEN OVER THE PREVIOUS UN-READ CHARACTER

word MOVE might be sent. What if it is to be a MOVES or MOVER command? Where do the S and R go?

To answer these questions, refer to Fig. 11-22. Notice that the program, after getting the next character, enters into a loop that looks for certain character values. The first is the "S" delimiter. If it finds an S after the M, it assumes it to be a MOVE Slow command, which sets one of the general-purpose flag bits. What does this do for us? Well, you'll see later that we will process information recalling whether that S flag has been set, so it is used as a marker, or a reminder. The same process goes on for the check of a RAMP command, except flag F1 is set as a result.

What if the host decides to send the word MOVE spelled out entirely? The way this loop is written, any characters not specifically needed in the command are automatically discarded. So we have a very flexible input command structure. The other thing the program tests for is the presence of a number. This indicates the motor device you wish to move. After detecting that, it goes on to process the offset you wish to travel.

Before it asks for the offset, the program takes the number received for the motor, and converts it into something called *position*. You should not confuse this with the position devices that are used to sense movement of the motors. This converted number, called position, is a character-to-binary bit-position converter. Let's look at how this is done, and shortly you will see why it is done.

Fig 11-25 details the operational flow of the GET POSITION subprogram. Basically, it retrieves the byte received last from the 8251A. It then enters a search loop that tests the value of the character. When it finds a particular match, it then sets the corresponding bit position in a general-purpose register. For instance if the character is an ASCII 6, then the bit assignments of that register are set as follows: 00100000. A three comes out as : 00000100. You see, each bit position carries a value of '1' starting from the right. We'll get back to this in a minute.

After the conversion to position, the controller calls another subprogram. This one is a bit more complicated than the previous ones. Fig. 11-26 shows the flow of the GET VALUE subprogram. For the uninitiated, this is what is called a BCD-to-binary converter-conversion program. What is BCD? It is the acronym for Binary Coded Decimal and includes the first ten codes of the hexadecimal table shown in Table 11-2. Only four bits are used to represent a value 0-9. When we specify the number of position marks to travel, we do so in decimal, e.g., +123 or −63. These numbers (there may be up to three) must be converted into one 8-bit binary number that can be stored in a motor register. This routine does this. It also allows flexible input as you may omit the plus sign if the value is to be positive, and you may enter any number up to three digits in the range of +128. It means that to enter the number 62 you don't have to say 062. The

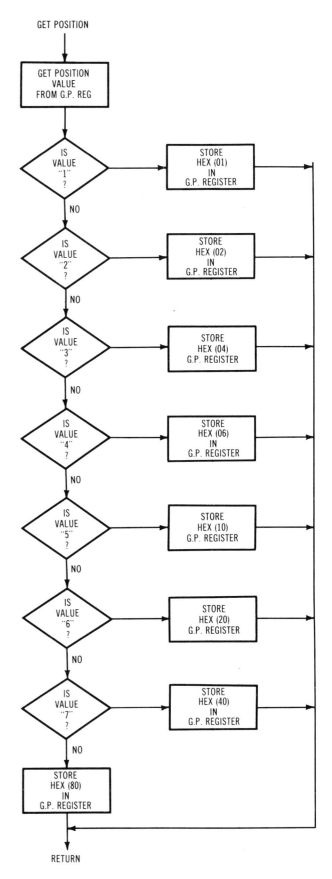

Fig. 11-25 Flowchart of Get Position subroutine.

164

program automatically adjusts to the number of digits received. When a negative number is received, the routine sets bit 8 of the value. This will tell the update run routine which motor device bit to enable, either forward or reverse.

With the motor defined and the offset value received, it is time to roll with the command. The first order of business is to check for the presence of Slow or Ramp flags. After all, if we are to move slowly, it is best to have set the speed before commanding the motor to move.

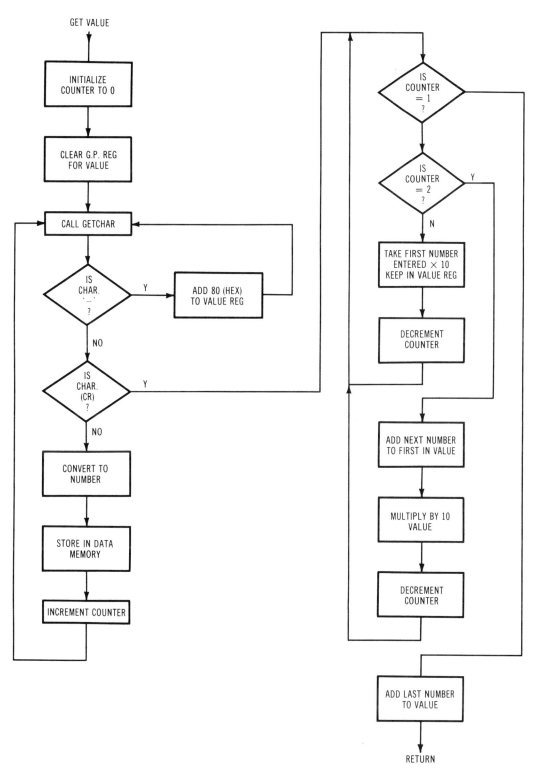

Fig. 11-26 Flowchart of Get Value subroutine.

Table 11-3. Assembly Language Code of Get Character Subroutine

Label	Mnemonic	Hex Code	Comments
CHECK	OUTL P2,#40	3A,40	Select 8251A control
	MOVX A,@R0	80	Get status word
	RRC A	67	Shift TX status into carry
	RRC A	67	Shift RX status into carry
	JNC CHECK	E6,CHECK	If no character go back to check
	OUTL P2,#00	3A,00	If character is present select data input
	MOVX A,@R0	80	Get character in receive register
	RETR	93	

Also, now is a good time to set Ramp bits according to the motor position. Both of these operations are performed before processing is done on the actual motion command, and with the use of the position information.

The register to load with the offset data compiled by the GET VALUE program is determined by the position

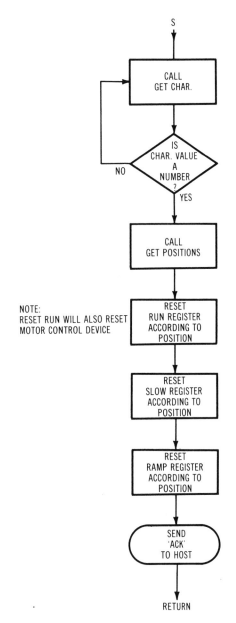

NOTE:
RESET RUN WILL ALSO RESET
MOTOR CONTROL DEVICE

Fig. 11-27 Stop command flowchart.

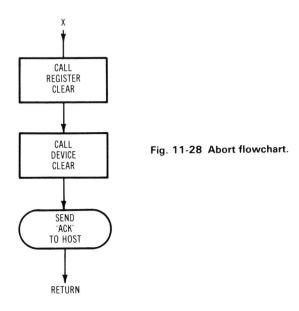

Fig. 11-28 Abort flowchart.

information. After loading is done, the RUN register is set according to position and the motor device is set to a forward or reverse-on position. That's all it takes to turn on a motor.

So, its running. How does it stop it?

STOP COMMAND

Stopping a motor manually, or by host instead of by automatic control, is very easy. After the Command Handler (Fig. 11-21) sees the command character S, it jumps to the STOP routine, Fig. 11-27. By now, the first three operations in this command ought to be familiar. Once again the input format is flexible, allowing the entire word STOP to be received. The motor number is received and its position determined.

This information is then used to reset the RUN bit and send a stop to the motor device. At this time, the Slow and Ramp registers are updated to reflect that this particular motor is no longer in the picture. With this and all other commands, the ACK character is then sent to the host to signify the completion of a command.

Notice that the author chose not to clear the motor register when a STOP command is processed. It might be desirable to the host if this information (number of

166

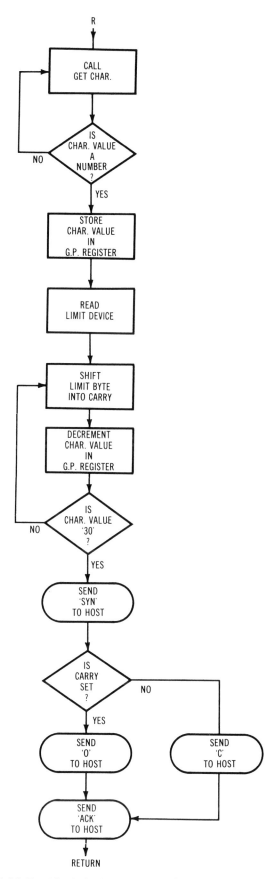

Fig. 11-29 Read Limit Switch command flowchart.

counts left) is kept intact. It can later be retrieved through a check command.

ABORT COMMAND

There is another way of stopping a motor. Except that this way halts the entire controller system. The X command signals an abort condition, which means that all motors should immediately stop and all general-purpose outputs should de-energize. The flowchart in Fig. 11-28 tells the story. This command may be used when an emergency situation exists and it is important to stop all operations at once.

READ COMMAND

At times when there are emergencies, it is nice to have a panic button close by to signal a call for action. The controller contains eight general-purpose limit-switch inputs. One of these could be used as an operator emergency stop button. Whenever the status of any of those switches changes (like the closing of the emergency button) the controller is obliged to signal the host and tell him who upset the apple cart. The READ command (Fig 11-29) could also be used to poll the status of a particular switch.

Looking at the figure, you can see that once we get the switch number, a READ of the current limit-switch status is instituted. Then the byte resulting from this READ is shifted serially one bit at a time (one switch position) into the carry bit. In between shifts, the controller is decrementing the number value received that denotes the particular switch. When the value equals character value 30 (0) the bit presently in the carry bit must be the one switch position we're looking for.

The carry is tested to determine the state of the switch C (closed) if it is a logic 0, and O (open) if it finds a logic 1. The message is reported upstream to the host in the SYN, O/C, ACK format.

CHECK COMMAND

Remember it was stated that after a motor had been stopped by an "S" command, the value remaining in the motor register may then be retrieved? Well, the Check command (Fig 11-30) does this. In fact, you can perform a CHECK even while the motor is running in case you want to gate some other action on the arrival of the motor to a certain position.

The operations in the flowchart are pretty straightforward. All you do is determine which motor you want and simply retrieve its current value. The message is then sent according to standard format.

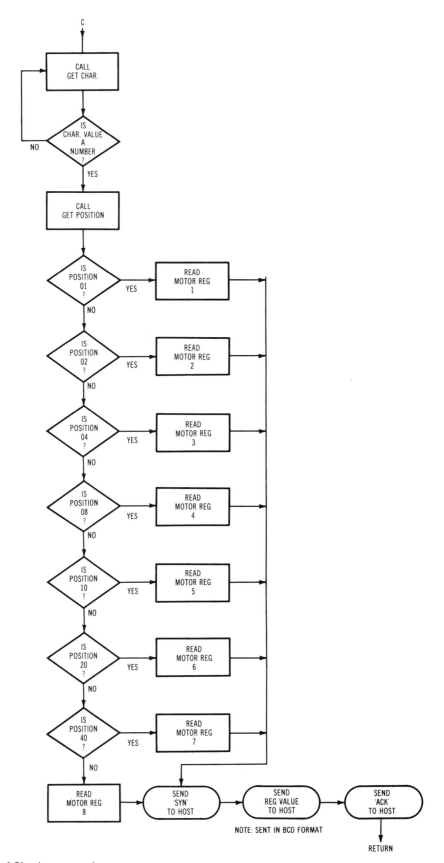

Fig. 11-30 Flowchart of Check command.

168

OUT COMMAND

The ability to control external devices, not associated with the actual movement of the robot, is useful. There are eight general-purpose outputs provided so that you may initiate actions such as conveyor control, work platform change, etc., on command.

The OUT command (Fig. 11-31) allows the host to address a particular output point and command it to turn ON (logic 0) or OFF (logic 1). Once again, flexible input format is used, in fact, you may enter the letter "N" to denote ON, or the letter "F" to denote OFF. This would shorten the message some. It is possible, however, to send the command string: OUTPUT 6, ON as the program will discard all nonessential input. After processing the command, the ACK message is passed to the host.

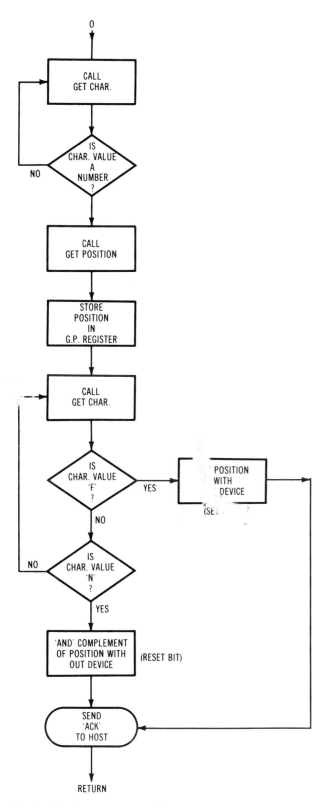

Fig. 11-31 Output command flowchart.

SENDING DATA

You know, throughout these discussions, we have been showing the controller communication with the host without revealing the way in which we accomplish transmission of data. Remember the flowchart regarding the reception of a character (Fig. 11-23)? Well, this is very similar except that we don't need to get status to determine if the transmitter is ready to accept a data transmission.

The 8748 has an input called T1 that may be tested with an instruction to determine its state. The transmit ready line from the 8251A is wired directly to this line. So, when the controller has determined that it wants to send a character upstream to the host, it must first test the status of the T1 input. If it is all right, it performs a MOVX @ R1/R1,A which takes the data out of the accumulator and places it into the 8251A. The C/D line must be in the Data position (logic 0), and the 8251A does all the rest.

THE HOST

Another subject not touched on here is the host. Who or what is he and where does he live? The author designed the communication command package to accept the output of a standard ASCII alphanumeric terminal. You could conceivably control a robot manipulator through this controller using such a terminal.

Actually, any computer may be used to act as host. This would be generally considered the brain of the robot. The controller is the muscle. It could reside within the manipulator structure or be separated by several thousand miles communicating over phone lines.

What type of programs can the host execute? Well, that's a topic in itself, and it happens to be the one next in line. So, without any further delay, let's move into that area.

Chapter 12

Robot Control
Languages

As you found evident from the last chapter, the programming side of a robot is by far the most involved. Like any microcomputer-based system, it's what you do with it in terms of software, rather than what hardware features it incorporates that matters. In keeping with this notion, this chapter is another "software mostly" discussion, although you'll find it on a much higher level here.

Robots, as you know by now, are used for a variety of tasks. Indeed we use the term robot to describe various types of mechanisms. The programmable microwave oven may be classified as a robot chef of a sort. The programming involved to implement the intelligence in the oven is very different from that of a pick and place robot arm used in the manufacturing facility of General Motors. Let's look at some of the kinds of programming methods used in today's robot systems and then we'll define and implement one of our own.

HISTORY

Robot programming languages got their start in the United States for control of the Unimate series of robots. Basically, this first language consisted of the ability to move to a point in space and perform an action. You, the operator, entered commands for motion that moved the arm to a desired point. On reaching that point, a "record" button was pushed. The controller then remembered the coordinates of all the joint positions. This type of move-set-record action goes on until the entire program is "learned." Then the operator pushed the "automatic" button which will recall each point from memory in the sequence it was entered, rather like a trained monkey.

This type of lead-through instant programming is still in use today. In fact, it has been found to be a very efficient way to program a small, short-run manufacturing manipulator. It requires no special programming skills, and the task is completed almost as fast as it takes to perform the job once. We will design a system that is close to this. It works on time activation, rather than position coordinates.

During the time this type of programming was first used, the U.S. government was heavily involved in funding research in robotic systems. Most of these projects involved the visual analysis of scenes. Some work was going on at Stanford University involving an arm that was programmed to sort through blocks, pick them up, and stack them in order. This system used a rather limited programming language that allowed the following functions:

1. Initialize
2. Servo
3. Open
4. Close

The *Initialize* command was used to initialize the arm to a known set of circumstances. *Servo* specified joint positions, in numbers, at which to set the six joints of the arm. It was used much like a move command. *Open* did just what it claims, opens a gripper, and *Close* did the opposite.

Each of these commands was called by a program and used like subroutines. All action within the program stopped until the called function was performed, then execution went on.

In 1971, a more advanced programmable system was developed whereby the operator or computer program need only tell the manipulator which object was to be grasped, and where to place it. The system was intelligent enough to search out the desired object, determine how to grasp it to avoid slippage and move it to the desired location before completing.

The first phase of this project (which came to be known as the Move Instance System) was implemented using a computer-graphics display system. On the screen, the operator could command the "cartoon" arm to move and stack objects. This worked well and was very impressive. The real world, however, posed much of a problem to the system and it was never finished. As we have seen, gravity, torque, friction, and all the elements that go along with our world each have their effect on robot design. To ignore any one of these spells disaster or, at least, frustration to the potential designer.

Over the years, several more programming languages were designed with varying degrees of success. The Wave System was developed to help manipulator-control programming by making use of various feedback information now being made available by the recent developments of touch and torque sensors. It had two modes of operation. In one, the planning phase, the operator entered high-level commands that were assembled and stored for later execution. This phase might be likened to the editor portion of a BASIC interpreter. The second phase was one where immediate execution would take place as the commands were entered. This language was used with some success controlling two manipulators. This was done by alternating control to one or the other so that simultaneous movement was emulated. However, this proved to be slow and very inefficient. A new, more capable language had to be developed.

The AL language was then designed to take up where Wave left off. At the time, the ALGOL language was a popular high-order tool, so it was decided to incorporate the Wave features into an ALGOL structure which would have the ability to control true simultaneous motions in two manipulators. ALGOL was an ancestor of today's ever popular PASCAL, which has become one of the most used languages for robot programming. It was found that the command structures of Wave conflicted with the ALGOL control philosophy. Although it was simpler to program various actions in AL than in Wave, the procedures that had to be defined became extremely time consuming and complex.

The next language developed was an outgrowth of the last two called PAL. Here, the language, also ALGOL based, overcame many of the shortcomings of both the AL and Wave implementations. It provided for a much more refined manipulator movement and control structure.

WHERE DO WE GO FROM HERE?

All these languages of the past and many more like them in the present are custom engineered to control one specific brand of manipulator. As an experimenter you might ask how can a high-level robot-programming language be applied to my garage-built household servant? Well, take comfort in realizing that you are where those university researchers were when they started. There is no off-the-shelf available robot operating systems for personal robots, nor will there be in the near future. Why? Because there is no hardware standardization in the "brains" being developed to control them.

This is why, throughout my experimentation, it was necessary to develop my own PAL languages. I would like to share two very limited adaptations of the BASIC language with you. The first is a teach and learn system, much like the initial Unimation systems described earlier.

ARM COMMANDER

This program is not a high-level language, but it does allow the storing and recall that programming languages use. Basically, it is made up of two modes: *manual* and *automatic*. Each mode works independently of the other. It is written with the ability to handle 12 execution codes. These codes are not labeled in English as your program requirements may differ greatly from mine. Each of these codes may be entered by the single depression of a key on the keyboard of a personal computer. The BASIC program will, depending on the mode selected, send the code assigned to this key out to an output port of some kind. The implementation specifically used in the provided listings is for the Radio Shack TRS-80 Color Computer. An output port was built at memory location 49152. Your output location may be different; therefore, take notice during the discussions regarding specific output destinations.

INITIALIZE

Look at Fig. 12-1. This figure shows the steps involved to set up the ARM Commander program. The first two operations involve setting aside space in memory to store the key codes and their durations when they're in the automatic "learn" mode. This is done by assigning each entity a specific one-dimensional array. The size of the array is determined by how many program steps you want to memorize. Arbitrarily, 25 steps were chosen for the program I implemented. It is really limited to how much memory your particular machine can spare.

Now comes the customization. The next job in the initialize routine is to make sure that the output port assigned to get the key codes as they are executed is set up properly. My system is an output-only port which requires no specific setup codes. Data delivered to

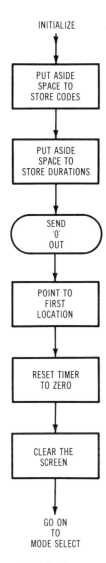

INITIALIZE

PUT ASIDE
SPACE TO
STORE CODES

PUT ASIDE
SPACE TO
STORE DURATIONS

SEND
'0'
OUT

POINT TO
FIRST
LOCATION

RESET TIMER
TO ZERO

CLEAR THE
SCREEN

GO ON
TO
MODE SELECT

Fig. 12-1   Flowchart of Intialization routine.

address 49152 simply exits the computer. This portion should be changed to reflect the needs of your computer.

Pointing to the first location will help the job of the memorizer later on in the program. It allows the memorizer simply to increment a variable that is assigned the job of remembering where to point next. It is this variable that we are now initializing to a value of 1. Another variable used in this way is the one to mark the time spent on a particular keypress. These times will later be stored in one of those arrays so it is a good idea to have a variable somewhere that can keep track of the time spent doing a specific task.

After all these areas are set, reset, and set aside, we find ourselves clearing the screen. This wipes clean any loading messages or system sign-on words that might have accumulated during the process of running the program.

Actual implementation of this routine is shown in Listing 12-1. Notice that the places set aside in memory

are arrays whose DIMensions match the number of codes I've allowed to be stored. These arrays are named for what they contain. In some forms of BASIC, you may not be able to use such long variable names. Check this out on the version you own before running into frustrating error problems.

Both the time and place variables are initialized and the null code of zero is sent to the unit we are commanding. After all that, the screen is cleared and its on to. . .

MODE SELECT

Here is where you, as the operator, notice that the program is working. A prompt message appears on the screen, asking you to select one of the following. There are two choices shown, one for manual mode, the other for automatic. Fig. 12-2 shows the flow of the routine. After viewing the prompt, you select the mode you wish to operate from. Selecting manual will branch you out to the manual mode routine. If automatic is your choice, the computer puts you in touch with that program. Notice that if neither is chosen, or if an erroneous code is entered, the program simply ignores it.

Listing 12-2 shows the implementation of this selection process. Using numbers to represent modes is the easiest to implement, however, you may choose to mod-

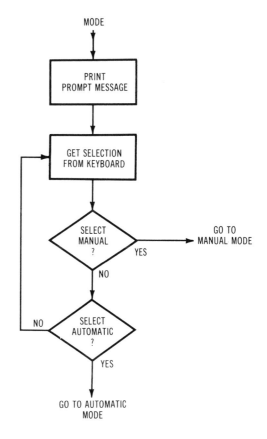

MODE

PRINT
PROMPT MESSAGE

GET SELECTION
FROM KEYBOARD

SELECT
MANUAL
?   YES → GO TO
MANUAL MODE

NO

NO   SELECT
AUTOMATIC
?

YES

GO TO AUTOMATIC
MODE

Fig. 12-2   Flowchart of Mode Select routine.

```
10 '
20 '    **  ARM COMMANDER  **
30 '
40 '
50 '      INITIALIZE
60 '
70 '
80 CLEAR 2000
90 DIM CODES$(25):DIM DURATION(25)
95 POKE 49152,0
100 PLACE=1:TIME=0:CLS
```

Listing 12-1 BASIC Code of Initialization Routine

```
110 PRINT"SELECT THE FOLLOWING"
120 PRINT"1) MANUAL MODE"
130 PRINT"2) AUTOMATIC MODE"
140 A$=INKEY$:IF A$="" THEN GOTO 140
150 IF A$="1" THEN GOTO 220
160 IF A$="2" THEN GOTO 310
170 CLS:GOTO 110
```

Listing 12-2 BASIC Code of Mode Select Routine

ify this to allow for the whole word, or portion thereof. The actual input sequence shown scans the keyboard for an entry. If none is found, it simply looks again. This is different than the normal INPUT statement common in BASIC programs. INPUT requires that the operator push ENTER, or carriage return, to signify that a code has been entered. The use of INKEY$ is essential to the design of this program. Later you will see where each time the computer scans the button in the down position, it will increment a value representing duration. This cannot be accomplished with INPUT.

MANUAL MODE

This mode allows you to control the robot in an immediate sense. Each command you enter is immediately sent to the robot. You have the option of stopping this action at any time by typing the letter "S." No command is stored in memory, therefore all actions are immediate and for nonprogrammed use.

Fig. 12-3 outlines the flow of operation involved with the manual mode. Notice that we first must wipe the screen clear of the selection data. Then we put up a sign saying that you are now in the manual mode of operation. At this time, we go, once again, to the keyboard looking for commands. These commands take the shape of single-key entries where the numerical value of the keys 1–9 are converted to actual decimal numbers and sent out. The zero key represents code 10 and the O and C keys (for open and close) are assigned codes 11 and 12, respectively. The call to the convert and send routine finds the computer operating as shown by the flowchart in Fig.

12-3. When the "S" key is detected, all execution is stopped and control is returned to the Mode Select routine. Listing 12-3 lists the BASIC code used to implement this program.

SUBPROGRAM: CONVERT AND SEND

Looking at the flowchart of the convert and send subprogram in Fig. 12-4, we see that the key code entered by us at the keyboard must be converted from its ASCII code to a usable code assigned to the robot system. If your system allows ASCII codes, there is no need for conversion at this time. In fact, you could eliminate this

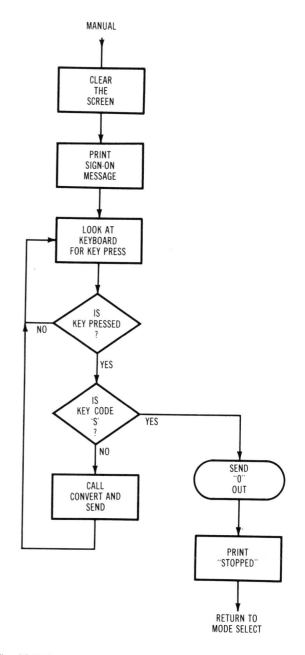

Fig. 12-3 Flowchart of Manual routine.

174

```
180 '
190 '    MANUAL MODE
200 '
210 '
220 CLS:PRINT"MANUAL INPUT MODE"
230 A$=INKEY$:IF A$="" THEN GOTO 230
240 IF A$="S" THEN POKE 49152,0:PRINT"STOPPED":GOTO 100
250 GOSUB 780   'CONVERT AND SEND
260 GOTO 230
```

Listing 12-3 BASIC Code of Manual Routine

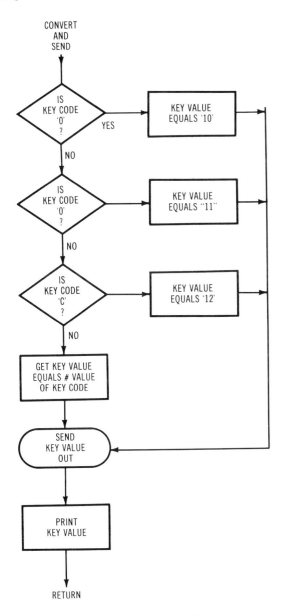

Fig. 12-4 Flowchart of Convert and Send subprogram.

subprogram altogether by simply putting an output instruction where the GOSUB was.

If you do require some conversion, this is the way to do it. Let's see what is involved. The digits 1 through 9 may

be converted to a decimal equivalent by the use of the VAL statement. See Listing 12-4 for the specific code used in this subprogram. Other codes of 0, O, and C must be converted by simple substitution. They never go through the VAL conversion portion of the program.

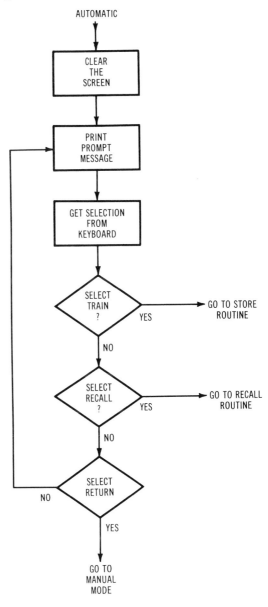

Fig. 12-5 Flowchart of Automatic routine.

175

```
740 '
750 '        CONVERT AND SEND SUBPROGRAM
760 '
770 '
780 IF A$="0" THEN KEYVALUE = 10:GOTO 820
790 IF A$="O" THEN KEYVALUE = 11:GOTO 820
800 IF A$="C" THEN KEYVALUE = 12:GOTO 820
810 KEYVALUE = VAL(A$)
820 POKE 49152,KEYVALUE:PRINT KEYVALUE
830 RETURN
```

Listing 12-4 BASIC Code of Convert and Send Subprogram

Once again, the particular output definition of your system might require some change in the POKE statement. And last, the code being sent out reflects on your screen to provide you with some feedback that the system is working.

AUTOMATIC MODE

Entering into the Automatic Mode you are once again faced with having to make a choice. Looking at Fig. 12-5, you see that after clearing the screen, this program asks you to choose one of three possible selections. Two of them deal with entering and recalling a program, while the other allows you to return to manual mode. Let's look at the design philosophy of the automatic operations.

First, the program allows you to enter up to 25 (remember the DIM statement?) commands into its memory. The key codes, as well as the time you spent holding each key down, is memorized. Remember now, all you have to do is press the key you desire; there is no need for pushing the ENTER key.

After storing your programmed commands, you will automatically return to the menu. At that time, you may elect to recall these commands from memory. When this is executed, the computer not only recalls, converts, and sends each key code, but it holds each code at the output for the same amount of time you held it down manually. Now this time is only approximate since the computer has limitations in that you may have lifted your finger a few milliseconds before the computer got around to noticing it. Listing 12-5 lists the codes used for this routine.

When all 25 preprogrammed actions have been output, the computer returns you to Mode Select. You can increase the number of program uter returns steps, as mentioned earlier, by changing the DIM statements at the beginning of the program.

STORE ROUTINE

This is the place where your key entries are put away for later execution. The flowchart in Fig. 12-6 shows that after clearing the screen the message "training" is displayed. Then it goes into its keyboard scanning mode. If it finds a key press, it immediately converts it and sends it out. Then it stores the key code, but not the converted key value. This code is placed in the code array (see Listing 12-6) and the time the key is down is marked with the variable "time." When the key is let up, this value is stored in the Duration array and the next place pointer is incremented, if you haven't reached the magic value of 25. If this end point is reached, however, a message is flashed on the screen indicating a full memory. Then you are transferred back to Mode Select.

RECALL ROUTINE

As was the case for all other routines, this one also clears the screen (Fig. 12-7) and notifies you of its func

```
270 '
280 '        AUTOMATIC MODE
290 '
300 '
310 CLS:PRINT"AUTOMATIC MODE"
320 PRINT"SELECT THE FOLLOWING"
330 PRINT"1) TRAIN"
340 PRINT"2) RECALL FROM MEMORY"
350 PRINT"3) RETURN TO MANUAL"
360 A$=INKEY$:IF A$="" THEN GOTO 360
370 IF A$="1" THEN GOTO 440  '      STORE SUBPROGRAM
380 IF A$="2" THEN GOTO 600  '      RECALL SUBPROGRAM
390 IF A$="3" THEN GOTO 220  '      MANUAL MODE
400 GOTO 310
```

Listing 12-5 BASIC Code of Automatic Routine

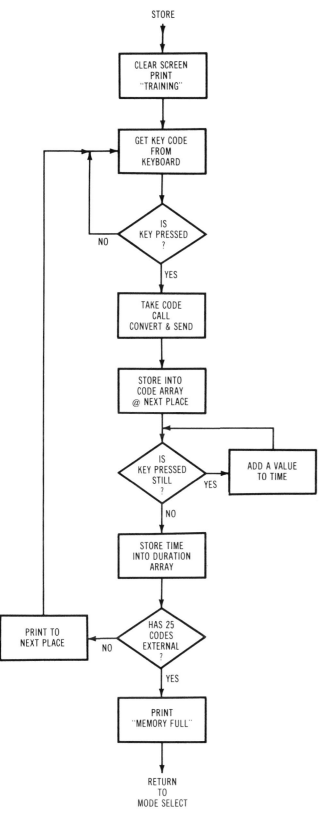

Fig. 12-6 Flowchart of Store subprogram.

tion. Then it gets key codes from the CODE array one at a time, converts them and sends them out to the machine you are controlling. It also extracts the duration information and counts down before getting the next code. If you reach the end of the codes by detecting a blank value, or if you've encountered the 25th value, the program stops the process by outputting a zero to the machine, printing "stopped," and returning to the Mode Select routine. Listing 12-7 lists the code.

That's it. That's all there is to programming a teach-learn robot system. I'm sure you could customize this a bit by adding command words, tape or disk storage, and a host of other features. In fact, an attempt to do just that is our next program example.

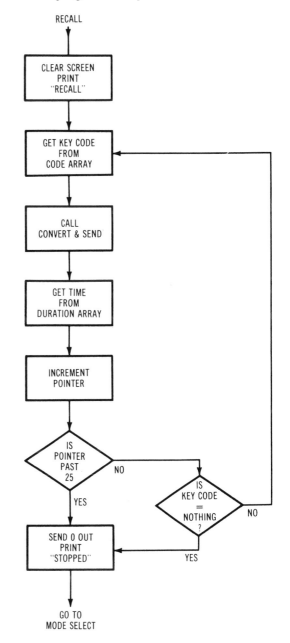

Fig. 12-7 Flowchart Recall subprogram.

```
410 '
420 '       STORE SUBPROGRAM
430 '
440 CLS:PRINT"TRAINING"
450 A$=INKEY$:IF A$="" THEN GOTO 450
460 GOSUB 780 '       CONVERT AND SEND
470 CODES$(PLACE)=A$
480 A$=INKEY$
490 IF A$="" THEN TIME=TIME + 1:GOTO 480
500 DURATION(PLACE)=TIME
510 PLACE=PLACE + 1
520 IF PLACE < 25 THEN GOTO 560
530 PRINT"MEMORY FULL"
540 FOR T=1 TO 250:NEXT T
550 GOTO 100
560 TIME=0:GOTO 460
```

Listing 12-6 BASIC Code of Store Subprogram

```
570 '
580 '       RECALL SUBPROGRAM
590 '
600 CLS:PRINT"RECALL FROM MEMORY"
610 A$=CODES$(PLACE)
620 GOSUB 780 '       CONVERT AND SEND
630 TIME=DURATION(PLACE)
640 IF TIME <> 0 THEN TIME = TIME - 1:GOTO 640
650 FOR T=1 TO 70:NEXT T
660 PLACE=PLACE + 1
670 IF PLACE < 25 THEN GOTO 710
680 PRINT"END OF PROGRAM"
690 FOR T=1 TO 200:NEXT T
700 POKE 49152,0:GOTO 100
710 A$=INKEY$
720 IF A$<>"" THEN POKE 49152,0:PRINT"STOPPED":GOTO 100
730 GOTO 610
```

Listing 12-7 BASIC Code of Recall Subprogram

MOTION BASIC

Wouldn't it be great to have a form of BASIC that includes not only all the popular statements used today but also have about twenty command statements that are directly robotic in nature? Imagine in line 20 the thrill you get from being able to say "MOVE 2 FEET"! Well, I thought it would be great, too. So I set out to design a special version of BASIC called Motion BASIC.

We would want all the normal statements of a good extended BASIC especially the higher order math functions, as robotics require quite a bit of number crunching. Added to that list are 21 other commands I thought useful. They are:

SCAN	RIGHT	LIFT	CLOSE	LISTEN
MOVE	PULSE	PITCH	SEE	
LEFT	REPEAT	YAW	COMPARE	
FORWARD	HOLD	ROLL	ROTATE	
REVERSE	LOWER	OPEN	SAY	

Some group, yes? Let's go over each one as it could pertain to a robot system.

The SCAN command would allow the robot, that has a vision system of some kind, to scan the area immediately in front of it. To this the system could

```
60000 ' MOTION SUBROUTINE PACKAGE
60001 '
60002 ' WRITTEN IN MICROSOFT BASIC
60003 ' SEPTEMBER,1982
60004 '
60005 '
60006 '    COMMAND AND VARIABLE ARE EXPECTED AS FOLLOWS:
60007 '
60008 '         C$="COMMAND,VARIABLE" GOSUB 60000
60009 '
60010 NC=1
60020 D$=MID$(C$,NC,1)
60030 IF D$="" OR D$=" " OR D$="," THEN 60050
60040 NC=NC+1:GOTO 60020
60050 CW$=LEFT$(C$,NC-1):GOTO 60072
60065 '
60066 '
60070 '
60071 '
60072 '    COMMAND INTERPRETER
60073 '
60074 ' COMMANDS "LOWER" TO "LISTEN" ARE FOR FUTURE ENHANCEMENT
60075 '
60076 '
60077 '
60078 '
60079 '
60080 IF CW$="SCAN" THEN GOTO 60290
60090 IF CW$="MOVE" THEN GOTO  60310
60100 IF CW$="LEFT" THEN DR=26:GOTO 60310
60110 IF CW$="FORWARD" THEN DR=17:GOTO 60310
60120 IF CW$="REVERSE" THEN DR=18:GOTO 60310
60130 IF CW$="RIGHT" THEN DR=10:GOTO 60310
60140 IF CW$="PULSE" THEN DR=9:GOTO 60310
60150 IF CW$="REPEAT" THEN DR=3:GOTO 60310
60160 IF CW$="HOLD"THEN DR=25:GOTO 60310
60170 IF CW$="LOWER"THEN GOTO 60290
60180 IF CW$="LIFT" THEN GOTO  60290
60190 IF CW$="PITCH" THEN GOTO  60290
60200 IF CW$="YAW" THEN GOTO 60290
60210 IF CW$="ROLL" THEN GOTO 60290
60220 IF CW$="OPEN" THEN GOTO  60290
60230 IF CW$="CLOSE" THEN GOTO  60290
60240 IF CW$="SEE" THEN GOTO 60290
60250 IF CW$="COMPARE" THEN GOTO  60290
60260 IF CW$="ROTATE" THEN GOTO 60290
60270 IF CW$="SAY" THEN GOTO  60290
60280 IF CW$="LISTEN" THEN GOTO 60290
60290 PRINT"ERROR-NO COMMAND":PRINT
60300 STOP
60305 '
60309 '
60310 '    COMMAND TRANSMITTER
60311 '
60312 '
60313 '
60314 ' POKE VALUE IS SET UP FOR A TRS-80 COLOR COMPUTER
60315 ' CARTRIDGE PORT
60316 '
```

Listing 12-8 Motion Subroutine Package

```
60317 ' CHANGE VALUE OF POKE FOR YOUR SYSTEM
60318 '
60319 '
60320 POKE 49152,DR
60330 FOR T=1 TO 5:NEXT T:POKE 49152,0
60340 '
60341 '
60342 ' COMMAND VARIABLE TRANSLATOR
60343 '
60344 ' GETS VARIABLE AFTER THE COMMA DELIMITER
60345 '
60346 '
60347 '
60348 '
60349 '
60350 NC=NC+1
60360 V$=MID$(C$,NC,1):IF V$="" THEN GOTO  60720 'FINISHED
60370 IF V$="A" THEN VA=A:GOTO 60630
60380 IFV$="B" THEN VA=B:GOTO 60630
60390 IF V$="C" THEN VA=C:GOTO 60630
60400 IF V$="D" THEN VA=D:GOTO 60630
60410 IF V$="E" THEN VA=E:GOTO 60630
60420 IF V$="F" THEN VA=F:GOTO 60630
60430 IF V$="G" THEN VA=G:GOTO 60630
60440 IF V$="H" THEN VA=H:GOTO 60630
60450 IF V$="I" THEN VA=I:GOTO 60630
60460 IF V$="J" THEN VA=J:GOTO 60630
60470 IF V$="K" THEN VA=K:GOTO 60630
60480 IF V$="L" THEN VA=L:GOTO 60630
60490 IF V$="M" THEN VA=M:GOTO 60630
60500 IF V$="N" THEN VA=N:GOTO 60630
60510 IF V$="O" THEN VA=O:GOTO 60630
60520 IF V$="P" THEN VA=P:GOTO 60630
60530 IF V$="Q" THEN VA=Q:GOTO 60630
60540 IF V$="R" THEN VA=R:GOTO 60630
60550 IF V$="S" THEN VA=S:GOTO 60630
60560 IF V$="T" THEN VA=T:GOTO 60630
60570 IF V$="U" THEN VA=U:GOTO 60630
60580 IF V$="V" THEN VA=V:GOTO 60630
60590 IF V$="W" THEN VA=W:GOTO 60630
60600 IF V$="X" THEN VA=X:GOTO 60630
60610 IF V$="Y" THEN VA=Y:GOTO 60630
60620 VA=VAL(V$):GOTO 60635
60629 '
60630 ' VARIABLE TRANSMITTER
60631 '
60632 IF VA>9 THEN C$=STR$(VA):NC=2:GOTO 60360
60635 RESTORE
60640 DATA 22,29,21,13,28,20,12,27,19,11
60650 FOR TA=0 TO 9
60660 READ DA
60670 IF TA=VA THEN GOTO 60690
60680 NEXT TA
60690 POKE 49152,DA
60700 FOR TA=1 TO 5:NEXT TA:POKE 49152,0
60710 GOTO 60342
60715 '
60717 '
```

Listing 12-8—cont. Motion Subroutine Package

```
60718 ' SEND OUTPUT COMMAND
60719 '
60720 POKE 49152,14:FOR TA=1 TO 5:NEXT TA:POKE 49152,0
60727 '
60728 ' SEND CHECK COMMAND
60729 '
60730 POKE 49152,5:FOR TA=1 TO 5:NEXT TA:POKE 49152,0
60732 '
60733 '
60750 ' IS PLATFORM FINISHED ROUTINE
60760 '
60770 '
60780 ' CHECKS THE STATUS OF SAME PORT FOR A HIGH BIT 6 FOR DONE
60790 '
60800 ' ALSO CHECKS FOR A HIGH BIT 5 WHICH INDICATES A BUMP CONDITION
60810 '
60820 ' ROUTINE TOGGLES BIT 7 TO RESET OTHER BITS
60830 '
60840 '
60850 DC=PEEK(49152)
60860 IF DC=96 OR DC=32 THEN BP$="Y":GOTO 60890
60870 IF DC=64 THEN BP$="N":GOTO 60890
60880 GOTO 60850
60890 POKE 49152,128:POKE 49152,0
60896 '
60897 '
60898 ' SEND CLEAR COMMAND
60899 '
60900 POKE 49152,1:FOR TA=1 TO 5:NEXT TA:POKE 49152,0
60910 RETURN
```

Listing 12-8—cont. Motion Subroutine Package

answer with a zero if there were no obstacles, or a −1 if there were something. You could use this as a function rather than a statement. A = SCAN might be a way to call the function where the value would end up in A. You could then test for it using an IF statement.

MOVE works from a relative base both in how far to travel and which direction. The other commands of FORWARD, RIGHT, LEFT, and REVERSE ask for specific distance information where MOVE would simply repeat the last motion command. PULSE could be used to step a motor one degree or possibly increment some electromechanical device. In the Big Trak example presented in Chapter 10, this could be used as the FIRE command. A number could be entered after PULSE which indicates how many times to turn a specific thing on and off.

REPEAT, I admit, I stole from the instruction repertoire of the Big Trak controller. This is useful in creating command loops. You simply provide the number of motion instructions you want repeated and it will execute them. HOLD is another Big Trak command that would be useful. It provides for a built-in pause in program execution.

Both the LOWER and LEFT commands would pertain to an arm or movable platform. These are pro-grammed with units indicating distance. PITCH, YAW, and ROLL are used in programming a wrist mechanism and OPEN and CLOSE pertain to the hand.

The SEE, COMPARE, and ROTATE commands could work with an imaging system. SEE would freeze a frame of video information. COMPARE could check the data representing the scene just viewed against that of previously stored scenes. This is also a function where a match would be signalled by a −1 and no match by a zero. ROTATE could shift the image scene 1° clockwise to prepare for another COMPARE. This would be necessary to match objects that are the same as those stored, yet seen in a different perspective.

The last two, SAY and LISTEN, could control the robot's vocal communications system. SAY would act just like a PRINT statement except the words output would be spoken instead of typed. LISTEN could take the place of the INPUT statement when voice commands are required. The voice input through a speech recognition device would be compared to prestored patterns and if there is a match, the ASCII equivalent command is entered.

No doubt, you have recognized, by now, that building this language is a tremendous task. In fact, many of the routines I have not implemented myself. I have written the set as callable subroutines, though, from an existing

```
10 CLS
20 PRINT"ROBOTIC DESIGN HELPER"
30 PRINT
40 PRINT"SELECT ONE OF THE FOLLOWING:"
50 PRINT:PRINT"1) GRIPPER FORCE EQUATION"
60 PRINT"2) WORK FORMULA"
70 PRINT"3) WORM GEAR DESIGN"
80 PRINT"4) LEAD SCREW DESIGN"
90 PRINT"5) MOTION MECHANICS"
95 PRINT"6) TORQUE MEASUREMENT"
100 A$=INKEY$:IF A$="" THEN 100
110 IF A$="1" THEN GOTO 200
120 IF A$="2" THEN GOTO 300
130 IF A$="3" THEN GOTO 400
140 IF A$="4" THEN GOTO 800
150 IF A$="5" THEN GOTO 900
155 IF A$="6" THEN GOTO 1000
160 CLS:GOTO 40
200 CLS: PRINT"GRIPPER FORCE EQUATION"
210 PRINT:PRINT"TO FIND GRIP FORCE REQUIRED:"
220 PRINT:PRINT"ENTER WEIGHT OF LIFTED OBJECT:"
230 INPUT"LBS";A
240 PRINT:PRINT"ENTER DISTANCE BETWEEN POINTS    OF CONTACT ON FINGER PAD:"
250 INPUT"(INCHES)";B
260 PRINT:PRINT"ENTER DISTANCE FROM CENTER OF    GRAVITY OF CONTACT:"
270 INPUT"(INCHES)";C
280 C=C/100:G=(A*B)/C
290 CLS:PRINT"GRIP FORCE= ";G;"POUND-INCHES"
295 PRINT:PRINT"<ENTER> FOR MENU,<SPACE> FOR    ANOTHER"
297 A$=INKEY$:IF A$="" THEN 297
298 IF A$=" " THEN GOTO 200 ELSE GOTO 10
300 CLS:PRINT"WORK FORMULA"
310 PRINT:PRINT"ENTER WEIGHT OF HAND ASSY:"
315 INPUT"LBS";A
320 PRINT:PRINT"ENTER WEIGHT OF OBJECT TO LIFT:"
330 INPUT"LBS"; B:W=A+B
340 PRINT:PRINT"ENTER DISTANCE BETWEEN DRIVER    SHAFT AND OBJECT:"
350 INPUT "INCHES";C
360 WK=W*C:CLS
370 PRINT"WORK = ";WK;" POUND-INCHES"
380 PRINT:PRINT"<SPACE> FOR ANOTHER,<ENTER> FOR    MENU"
390 A$=INKEY$:IF A$="" THEN 390
395 IF A$=" " THEN GOTO 300 ELSE GOTO 10
400 CLS:PRINT"WORM GEAR DESIGN"
410 PRINT:PRINT"SELECT THE FOLLOWING:"
420 PRINT:PRINT"1) WORM SPEED"
425 PRINT"2) WORM WORK FORMULA"
430 PRINT"3) PITCH ANGLE FORMULA"
440 A$=INKEY$:IF A$="" THEN 440
450 IF A$="1" THEN 500
455 IF A$="2" THEN 600
460 IF A$="3" THEN 700
470 GOTO 400
500 CLS:PRINT"WORM SPEED"
510 PRINT:PRINT"ENTER WORM DRIVE SPEED:"
520 INPUT"RPM";A
530 PRINT:PRINT"ENTER NUMBER OF TEETH IN DRIVEN GEAR:"
540 INPUT B:S=A/B
550 CLS:PRINT"WORM DRIVE SPEED=";S;"RPM"
```

Listing 12-9 BASIC Program of Robot Design Calculations

```
560 PRINT:PRINT"<SPACE> FOR ANOTHER,<ENTER> FOR MENU"
570 A$=INKEY$:IF A$="" THEN 570
580 IF A$=" " THEN GOTO 400 ELSE GOTO 10
600 CLS:PRINT"WORM WORK FORMULA"
610 PRINT:PRINT"ENTER DIAMETER OF DRIVE SCREW:"
620 INPUT"INCHES";A:R=A/2
630 PRINT:PRINT"ENTER PITCH OF THREADS:"
640 INPUT"INCHES";P
650 FW=(6.28*R)/P
660 PRINT:PRINT"ENTER PITCH ANGLE:"
670 INPUT"DEGREES";PA
680 W=FW*R*TAN(PA)
690 CLS:PRINT"WORK=";W;"INCH-POUNDS"
692 PRINT:PRINT"<SPACE> FOR ANOTHER,<ENTER> FOR MENU"
695 A$=INKEY$:IF A$="" THEN 695
697 IF A$=" " THEN GOTO 400 ELSE GOTO 10
700 CLS:PRINT" PITCH ANGLE FORMULA"
710 PRINT:PRINT"ENTER DIAMETER OF DRIVE SCREW:"
720 INPUT"INCHES";A:R=A/2
730 PRINT:PRINT"ENTER PITCH OF THREADS:"
740 INPUT"INCHES";P
750 PRINT:PRINT"ENTER WORK AMOUNT:"
760 INPUT"INCH-POUNDS";W
770 PA=(((6.28*R)/P)*R)/W
780 CLS:PRINT"PITCH ANGLE=";PA;"DEGREES"
790 PRINT:PRINT"<SPACE> FOR ANOTHER,<ENTER> FOR MENU"
795 A$=INKEY$:IF A$="" THEN 795
797 IF A$=" " THEN 400 ELSE GOTO 10
800 CLS:PRINT"LEAD SCREW MECHANICS"
810 PRINT:PRINT"ENTER WEIGHT OF PAYLOAD:"
815 INPUT"LBS";W
820 PRINT:PRINT"ENTER DISTANCE OF TOTAL TRAVEL:"
825 INPUT"INCHES";D
830 PRINT:PRINT"ENTER SCREW THREAD TYPE:"
835 INPUT ST
840 GR=ST*D
850 F=((W*D)/(GR*6.28))*16
860 CLS:PRINT"TORQUE REQUIRED=";F;"OUNCE-INCHES"
870 PRINT:PRINT"<SPACE>FOR ANOTHER,<ENTER> FOR MENU"
880 A$=INKEY$:IF A$="" THEN 880
890 IF A$=" " THEN 800 ELSE GOTO 10
900 CLS:PRINT"MOTION MECHANICS RESISTANCE"
910 PRINT:PRINT" ENTER TORQUE OF DRIVE MOTOR:"
920 INPUT"INCH POUNDS";F
930 PRINT:PRINT"ENTER DIAMETER OF WHEEL"
940 INPUT"INCHES";D:R=D/2
950 PRINT:PRINT"ENTER WEIGHT OF ROBOT"
960 INPUT"LBS";W
970 RE=(F*R)/W
980 CLS:PRINT"RESISTANCE TO MOTION=";RE;"LBS"
990 PRINT:PRINT"<SPACE> FOR ANOTHER,<ENTER> FOR MENU"
995 A$=INKEY$:IF A$="" THEN 995
997 IF A$=" " THEN GOTO 900 ELSE GOTO 10
1000 CLS:PRINT"TORQUE MEASUREMENT SYSTEM"
1010 PRINT:PRINT"DO YOU WANT TO:"
1020 PRINT"1) FIGURE TORQUE"
1030 PRINT"2) MEASURE TORQUE"
1040 A$=INKEY$:IF A$="" THEN GOTO 1040
1050 IF A$="1" THEN GOTO 1100
```

Listing 12-9—cont. BASIC Program of Robot Design Calculations

```
1060 IF A$="2" THEN GOTO 1200
1070 GOTO 1000
1100 CLS:PRINT"ENTER WEIGHT TO BE LIFTED"
1110 INPUT"(LBS)";A
1120 PRINT"ENTER DISTANCE BETWEEN WEIGHT   AND SHAFT"
1130 INPUT"(INCHES)";B
1140 PRINT:PRINT"TORQUE MUST =";A*B;"POUND-INCHES"
1150 PRINT:PRINT"<SPACE> FOR ANOTHER,<ENTER> FOR MENU"
1160 A$=INKEY$:IF A$="" THEN 1160
1170 IF A$=" " THEN GOTO 1000 ELSE GOTO 10
1200 CLS:PRINT"TORQUE MEASURER"
1210 PRINT:PRINT"ENTER DIAMETER OF PULLEY"
1220 INPUT"(INCHES)";A
1230 PRINT"ENTER STALL WEIGHT"
1240 INPUT"(LBS)";B
1250 PRINT:PRINT"TORQUE =";(.5*A)*B;"POUND-INCHES"
1260 PRINT:PRINT"<SPACE> FOR ANOTHER,<ENTER> FOR MENU"
1270 A$=INKEY$:IF A$="" THEN GOTO 1270
1280 IF A$=" " THEN GOTO 1200 ELSE GOTO 10
```

Listing 12-9—cont. BASIC Program of Robot Design Calculations

BASIC program. The ones that are implemented simply output codes to a hardware device that performs the action. The device in this case was the Big Trak. Listing 12-8 is the lengthy listing of the program as it now exists. I hope you will take up the challenge to implement the complete package and adapt it to your own needs.

With these commands out of the way, let's touch on a program I've been referring to for many chapters. Way back in the early chapters there were many short design programs shown with the promise of an all-encompass-

ing program later down the road. Well, the road ends here. Listing 12-9 lists the entire robot design package program with the ability to call up any program from a main menu.

The subject of programming robots could go on forever. We can't. So, it's left to you to implement the program you think best and we'll go on to the interface between the control computer and the robot. After seeing how a cord wraps up a wandering robot, you'll appreciate the remote-control circuitry presented next.

Section V:
COMMUNICATION/CONTROL

Chapter 13

Remote Command Links

There are few things that are as fantastic as seeing a piece of machinery react to your command where there is no apparent connection between it and you. Touching the button on a tv remote controller in a store where instantly you have returned two dozen sets gives one a feeling of immense power. So, too, with remote command of robots.

In this chapter, you will be introduced to using light, sound, and radio waves to command a robot. By command, I do not merely mean on and off. The emphasis will be on an intelligent communication between the two of you.

BACKGROUND

The three most popular ways of remotely controlling a machine without the use of wires are by infrared light beam, ultrasonic, and radio transmission. We have seen the use of light in many applications in this book. Ultrasonic control involves the use of high-frequency (so high we can't even hear it) sounds. The last, radio, is familiar to us all.

You've probably heard all this before. No doubt you've thought of giving your robot the ability of slipping away without a command umbilical cord. Perhaps you've decided to provide on-board computer control. So what's this chapter got for you?

Well, I think I've managed to get a little bit for everybody here. Two complete remote-command systems will be presented. The first directly controls each function, much like a bundle of wires. The second communicates with that on-board intelligence to program the robot.

But, before we get into the systems, let's view the components.

REMOTE ON-OFF

You've got to start somewhere, right? The first component that we should examine is the remote transmitter. This is the device that delivers your command to the robot. In the case of the infrared and ultrasonic versions, this may be the same circuit. Let's define what we want. First, we want range. After all, what good is remote control if it can't be remote? The next item is information. What kind of information will activate the other side? In the case of an on-off system, this may simply be a tone of a precise frequency.

So far, we have a long-range beeper. Add small size and battery operation, and you have a very plausible system. Fig. 13-1 shows a complete schematic of a transmitter that will, when powered, emit a 40-kHz tone that oscillates either the ultrasound transducer or an infrared LED. The frequency is variable by the potentiometer; however, the ultrasonic transducer is tuned to only 40 kHz. This circuit has a working range of approximately 20 feet.

Basically the transmitter is made up of a 555 timer IC that is connected as an oscillator. The frequency determining components are set to provide the correct frequency. The output drives the ultrasonic transducer directly. Transmission is keyed by interrupting the power to the circuit. Although this is crude, it works well for on-off applications.

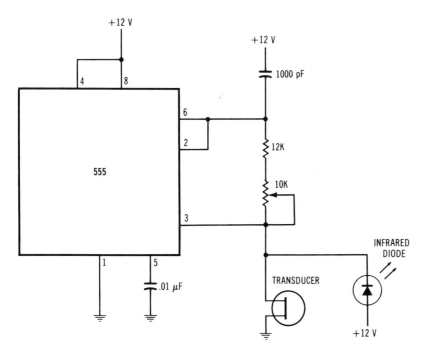

Fig. 13-1 Simple infrared or ultrasonic transmitter.

As you can see, there isn't much to a remote transmitter. The receiver end is not really much more of a challenge. Fig. 13-2 shows one way to amplify the signal being received. This approach uses a two-transistor circuit that amplifies the signal and presents it to a tone decoder IC. This IC (567) is tuned to detect the 40-kHz signal. An alternate amplifier circuit is shown in Fig. 13-3.

Using the two of these circuits, you should be able to transmit a control signal the length of a room. Today's tv remote-control equipment uses custom designed integrated circuits to act as the transmitter and receiver. Most

of these circuits are available now as standard products. They range from simple on-off controllers to sophisticated multichannel control units that have the capability to output analog control signals. Let's look at a few of these ICs and find out how to apply them to our needs.

AMI 2743/2742

This is a two-chip remote encoder/decoder pair. They are constructed using PMOS technology and run on 9-volt levels. The 2743 encoder replaces the 555 oscillator

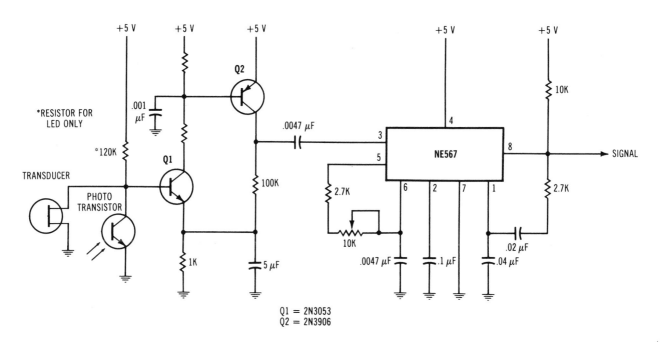

Fig. 13-2 Ultrasonic or infrared receiver using discrete amplifier.

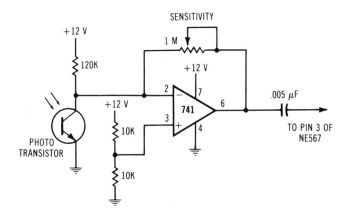

Fig. 13-3 Alternate integrated circuit amplifier for use with Fig. 13-2.

shown in Fig. 13-1. Instead of emitting one tone, this encoder employs a method called *frequency shift keying*. Each tone message actually consists of 16 data bits of information. Why data bits at all? Well, this IC has the capability of sending out a unique code that will address or select only one receiver. There are 9 address input pins which are tied either high or low that determine the value of the address being output. Every data bit has a length of 32 cycles of the high-frequency clock. The entire data message will consist of 512 cycles of half the oscillator frequency length. Confused? Let's go through that more definitively.

A logic 1 is 32 cycles of the higher frequency. This frequency is a derivative of the master oscillator that is controlled by an external RC network. Fig. 13-4 shows the pin configuration and block diagram. A logic 0 consists of 16 cycles of the same high frequency followed by 8 cycles of a frequency that is one-half of the higher. There is a synchronization pulse that is 16 cycles of the lower frequency. This comes first.

The pair is used primarily in on-off control of garage-door openers. Let's look at the receiver. Fig. 13-5 shows the pin connection and internal block diagram of the 2742 decoder. An external amplifier must be connected in front of this device. It replaces the 567 tone decoder. It, too, has 9 address input pins. So it's conceivable that you could have one transmitter that is connected to a parallel port. Over the port you program which receiver you want to address. Each receiver could be configured to a unique address, i.e., one for the right hand, left hand, right elbow, etc.

When the signal is detected by the receiver, it compares the code with its own externally selected code. The correct code must be present for three consecutive passes before the receiver will validate a good message. If a good message is detected, the signal valid output will pulse. You have the ability of selecting the time period of this pulse through external components. That's all there is to it. There is, however, a more detailed description available from AMI in their applications note #79C06.

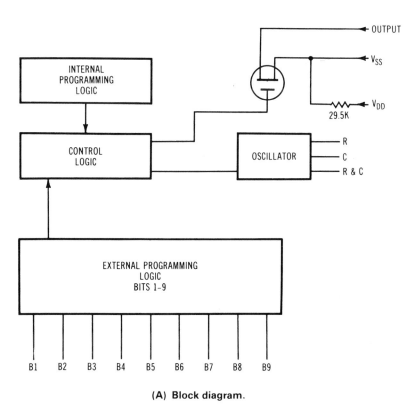

(A) Block diagram.

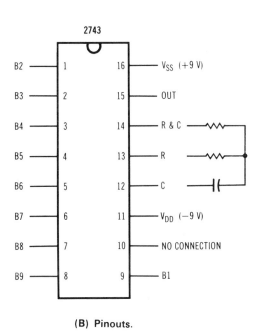

(B) Pinouts.

Fig. 13-4 Block diagram and pinouts of the AMI 2743 transmitter.

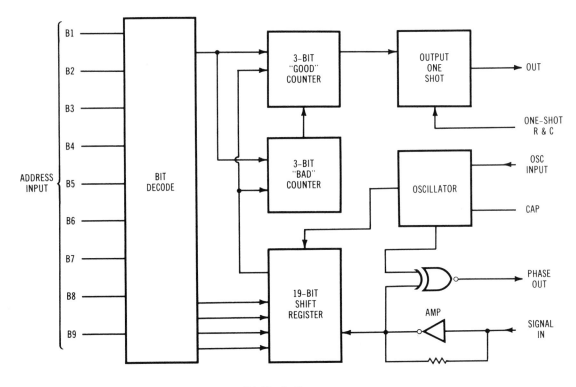

(A) Block diagram.

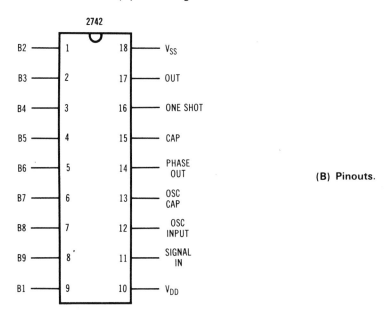

(B) Pinouts.

Fig. 13-5 Block diagram and pinouts of the AMI 2742 receiver.

MOTOROLA MC14457, 14458

Here we have yet another chip set. However, you may find this pair more to your liking. It consists of a transmitter (MC14457) which operates from a 9-volt battery, encodes a 20-key keypad, and transmits the signal directly to an ultrasonic or infrared element. The receiver works on the familiar 5-volt power level and its inputs and outputs are TTL levels.

This pair has the capability of sending and receiving up to 256 separate codes. One of those is an analog-control signal that increases or decreases the receiver analog output level.

The MC14457 transmitter circuit encodes keyboard position into frequency-modulated biphase data. You can directly attach a 20- or 32-key keypad to the IC to provide either channel select or analog information. When it is used with the MC14458 receiver, the transmit-

190

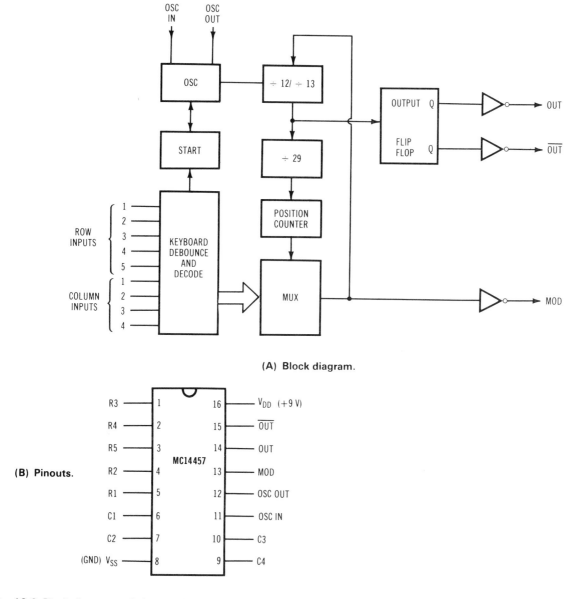

(A) Block diagram.

(B) Pinouts.

Pinout labels:
R3 — 1 ... 16 — V_DD (+9 V)
R4 — 2 ... 15 — $\overline{OUT}$
R5 — 3 ... 14 — OUT
R2 — 4 ... 13 — MOD
R1 — 5 ... 12 — OSC OUT
C1 — 6 ... 11 — OSC IN
C2 — 7 ... 10 — C3
(GND) V_SS — 8 ... 9 — C4

MC14457

Fig. 13-6 Block diagram and pinouts of the Motorola MC14457 transmitter.

ter can send any single or two-digit channel select up to 256 channels. Fig. 13-6 shows the block diagram and pinouts of the transmitter.

The master oscillator (pins 11 and 12) is included on-chip, and all that is required for operation is to attach a frequency determining element. For ultrasonic operation, you will want the output frequency to be in the neighborhood of 40 kHz. As you can see from the diagram, this master frequency is divided by 12 and by 13. A data 0 consists of 256 periods of frequency divided by 12. The output of data 1 will be the reverse.

It turns out that a master oscillator frequency of 500 kHz operates sufficiently because the higher frequency (/ 12) is 41.66 kHz and the lower (/ 13) equals 38.46 kHz. You will find, however, that it is not easy to find a 500-kHz crystal in your local supply store. There is

another device that is being used in many applications where frequency references are needed. This device is called a *ceramic resonator*. The MC14457 has been designed to handle both crystals and resonators. It is easier to obtain a ceramic resonator at that low a frequency. However, you could take a higher frequency crystal and divide it down through an external circuit and apply it to the OSC IN pin.

Looking back at the block diagram, we see that the keyboard debounce circuitry and decoder are built into the chip. Now, this circuit works slightly different from the methods we have previously discussed. Yes, it does use a matrix (x − y) in the keypad, but it requires that both x and y be low when read. Therefore, there must be three contacts per switch. Fig. 13-7 shows a typical hookup of the MC14457.

This schematic shows the use of the 500-kHz crystal, or resonator. The output is directly connected to an ultrasonic transducer. Notice that the plunger portion of each key is attached to ground. Pressing any key will ground one row and one column line. The internal decoder locates a 5-bit code for this situation. The transmitter then sends out a start code of a data 0, then data 1. After this code is the 5-bit code, then a low-frequency burst. Seven bits in all are transmitted in approximately 100 milliseconds. Table 13-1 shows the codes produced for each key pressed.

At the other end (robot side) you would have the receiver. The MC14458 has been designed to fit into typical logic applications. It runs on a 5-volt supply and requires an external frequency source. There also is no internal amplifier so this will have to be provided. Let's look at the structure of the device.

Fig. 13-8 provides us with a block diagram of the receiver. An amplified signal is applied to the DATA input of the receiver. From here it is decoded from frequency information into ones and zeros. The start bit combination is stripped off and the five remaining data bits are shifted into a shift register.

There are two methods of reception: single digit and double digit. In the single digit mode, only the L1 through L8 outputs are used. A valid data ready pulse occurs after the reception of only five bits of data (one digit). When in double digit mode, both the L and M outputs are active. The data-ready pulse does not occur until two buttons are pressed. The receiver automatically enters single-digit

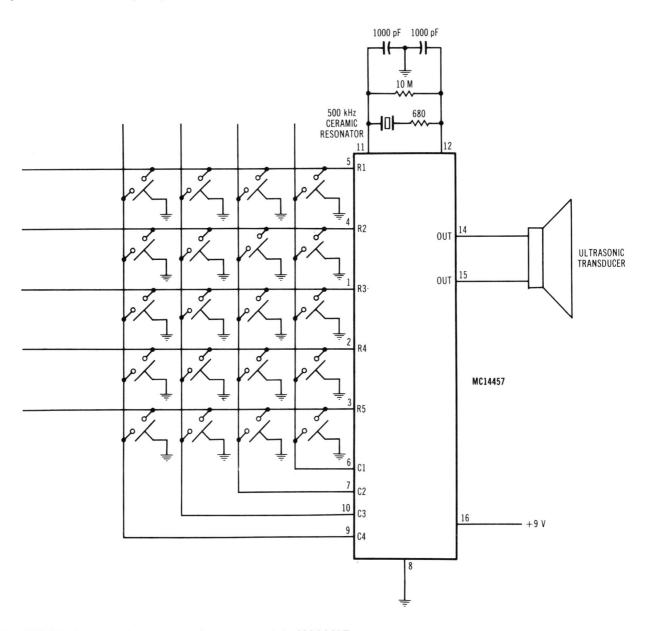

Fig. 13-7 Simple connections necessary for operation of the MC14457.

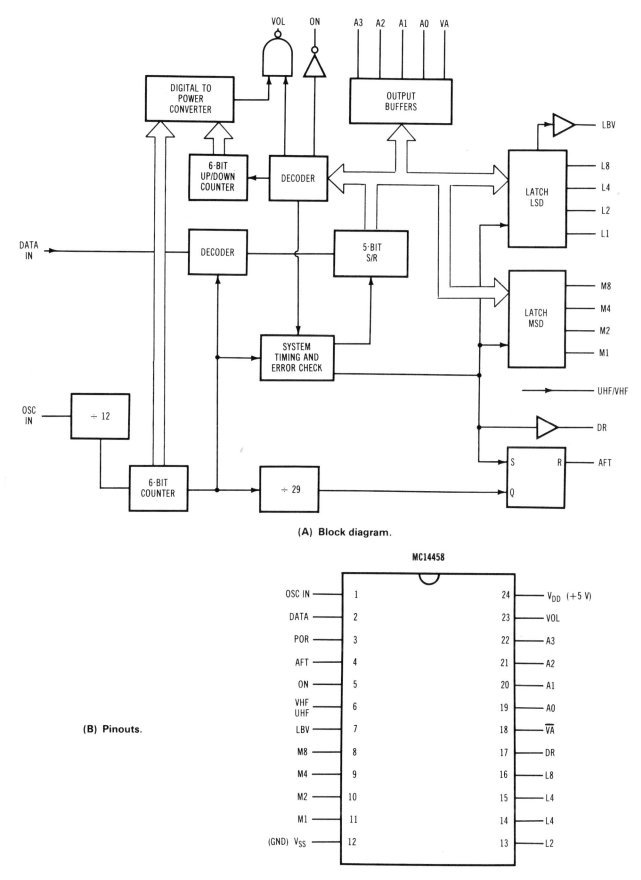

(A) Block diagram.

MC14458

OSC IN —	1	24 — V_DD (+5 V)
DATA —	2	23 — VOL
POR —	3	22 — A3
AFT —	4	21 — A2
ON —	5	20 — A1
VHF UHF —	6	19 — A0
LBV —	7	18 — $\overline{VA}$
M8 —	8	17 — DR
M4 —	9	16 — L8
M2 —	10	15 — L4
M1 —	11	14 — L4
(GND) V_SS —	12	13 — L2

(B) Pinouts.

Fig. 13-8 Block diagram and pinouts of the Motorola MC14458 receiver.

recognition when the M4 data output is tied to +5 volts and the UHF output is tied to ground.

What about all these other outputs? Well, if the channel number transmitted (the chip set was designed for tv use) is 2 through 6, the LBV output will go high. When the channel is 0,1, or 7 to 99 it will go low. If the channel number is between 14 and 83 the UHF output will go high. There is an ON pin that could disable your robot when an OFF command code (1001) comes in. This output is high when a valid channel number is received. Off resets it to a zero.

Other outputs include AFT pin 4. This goes low for approximately one-third of a second following a change in channel. Also, certain commands (0000,0001, 0010,

Table 13-1. Motorola Transmitter Output Codes

Key Number	Operation	Row (Active Low)	Column (Active Low)	Transmitter Data & Receiver Output Address					VA Pulse	Notes
				MSB/A3	LSB+2/A2	LSB+1/A1	LSB/A0	Function		
1	Digit 0	R1	C1	0	0	0	0	0	–	1
1	Digit 1	R1	C2	0	0	0	1	0	–	1
3	Digit 2	R2	C1	0	0	1	0	0	–	1
4	Digit 3	R2	C2	0	0	1	1	0	–	1
5	Digit 4	R3	C1	0	1	0	0	0	–	1
6	Digit 5	R3	C2	0	1	0	1	0	–	1
7	Digit 6	R4	C1	0	1	1	0	0	–	1
8	Digit 7	R4	C2	0	1	1	1	0	–	1
9	Digit 8	R5	C1	1	0	0	0	0	–	1
10	Digit 9	R5	C2	1	0	0	1	0	–	1
11	Spare	R1	C3	0	0	0	0	1	√	2
12	Spare	R1	C4	0	0	0	1	1	√	2
13	Fine Tuning	R2	C3	0	0	1	0	1	√	3
14	Fine Tuning	R2	C4	0	0	1	1	1	√	3
15	Spare	R3	C3	0	1	0	0	1	√	3
16	Spare	R3	C4	0	1	0	1	1	√	3
17	Vol ↓	R4	C3	0	1	1	0	1	√	3
18	Vol ↑	R4	C4	0	1	1	1	1	√	3
19	Mute	R5	C3	1	0	0	0	1	√	2
20	Off	R5	C4	1	0	0	1	1	√	2
21	Digit 10	R2 + R5	C1	1	0	1	0	0	–	1
22	Digit 11	R2 + R5	C2	1	0	1	1	0	–	1
23	Digit 12	R3 + R5	C1	1	1	0	0	0	–	1
24	Digit 13	R3 + R5	C2	1	1	0	1	0	–	1
25	Digit 14	R2 + R3 + R5	C1	1	1	1	0	0	–	1
26	Digit 15	R2 + R3 + R5	C2	1	1	1	1	0	–	1
27	Spare	R2 + R5	C3	1	0	1	0	1	–	3
28	Spare	R2 + R5	C4	1	0	1	1	1	–	3
29	Spare	R3 + R5	C3	1	1	0	0	1	–	3
30	Spare	R3 + R5	C4	1	1	0	1	1	–	3
31	Spare	R2 + R3 + R5	C3	1	1	1	0	1	–	3
32	Spare	R2 + R3 + R5	C4	1	1	1	1	1	–	3

Notes:
1. Channel Select Keys (Function Bit = 0). Data is transmitted once each time a key is activated.
2. Toggling type On/Off or counter advance type keys. Data is transmitted once each time a key is activated.
3. Analog Up/Down or On/Off keys.i.e., one key for Down or Off and another key for Up or On. Data transmission is repeated as long as the key is operated.

In Table 13-1 all channel select data is noted by the function bit equal to zero. For functions other than channel, the function bit equals one.

The four toggling or counter advancxe type keys that transmit data once each time a key is activated are Mute, Off, Channel Search Up, and Channel Search Down.

The twelve remaining analog keys (Vol, Tint, Color, etc.) transmit data as long as the key is activated. The keys' functions are arranged to provide the most typical application without grounding of multiple row or columns required.

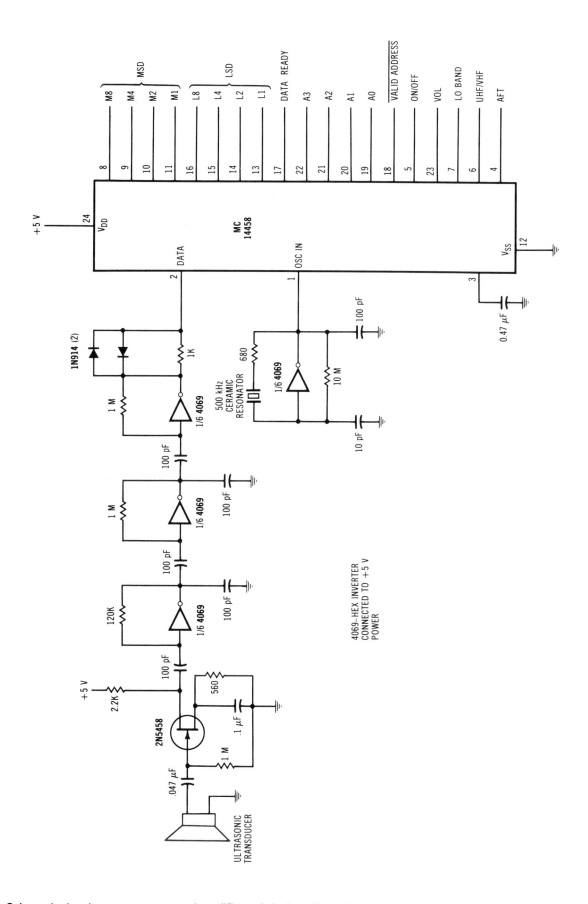

Fig. 13-9 Schematic showing necessary external amplifier and clock oscillator for use with the MC14458.

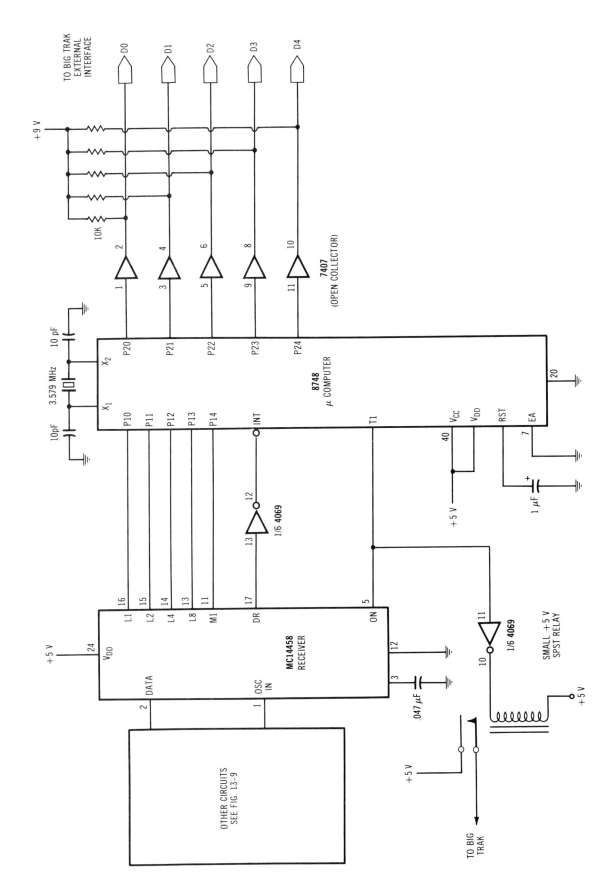

Fig. 13-10 Schematic of the 8748-based remote-command controller.

196

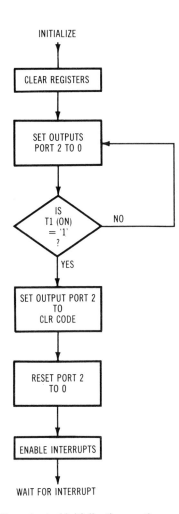

Fig. 13-11 Flowchart of initialization routine.

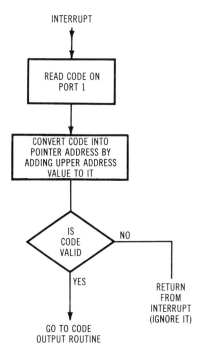

Fig. 13-12 Flowchart of routine that receives codes from the Motorola receiver.

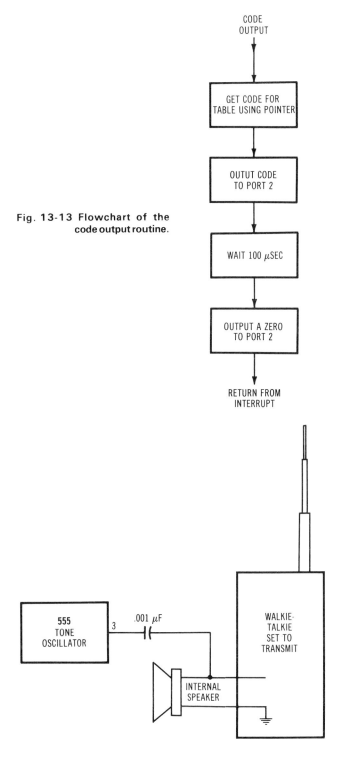

Fig. 13-13 Flowchart of the code output routine.

Fig. 13-14 Simple connection of a tone oscillator to radio walkie-talkie.

we clear everything inside the unit, then it is necessary to deselect any keys on the Big Trak unit. Then sit in a loop waiting for an ON command. After the receipt of this ON command, it sends a CLR to Big Trak. We now go into a program loop looking for an interrupt that will signal an input from the receiver. When a valid data received pulse

and 0011) cause this output to pulse low. Address outputs and a valid address pulse occur when selected analog and control functions are keyed.

The analog output varies between zero and +5 volts when connected to an external integrater/filter. Its value may be incremented or decremented by pushing either the volume-up or volume-down keys. This output is shut off by operating the mute key. Fig. 13-9 shows a typical hookup of the MC14458 receiver. The amplifier consists of portions of a CMOS hex inverter wired as gain stages.

You can see that by experimenting with these devices it is possible to set up a fairly complex remote controller. It is possible to label the keys as robot commands, such as forward, reverse, open, close, etc. The coded outputs of the receiver would be decoded by microprocessor into actual commands. At this time, let's embark on defining what it is we might want to command remotely. Let us also decide the protocol used and the results an on-board micro must provide.

COMMAND CONTROLLERS

Looking back at Chapter 10, we see that the motion controller presented was based on a modification of the Milton Bradley Big Trak. This programmable tank had a series of commands that could be stored sequentially, then executed just as they were stored. We first built a simple parallel interface to the unit, then added a sophisticated local-control computer.

If we drop back to the simple parallel interface, we see that there must be a separate code for the digits 0 through 9 and one for each of the commands. Using the MC14457/MC14458 chip set selected for single-digit entry, we should be able to enter commands remotely into Big Trak's memory. It would require some code conversion but what easier job could there be for a single-chip microcomputer?

We have already learned and applied the 8748 in other systems. Here we will use it again. I have condensed the output-codes chart seen previously into just what the micro sees from the receiver output. Table 13-2 shows these outputs. When one code is received, the micro must simply look up which one it is, and output the applicable Big Trak code. Fig. 13-10 shows a way of hooking up the 8748 into the receiver circuit.

As you know by now, it is time to get into the programming. First, let's start with an initialization. Fig. 13-11 shows the flowchart of the INIT routine. As usual,

Table 13-2. Motorola Receiver Output Codes

Function Bit	MSB	MSB-1	LSB+1	LSB	Command
0	0	0	0	0	Channel Digit 0
0	0	0	0	1	Channel Digit 1
0	0	0	1	0	Channel Digit 2
0	0	0	1	1	Channel Digit 3
0	0	1	0	0	Channel Digit 4
0	0	1	0	1	Channel Digit 5
0	0	1	1	0	Channel Digit 6
0	0	1	1	1	Channel Digit 7
0	1	0	0	0	Channel Digit 8
0	1	0	0	1	Channel Digit 9
0	1	0	1	0	Channel Digit 10
0	1	0	1	1	Channel Digit 11
0	1	1	0	0	Channel Digit 12
0	1	1	0	1	Channel Digit 13
0	1	1	1	0	Channel Digit 14
0	1	1	1	1	Channel Digit 15
1	0	0	0	0	Channel Search Down
1	0	0	0	1	Channel Search Up
1	0	0	1	0	Fine Tuning Down
1	0	0	1	1	Fine Tuning Up
1	0	1	0	0	Miscellaneous Command Spare
1	0	1	0	1	Miscellaneous Command Spare
1	0	1	1	0	Volume Down
1	0	1	1	1	Volume Up
1	1	0	0	0	Mute On/Off
1	1	0	0	1	Set Off
1	1	0	1	0	Miscellaneous Command Spare
1	1	0	1	1	Miscellaneous Command Spare
1	1	1	0	0	Miscellaneous Command Spare
1	1	1	0	1	Miscellaneous Command Spare
1	1	1	1	0	Miscellaneous Command Spare
1	1	1	1	1	Miscellaneous Command Spare

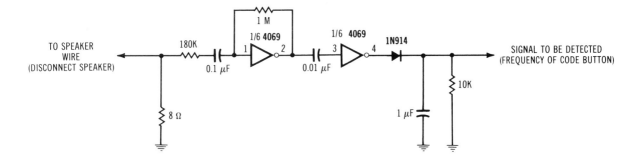

Fig. 13-15 Circuit connected to output walkie-talkie provides tone receiver.

is seen, the code presented is input. Fig. 13-12 shows the flowchart for the code-process loop. Fig. 13-13 completes the system by outputting the correct code. Well, it definitely is a much simpler way of transmitting and receiving coded information without the use of these specialized chip sets.

For the last few chapters, we have been using regular serial ASCII communications to control systems. This involved the readily available UAR/T chips only. Since we have developed a reliable transmitter and receiver circuit (Figs. 13-1 and 13-2), why not hook up the transmitter to the output of a UAR/T and the receiver the same way? Figs. 13-14 and 13-15 show these circuits, respectively. That's all there is to it! The software that you have developed for communications will still work.

When tuning the remote link, place the transmitter and receiver about 1 foot apart (facing each other). Before attempting to receive the signal from the transmitter, turn on the receiver and measure the frequency of the tone decoder on pin 6. Adjust the potentiometer until it oscillates at 40 kHz. Now, do the same for the transmitter while reading the frequency out of pin 3. With these frequencies about the same, try pointing them at each other. Adjust the receiver potentiometer until its output is a steady low on pin 8. When this is accomplished, you now have a remote command loop.

The local-control computer built into Big Trak is expecting serial ASCII so this could be used with the receiver circuit. Are there any other forms of control we haven't touched on yet? Yes, radio transmission has not been covered. The circuits used so far simply emit light or sound and require precise positioning. Radio, however, may be used almost anywhere.

RADIO

Radio transmitters and receivers can be tricky circuits to construct. The power levels must be carefully watched to avoid interference with other forms of communication. The easiest way to experiment with radio is to purchase a small remote-controlled toy car. These units usually include only one channel and yet can transmit reliably a good 50 feet, even through house walls!

How do you get these units to transmit ASCII command data? Well, let's go back to the tone generator. If we hook up a 555 oscillator that emits an audible tone, we could couple it to the transmitter circuit as shown in Fig. 13-14. It is even easier if you purchase one of those walkie-talkies with an integral morse code button. One of these set up as a transmitter could interface very easily.

On the receive end, you must decouple the tone from the carrier. This is easily done at the speaker connection. Here we clean up the signal and present it to the receive input of the tone decoder (Fig. 13-15). Voila, an RF link! What could be more versatile? Of course, just saying the commands to the robot would be like living in the future. In the next chapter, we will investigate and build several voice-recognition interfaces for robot control. So much for the future!

Chapter 14

Voice Command Design

Communicating ideas between people is easy. Getting them into machines has become an art. We take for granted all the control signals we receive in a given day.

First, there is the alarm clock in the morning; then our automatic speed increases when we notice that the clock says we're late. Traffic lights and street signs direct our motion along a path. During the day, written information directs our thought processes. At the conclusion of the day, the reverse happens.

If we work at the same job every day, we are actually performing a set control program that operates automatically. Did you ever get to work and realize that you didn't see half the landmarks on the way to work? That's because your program drove you to work.

Communications, in the form of control statements, are passed to machines in hundreds of different ways, too. Some machines require pushing buttons while others need the combination of a magnetic card and buttons, as in the automatic teller system at the bank.

Remote control airplanes use radio signals to tell them to climb, turn, or dive. The newer television sets use infrared light to communicate your program desires from a small control panel held in your hand.

BUTTONITIS

Mrs. Jetson of the old cartoon series once was afflicted by buttonitis, a disease caused from having to push too many buttons. That day may soon be here. Look at all the hand-held button-covered gadgets there are. Even the Big

Trak motion platform from Chapter 10 had 23 buttons on its keypad. How can we convert those button presses from a remotely located controller into commands at the machine? Let's look at some ways to do this.

As I see it, there are three really good ways to do it. They are radio, light, and sound. Radio has the capability to pass through nonmetallic walls and over great distances outside. Light can be bounced off of walls and is necessarily confined to "same-room" or line-of-sight control. Sound depends on the volume of the controller, and the sensitivity of the listener. Fig. 14-1 depicts these three varied methods.

I can foresee robots configured so that a small receiver mounted on their waist would decode position information from a controlling host computer several feet away. One command could lift an arm, another could move the robot forward.

Limit sensors located on the robot could report their status back to the host through a small transmitter. There is a versatile two-way link!

A simple radio-communication link can be constructed using standard walkie-talkies. Figs. 13-14 and 13-15 in Chapter 13 showed a method of connecting them to a typical control system. You will notice that tone encoding of signals was chosen. This is the easiest system to implement. The NE567 is tuned to the frequency of the 555 timer so that on receipt of a burst of tone, its output goes low, signalling some external system or switch.

More complex methods of radio control can be implemented using a variable-frequency source and

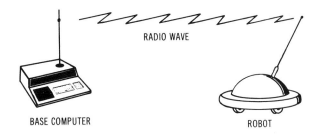

(A) Radio link.

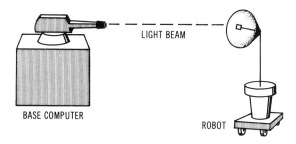

(B) Light path control.

(C) Sound control.

Fig. 14-1 Three most popular remote-control methods.

multiple-receiver decoders, or perhaps a pulse-counting scheme would work. Here the output of the NE567 would be connected to a counter whose outputs control other systems.

LED THERE BE LIGHT

The circuit and applications we just went over could be handled by replacing the radio link with an optical beam. Typical communications systems utilizing light as the means for transmission use infrared light. That way normal ambient light does not trigger the receiver.

There are many infrared ICs available that will handle the modulation and demodulation of the signal. Of course, you could use these with the radio link, as well.

In my experience, I have found light systems to be very tricky to align. The key is in the type of lens system you use. There is a more appealing approach to remote control: sound input.

Communications with an intelligent machine implies that the party on the receiving end should be able to determine what you mean by the command you sent. Sounds come in many varieties. First, there is the "clap" or one-time sharp burst of noise. Then, there are tones or constant frequency signals. Don't forget the most universal of all — the voice. Our machine must be configured to understand the type of sound we choose to use for command.

Fig. 14-2 shows two simple sound-detector circuits. Both utilize a crude microphone preamplifier which triggers a timer or one-shot multivibrator on detection of a noise. These circuits work well as "clap" detectors. You could connect the output of the timer to a counter. Thus one clap means start; two means stop . . ., etc. In fact, there are a couple of "voice-controlled" cars or vans on the toy shelves that actually utilize this type of circuitry. Any sound can activate the circuit, even tones.

If you are thinking of tone control, however, it would be wasteful to use such a crude approach when so many other sophisticated circuits exist. You see, that tone carries a lot of useful information with it. It has a frequency that can differentiate it from another if it is counted, and it has a duration.

Tone control is not new. If you own a touch tone telephone you are using probably the most sophisticated tone-signalling system developed. Touch tone actually uses two frequencies per button (command) specially mixed to sound like one tone. A touch-tone receiver must first split the two tones, then count them. The combination of the two frequencies determines the button pushed. Fig. 14-3 depicts a complete touch-tone system.

This circuit can be connected into any of the transmission mediums previously described. Radio, of course, allows you the most range, unless you connect the output of the tone generator to a PA system and have the receiver connected to one of those sensitive "ear" systems with the parabolic dish like those used in spy movies. I don't recommend light transmission for robotics. The highly directional nature of the medium makes it an "iffy" type of system

The touch-tone decoder ICs are available from two sources, Mitel Semiconductor and GTE Semiconductor. Any touch-tone generator IC or tone pad may be used, providing that it mixes both the tones (some have separate outputs).

OPEN SEZME

Tones can do a lot. The circuit previously described allows up to 16 control functions. But what do you do if you need more? Like the detergent commercial used to say: "Shout-it-out!"

Your voice has the ability to mimic many frequencies and create a few of its own. There is nothing more natural

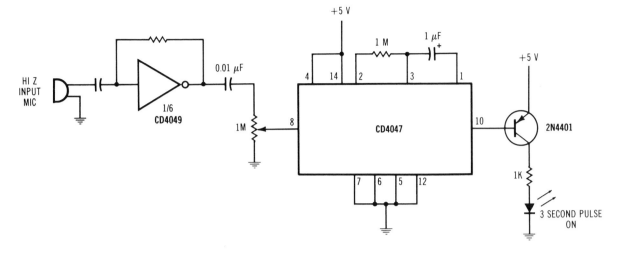

(A) One-shot multivibrator circuit.

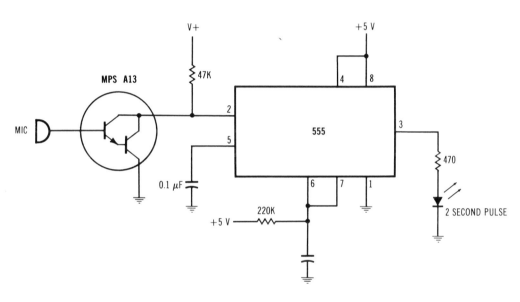

(B) 555 timer circuit.

Fig. 14-2 Two simple sound-detector circuits.

for control than to speak the command. With voice control you open up a world of new and exciting possibilities that used to be only written about in science-fiction books. This book is about science fact, so let's see how to construct a few voice recognition systems for relatively low cost. There is even a very low-cost system for the home experimenter.

Speech recognition presents many problems to potential circuit developers. Over the years, we humans have learned the limits of our own sound recognition systems (ears) and unfortunately have endeavored to stretch our speech patterns to these limits. We have many hundreds of accents, dialects, and languages. Some of us talk fast, others extremely slow. Which standard do we use when designing a speech recognizer?

Today's technology does not accommodate the development of a recognizer that will understand multiple languages from multiple speakers. Some more recent systems recognize a small number of phrases from a large number of different speakers, others can understand a large amount of words from a small number of speakers. These categories form the basis of comparison between speech-recognition systems. They are:

1. Speaker Independent: isolated word
2. Speaker Independent: connected word
3. Speaker Dependent: isolated word
4. Speaker Dependent: connected word

The speaker independent systems do not necessarily mean any number of speakers; they may mean two out of

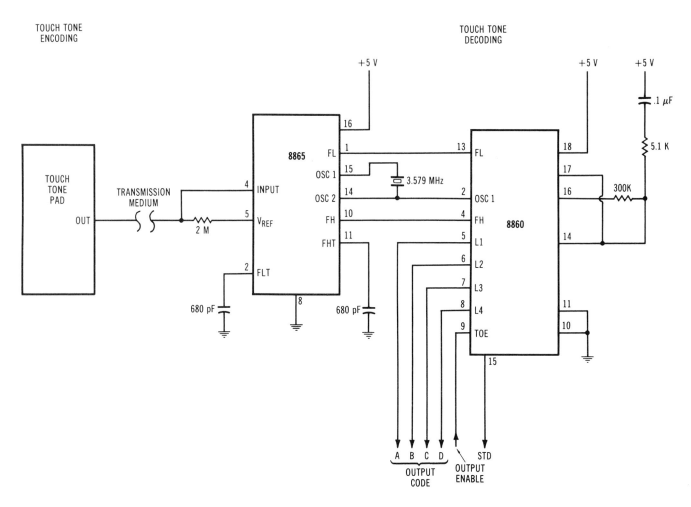

Fig. 14-3 Schematic of a touch-tone signalling system.

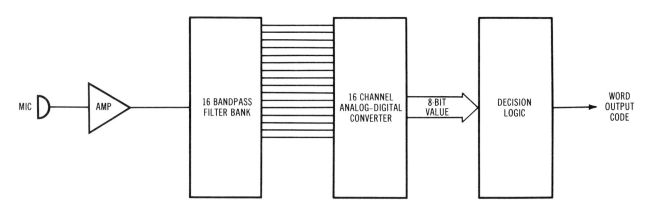

Fig. 14-4 Block diagram of frequency spectral-analysis voice-recognition system.

three speakers would work. On the other hand, speaker dependent usually means the system must be "trained" by the user, and this person is probably the only one it will recognize. Training is accomplished simply by speaking the vocabulary of control commands a number of times, so that the system can learn the voice pattern. These patterns are used as the basis for comparison against incoming patterns on recognition time. They are commonly referred to as *templates*.

Just as there are many categories of recognition sys-

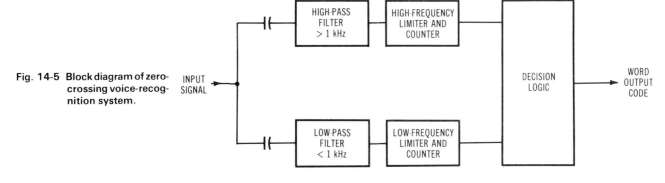

Fig. 14-5 Block diagram of zero-crossing voice-recognition system.

tems, there are as many different methods of sampling the voice input to the recognizer. There are, however, two very popular methods in use today and they are finding their way into monolithic ICs.

1. Frequency-Spectral Analysis
2. Zero-Crossing Analysis

The first method splits the incoming speech waveform into many frequency bands or groups. Each frequency filter is tuned to only allow a certain range to pass. Normally 16 filter banks are used. Fig. 14-4 depicts a typical block diagram of this technique.

The output of the filters is brought to an analog multiplexer that acts like a 16-pole selector switch. Sequentially, each filter output is passed to the analog-to-digital converter which converts the energy level of that particular frequency band into some value. This number is then stored as part of the template. You can see that by doing this method we get a picture of the different frequencies (up to 16) encoded within the spoken utterance, as well as a pattern of timed levels where we are controlling the sampling rate. Basically we are setting 16 frequency counters with time logging capability.

The other method, zero-crossing, has been around from day one. Fig. 14-5 illustrates the circuitry blocks necessary to count zero crossings. As you can see, this method is by far the least complex of the two and, as far as hardware goes, the least reliable of both.

Notice, I said *as far as hardware goes*. You see, zero crossings also count frequency. In fact, they count both frequency and time because you sample the output of the detector. The only difference is that you are looking at only the low frequencies and the high frequencies: two instead of sixteen. It's what you do with these two that counts.

Fig. 14-6 illustrates the basic algorithm used by some zero-crossing systems. Let's go over it. First, the key is to sample the output of both the low- and high-pass filters every 160 microseconds. When you sample at this time, you compare what you read with what was obtained 160 microseconds ago. If the input sample shows a change from the last sample, you increment a counter. You must

have a separate counter for each filter. We do this sampling-compare-increment sequence 100 times, or for a total of 16 milliseconds.

It gets complicated. Now we take the count values of both counters and classify their content into five categories for the high-pass counter and into six different categories for the low-pass output. The actual counter values and their associated category numbers are shown in Fig. 14-7. Also shown in this figure is the five by six pattern of bytes that we use to store these categories.

If your utterance produced a high-pass counter value in 16 milliseconds of 59, then you qualify for a category 3, according to the figure. At this time, go look at the low-pass counter (don't forget the high-pass category number). Let's use a low-pass value of 18, or a category 3, also. Now go to the 30-byte pattern and find the intersection where category 3 of the high-pass and 3 of the low-pass meet. This is a location in memory denoted by the number in the upper half of that block. What you do now is increment the value of that location. On initialization, you will want to clear, or zero out, every location in the table to start a fresh pattern.

Now what? Do it again. Start another 100 samples, but don't forget to clear the high and low counters first. Don't clear the pattern locations though. Go through the same operation for a total of 60 pattern updates. This should bring you to 0.96 second or almost one full second. Therefore, this recognizer listens to your voice, after it notices it is there, for about one second. It doesn't seem very long, but here's where the limitations come in. This method is speaker dependent isolated word, but could be modified to listen for longer periods of time.

What we have just created is a template for the word spoken. Those 30 bytes will be compared to an incoming pattern of 30 bytes to determine the word spoken. Of course, both patterns will never be exactly byte for byte the same, so some error threshold must be built in when the compare is done.

I have built an actual circuit utilizing the techniques described. Fig. 14-8 is the schematic. Notice the use of a single-chip microcomputer to do the scanning.

Have no fear, there is more to come!

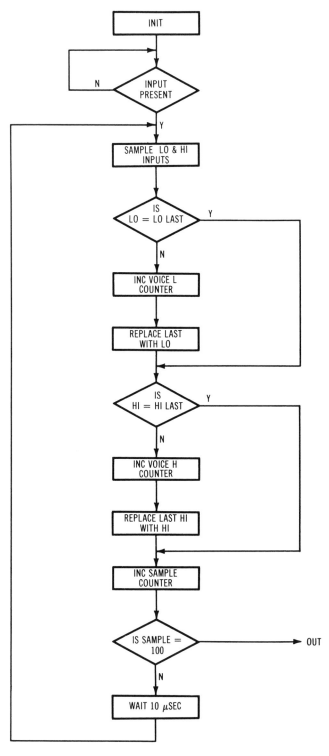

Fig. 14-6 Flowchart of an input scanning routine for zero-crossing recognizer.

ONE-CHIP VOICE RECOGNITION

When, 1990? No . . . right now! There is a company called Interstate Electronics of California that has been involved with voice recognition for many years. They also were the first company to announce IC voice recognizers. Their latest product is a single-chip version that recognizes up to 16 words from any speaker. The part, however, is being targeted at high volume applications such as toys and appliances. They do have an evaluation unit which is preprogrammed to accept 12 words. The words programmed are the following:

MODE 1:	STOP
	GO AHEAD
	SEARCH
	FASTER
	SLOWER
	REPORT
MODE 2:	ALARM
	LIGHTS
	SENSOR
MODE 3:	TRUE
	FALSE
	REPEAT

Actually, they sound like robotic application oriented words don't they? I have built a circuit using their part (VRC-08). It's shown in schematic form in Fig. 14-9. Fig 14-10 shows the board.

The program asks which group of words or mode number you want, then it tells you which words are available in that mode. The chip outputs a binary code for each word recognized, which is unique. Comparing the received code with the codes of the word list reveals the spoken word which is then displayed.

There are two versions of the device available, one NMOS and the other a low-power CMOS. Both are only 28-pin devices. Not bad!

COULD THERE BE ANYTHING BETTER?

You bet. There are a number of products from boards to ICs. The real accurate recognizers now come in chip sets, also. Interstate announced last year the VRC-100 two-chip recognizer which makes use of the spectral-analysis technique described earlier. There are two different ICs in the set: one analog, the other digital.

The analog IC is a 28-pin 16-filter channel bank with 16-channel analog multiplexer built in. All you need to add is a microphone pre-amp and the 8-bit analog-to-digital converter.

The digital component is a preprogrammed Motorola 68701 single-chip computer (sound familiar?) which contains the program to control the multiplexer, sample the A/D, generate templates during training, and compare them during recognition. The addition of some address

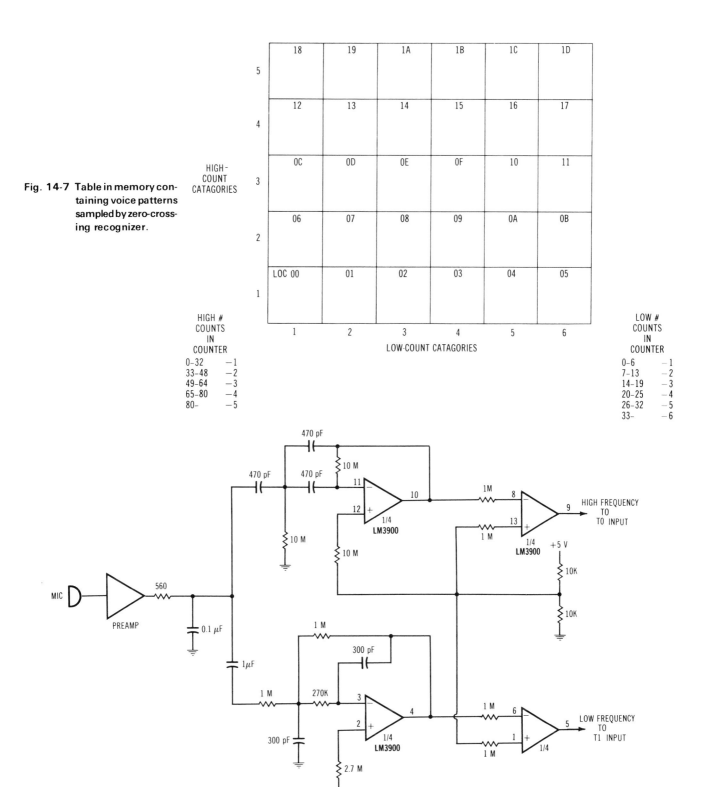

Fig. 14-7 Table in memory containing voice patterns sampled by zero-crossing recognizer.

	1	2	3	4	5	6
5	18	19	1A	1B	1C	1D
4	12	13	14	15	16	17
3	0C	0D	0E	0F	10	11
2	06	07	08	09	0A	0B
1	LOC 00	01	02	03	04	05

HIGH-COUNT CATAGORIES

LOW-COUNT CATAGORIES

HIGH # COUNTS IN COUNTER

0-32	-1
33-48	-2
49-64	-3
65-80	-4
80-	-5

LOW # COUNTS IN COUNTER

0-6	-1
7-13	-2
14-19	-3
20-25	-4
26-32	-5
33-	-6

Fig. 14-8 Schematic of zero-crossing filters which connect to 8748 to provide a low-cost recognition system.

selectors and external template RAM (up to 4K) allows for the storage of the 100 word templates used. Fig. 14-11 shows the chip set.

The VRC-100 set falls under the category of speaker dependent isolated word recognition. You must train the recognizer by repeating each word a predefined number of times. In the basic chip set, there are 15 commands. They are

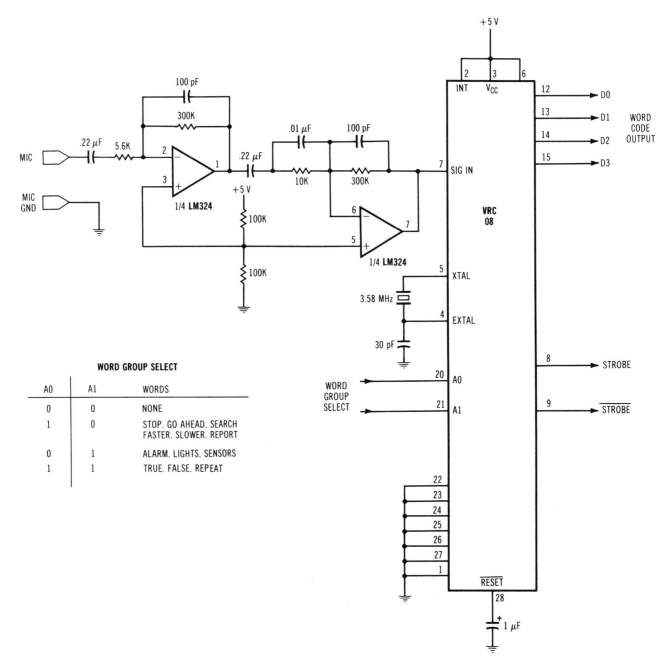

Fig. 14-9 Schematic of circuitry necessary to use the Interstate Electronics single-chip voice recognizer.

WORD GROUP SELECT

A0	A1	WORDS
0	0	NONE
1	0	STOP, GO AHEAD, SEARCH FASTER, SLOWER, REPORT
0	1	ALARM, LIGHTS, SENSORS
1	1	TRUE, FALSE, REPEAT

Train
Update
Reset
Set Reject Threshold
Read Reject Threshold
Download Reference Patterns
Upload Reference Patterns
Recognize
Write Parameters
Read Parameters
Download Object Code and Execute
Set/Read Mode

Set Gain
Read Gain
Adaptation Stability Test

The Train and Update commands are virtually the same, except that Update does not erase the reference-template patterns before operation. It merely averages the sample with the prestored pattern for that word.

When the recognizer is determining which word it has heard, it compares the reference pattern stored with that of the incoming sample. As mentioned earlier, the two patterns will never be exactly the same, therefore some

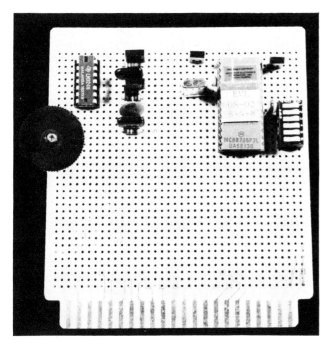

Fig. 14-10 Photograph of project board used to build circuit of Fig. 14-9.

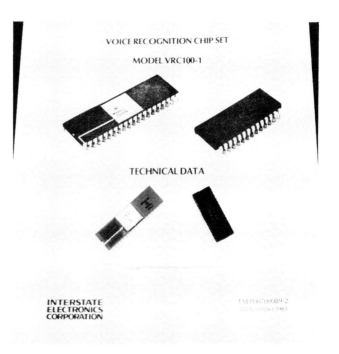

Fig. 14-11 Interstate Electronics high-performance recognition-chip set.

threshold or maximum number of wrong bytes must be determined. The two commands referring to the reject threshold perform this function.

After training it to a particular vocabulary, you can transfer the voice patterns back to a host computer for storage, then later retrieve them using the Upload and Download commands.

The Recognize command puts the system into a mode where every utterance entering the chip set is compared against the reference patterns and the closest match is then output.

Other commands help set the gain of the programmable microphone pre-amp, reset the chip set, and perform various setup instructions. The documentation supplied with the chip set fully explains their operation.

Many commercial products are being designed today utilizing these chip recognizers. Some companies, including most of the major IC manufacturers, are planning chip sets. The push for the talk and listen intelligent machine is well underway.

Communication with these machines will become second nature and before you know it, people will be using pet names for their machine-slaves. Mechanical robots that wash windows, do dishes, clean the house, mow the lawn, and play with the kids will be conversing . . . maybe even between themselves!

Parts Suppliers

Interstate Electronics Corp.
1001 E. Ball
P.O. Box 3117
Anaheim, CA 91803
(714) 635-7210

Mitel Semiconductor   —touch-tone ICs
P.O. Box 13320
360 Legget Drive
Kanta, Ontario, K2K1X5
(613) 592-5630

GTE Microcircuits   —touch-tone ICs
2000 West 14th Street
Tempe, AZ 85281
(602) 968-4431

Intel Corporation   —8748 Single-Chip
3065 Bowers Avenue   Micro
Santa Clara, CA 95051
(408) 987-8080

Sprague Electric   —Stepper drivers
70 Pembroke Road   Hall-effect ICs
Concord, NH 03301   motor drivers

Signetics   —motor drivers
811 E. Arques Avenue   servo systems
Sunnyvale, CA 94016   speed controls

Texas Instruments   —motor drivers
P.O. Box 225012   Hall-effect
Dallas, TX 75265   sensors

Zilog
1315 Dell Drive
Campbell, CA 95008
(408) 370-8000

Ball Brothers Research
  Corporation
Electronic Display Division
1633 Terrace Drive
St. Paul, MN 55113
(612) 633-1742

Edmund Scientific
101 E. Glaucester Pike
Barrington, NJ 08007
1-800-257-6173

Bishop Graphics, Inc.   —E-Z Circuit
5388 Sterling Center Drive   adhesive etch
P.O. Box 5007   patterns
Westlake Village, CA 91359
(213) 991-2600

National Semiconductor
  Corporation
2900 Semiconductor Drive
Santa Clara, CA 95051
(408) 737-5000

Motorola
Semiconductor Products, Inc.
3501 Ed Bluestein Blvd.
Austin, TX 78721

Hewlett Packard   —optoelectronic
  Components   components
640 Page Mill Road
Palo Alto, CA 94034

Standard Microsystems   —Communications
  Corporation   circuits
35 Marcus Blvd.
Hauppauge, NY 11787
(516) 273-3100

Robot Suppliers

Mircobot, Inc. —Mini Mover Arm
453-H Ravendale Drive
Mountain View, CA 94043

Sandhu Machine Design, —Rhino XR-1 Arm
 Inc.
308 S. State
Champaign, IL 61820
(217) 352-8485

Tomy Toys, Inc. —Armatron Toy
901 East 233 Street Robot Arm
Carson, CA 90745

Books and Magazines

Books About Voice Recognition

Trends in Speech Recognition
Wayne A. Lea 1980
Prentice-Hall

Teaching Your Computer to Talk
Edward Teja 1981
TAB Books #1330

Books About Computers

Basic Microprocessors and the 6800
Ron Bishop
Hayden Books

Handbook of Microprocessor Applications
John Kuecken
TAB Books

6801, 68701, & 6803
Microcomputer Programming & Interfacing
Andrew C. Staugaard, Jr.
Howard W. Sams & Co., Inc.

Motor Control Books

Solid State Motor Controls
John Kuecken
TAB Books

Introduction to Servo Mechanism System Design
W. Humphrey
Prentice-Hall Books

Basic Electronic Books

Understanding Solid State Electronics
Texas Instruments Learning Center
Radio Shack Books #62-2035

Transistor Circuit Design
Texas Instruments
McGraw-Hill Books

Vision Books

Computer Vision Systems
Allen R. Hanson and Edward M. Riseman
Academic Press

Robot Magazines

Robotics Age
Division of North American Technology
174 Concord Street
Strand Building
Peterborough, NH 03458
(603) 924-7136

Robotics Today
One S.M.E. Drive
P.O. Box 390
Dearborn, MI 48128

INDEX